IN AMERICA

by Peter Matthiessen

PENGUIN BOOKS

Penguin Books Ltd, Harmondsworth,
Middlesex, England
Penguin Books, 625 Madison Avenue,
New York, New York 10022, U.S.A.
Penguin Books Australia Ltd, Ringwood,
Victoria, Australia
Penguin Books Canada Limited, 2801 John Street,
Markham, Ontario, Canada L3R 1B4
Penguin Books (N.Z.) Ltd, 182–190 Wairau Road,
Auckland 10, New Zealand

First published in the United States of America by
The Viking Press 1959
First published in England by Andre Deutsch Ltd. 1960
Viking Compass Edition published 1964
Reprinted 1966, 1967, 1969 (twice), 1972, 1975
Published in Penguin Books 1977
Reprinted 1978

LIBRARY OF CONGRESS CATALOGING IN PUBLICATION DATA
Matthiessen, Peter.
Wildlife in America.
Bibliography: p. 289.
Includes index.
1. Zoology—North America. 2. Hunting—North America.
3. Fishing—North America. 4. Wildlife conservation—
North America. I. Title.
[QL151.M37 1977] 596'.097 77-11995
ISBN 0 14 00.4793 X

Printed in the United States of America by
The Murray Printing Company, Westford, Massachusetts
Set in Linotype Electra

Portions of the text appeared in *Sports Illustrated*

For Elizabeth C. Matthiessen and Erard A. Matthiessen
with love and many thanks

Contents

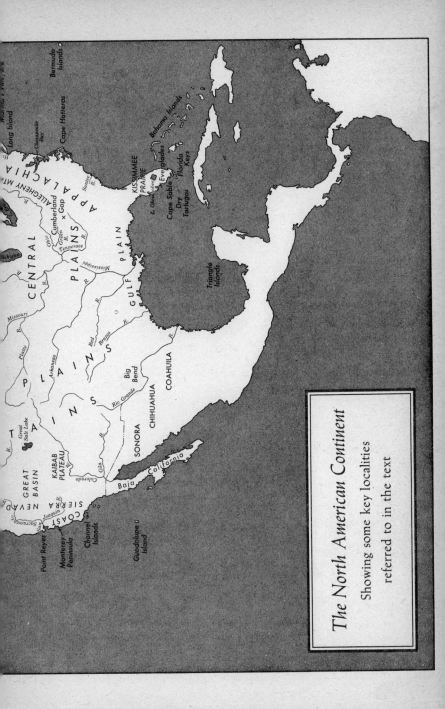

The North American Continent

Showing some key localities
referred to in the text

ACKNOWLEDGMENTS

Much of the information necessary for the preparation of this book was drawn from the works of naturalist-writers, past and present, to whom this crucial debt is hereby gratefully acknowledged; a selected list of the most important reference material may be found in the Bibliography. Among active writers, I would like especially to thank the following: Durward L. Allen, Daniel B. Beard et al., Paul R. Cutright, James Fisher, James C. Greenway, Jr., Roger Tory Peterson, A. W. Schorger, Paul B. Sears, Edouard A. Stackpole, Edwin Way Teale, and Robert Henry Welker.

In addition, generous personal assistance was received from the following conservationists, biologists, and others:

Mr. Richard H. Pough read and criticized the entire manuscript, offering a great many helpful suggestions and corrections, particularly in regard to the sections on conservation.

Reference material pertaining to the fishes remains regional and relatively uncoordinated, and research in this field was performed almost entirely through personal interview and correspondence: I am particularly indebted to Dr. Carl L. Hubbs, of the Scripps Oceanographic Institute, La Jolla, California, whose kind interest and assistance formed the basis for research in this field; I also received invaluable cooperation and information from Dr. Reeve M. Bailey (University of Michigan), Dr. W. Harry Everhart (University of Maine), Dr. W. I. Follett (California Academy of Sciences), Dr. Robert R. Miller (University of Michigan), Dr. James W. Moffett (U. S. Fish and Wildlife Service), and Dr. Edward C. Raney (Cornell University).

For valuable information in regard to the amphibians and reptiles, I am indebted to the following: Benjamin Banta (Stanford University), Charles M. Bogert (American Museum of Natural History), Dr. Robert F. Inger (Chicago Natural History Museum), Alan Leviton (California Academy of Sciences), Dr. Robert C. Stebbins (University of California).

Information on North American birds is generally available in many excellent books and magazines. For assistance in observing the California condor, white-tailed kite, and Kirtland's warbler in the field, I am grateful, respectively, to

Sidney Peyton, James B. Dixon, and Dr. Sewall Pettingill. Dr. Dean Amadon of the American Museum of Natural History answered a number of questions, and Robert Porter Allen, Research Director of the National Audubon Society, was kind enough to read over my notes in regard to rare and vanishing American birds, making certain important corrections.

As in the case of the birds, general information in regard to North American mammals is generally available. Specific information and advice was supplied by Dr. Harold E. Anthony (American Museum of Natural History), Dr. Clarence Cottam (Welder Wildlife Foundation), Dr. Ira Gabrielson (Wildlife Management Institute), and Lewis Wayne Walker (Arizona-Sonora Museum).

Dr. Richard Van Gelder of the American Museum of Natural History was kind enough to read over my notes in regard to the rare and vanishing North American mammals, and, like Mr. Allen, made a number of important suggestions.

I would also like to thank Mrs. Richard Kimball, Dr. Mont Cazier, and Miss Ruth Norton of the American Museum of Natural History for their cooperation in arranging a most profitable stay at the Museum's Southwestern Research Center in Arizona; Mr. John H. Baker and Miss Amy Clampitt of the National Audubon Society have also been very helpful, making available the excellent library of the National Audubon Society.

The biologists and field men of the Fish and Wildlife Service offered unfailing interest, courtesy, and hospitality during the course of a research trip undertaken in 1957 for this book; I am particularly indebted to the following: Philip Dumont, Richard Griffith, and Seton Thompson, of the Fish and Wildlife Service offices in Washington, and the personnel of many National Wildlife Refuges and Game Ranges, especially Claude Lard and Hal Irby (Aransas), Luther Goldman, Russ Clapper, and George Unlin (Laguna Atascosa, Santa Ana), Cecil Kennedy (San Andres), Gale Monson and Chuck Kennedy (Kofa, Imperial), Ben Hazeltine (Charles Sheldon), Leroy Giles and Thomas Horne (Lower Klamath, Tule Lake), Jim Johnson (Kenai), Dave Spencer (Supervisor, Alaskan Refuges), Gordon Watson (Alaska Fisheries), Jim Branson and Ray Tremblay (Alaska Game Agents-Pilots), Joe Miner (Alaska Predator Control Agent), John Schwartz (National Bison Range), Winston Banko (Red Rock Lakes), Cordia Henry (Seney).

Also, park naturalists Jim Reid (McKinley National Park) and Dave Beal (Yellowstone National Park).

Also, California Park Rangers Jack Rhodes and Jim Whitehead.

The people who have made contributions of time and hospitality are too numerous to list, but the following should be mentioned: Scotty Anderson, Louis Blachly, Guy Miller, Mr. and Mrs. Dave Leach, Mr. and Mrs. Dan Kilgore, Mr. and Mrs. Charles Michael, George Guilsher, Peter Gimbel, Erard A. Matthiessen, G. C. Matthiessen, C. R. Gutermuth, Senator Richard Neuberger, Mrs. Charles Kennedy, Mrs. James Branson, Mrs. Ray Tremblay, and Mrs. John Schwartz.   —P. M.

Introduction

IT IS ODD, one reflects after reading this book, that what it does has never been done before. We have long needed a historical survey that would give us the whole story of the white man's effect on wildlife in North America, from the earliest records to the present day. Mr. Matthiessen's book is precisely this, and its fulfillment of this need, its excellent documentation and engaging style of writing, make it an outstanding contribution to the literature in the field.

To begin with, the author provides a vivid picture of the original abundance of wildlife in America. This abundance, which incidentally proved to be an accurate portent of the richness of the continent's natural resources, demonstrated that fertile land could support enormous numbers of animals when nature's food chains and the wildlife pyramids they created were intact. One of the aspects of the book that is unique, in my view, is this: for the first time we have in a single volume information gathered from the widely scattered writings of early explorers and settlers. This particular part of the record is immensely interesting to people who want to understand the original status of our wildlife, in order to be able to evaluate better our efforts today to conserve it, to restore it.

The reader, for instance, will see references by early writers to the lack of "wildness" in animals we now regard as extremely shy; the frequency of these references indicates how man's behavior toward animals has been responsible for their present tendency to make a hurried departure when he appears on the scene. Today, in some of our great national parks where both predator and prey are equally protected, we see that some of the tameness observed by the first settlers is returning. We see it also in and around cities, where terns and skimmers nest in the loops of highway clover-leafs and wild ducks and geese winter in park ponds; these are manifestations of the remarkable willingness of wildlife to live in close association with man on a live-and-let-live basis if man permits.

The story of what the white man has done to the continent's wealth of wildlife is not a pleasant one. Among America's explorers, no consideration was given to the ability of animals, or their lack of it, to replenish themselves. Today's concepts of sustained yield and carrying capacity of land were wholly foreign to the thinking of the times. These concepts were extremely slow to develop in the ensuing years and, as exploration and settlement spread across the continent in the nineteenth century, such ideas as did develop met with an indifference that remained maddeningly obdurate. Even now, when interest in the preservation of the wildlife that remains to us has risen encouragingly, a far greater understanding of the whole picture is necessary. It is to be hoped that Mr. Matthiessen's eloquent book will do service toward this end, especially among the large general public that does not realize the full and dramatic import of what has happened to our wildlife over the past three and a half centuries.

In instance after instance, the reader will see how reluctant everyone was to recognize that a species was declining. Some animals were already extinct before any note of alarm was expressed, even by scientists. "They must have gone elsewhere this year" is still a stock explanation for any decline in wildlife numbers, even though we have overwhelming proof that migratory forms cling tenaciously to specific breeding and wintering areas and to closely circumscribed routes between them. Once the dwindling of a species can no longer be ignored, a scapegoat is always sought. The Indians were the first to be blamed, and then, as their numbers decreased, the blame was shifted to the predators. This theory persists, in the form of bounties on predators, although we now know that the practice aggravates the situation by further disrupting the equilibriums of the wildlife community.

The material in this book is the best possible answer to today's final folly: the clamor for the introduction of exotic species from other lands. To believe that animals from different lands and climates will be better adaptable to American conditions than our native species, which have been molded to them by millions of years of evolutionary development, is to go against the findings of science since Darwin's day. All the evidence we have shows that our own species are superbly suited to their environment, and are capable of maintaining healthy populations if man will only give them a chance.

The value of the volume is enhanced by a full bibliography and carefully compiled appendices. Lists of rare and extinct forms of wildlife have an unhappy tendency to grow longer; the author's own list is noteworthy because it is, at this writing, the most up-to-date, and because it covers not one group of animals but all North American forms—fish, amphibians, reptiles, birds, and mammals—that are extinct or so rare as to be endangered. Equally useful is the chronological record of the effort to conserve America's wildlife through laws, which started with legislation in Bermuda, around 1616, to protect the cahow and the green turtle. This legal record makes striking reading in connection with the text proper, for it points up how frequently legislation and international agreements have been either "too little or too late," or virtually unenforceable. The present sorry plight of the world's last great whale population, that of the Antarctic, is a reminder that we are not fully aware of what we can learn from the past.

The drawings of Bob Hines are an accurate and artistic complement to Mr. Matthiessen's text. They lend force and persuasion, if such are needed, and they also provide for readers, be they laymen or specialists, a valuable visual record. The most useful thing a book such as this can do is to point the way to a better treatment of wildlife in the future. The lesson it teaches above all others is that nature can produce abundant wildlife populations if we give back to her the exclusive use of a few patches of land here and there, the land that once supported the fabulous wildlife of which the author gives us such a clear and impressively documented story.

—RICHARD H. POUGH

Pelham, New York, June 1959

WILDLIFE IN AMERICA

And, in the isolation of the sky,
At evening, casual flocks of pigeons make
Ambiguous undulations as they sink,
Downward to darkness, on extended wings.

—WALLACE STEVENS, "Sunday Morning"

And I brought you into a plentiful country, to eat the fruit thereof
and the goodness thereof; but when ye entered, ye defiled my land,
and made mine heritage an abomination.

—Jeremiah 2:7

These Penguins are as bigge as Geese, and flie not . . . and they multiply so infinitely upon a certain flat Iland, that men drive them from thence upon a boord into their Boates by hundreds at a time; as if God had made the innocencie of so poore a creature to become an admirable instrument for the sustenation of man. —RICHARD WHITBOURN (1618)

1 : The Outlying Rocks

IN EARLY JUNE OF 1844, a longboat crewed by fourteen men hove to off the skerry called Eldey, a stark, volcanic mass rising out of the gray wastes of the North Atlantic some ten miles west of Cape Reykjanes, Iceland. On the islets of these uneasy seas, the forebears of the boatmen had always hunted the swarming sea birds as a food, but on this day they were seeking, for collectors, the eggs and skins of the garefowl or great auk, a penguin-like flightless bird once common on the ocean rocks of northern Europe, Iceland, Greenland, and the maritime provinces of Canada. The great auk, slaughtered indiscriminately across the centuries for its flesh, feathers, and oil, was vanishing, and the last birds, appearing now and then on lonely shores, were granted no protection. On the contrary, they were pursued more intensively than ever for their value as scientific specimens.

At the north end of Eldey, a wide ledge descends to the water, and, though a sea was running, the boat managed to land three men, Jon Brandsson, Sigourour Isleffson, and Ketil Ketilsson. Two auks, blinking, waddled foolishly across the ledge. Isleffson and Brandsson each killed a bird, and Ketilsson, discovering a solitary egg, found a crack in it and smashed it. Later, one Christian Hansen paid nine pounds for the skins, and sold them in turn to a Reykjavik taxidermist named Möller. It is not known what became of them thereafter, a fact all the more saddening when one considers that, on all the long coasts of the northern ocean, no auk was ever seen alive again.

The great auk is one of the few creatures whose final hours can be documented with such certainty. Ordinarily, the last members of a species die in solitude, the time and place of their passage from the earth unknown. One year they are present, striving instinctively to maintain an existence many thousands of years old. The next year they are gone. Perhaps stray auks persisted a few years longer, to die at last through accident or age, but we must assume that the ultimate pair fell victim to this heedless act of man.

One imagines with misgiving the last scene on desolate Eldey. Offshore, the longboat wallows in a surge of seas, then slides forward in the lull, its stem grinding hard on the rock ledge. The hunters hurl the two dead birds aboard and, cursing, tumble after, as the boat falls away into the wash. Gaining the open water, it moves off to the eastward, the rough voices and the hollow thump of oars against wood tholepins unreal in the prevailing fogs of June. The dank mist, rank with marine smells, cloaks the dark mass, white-topped with guano, and the fierce-eyed gannets, which had not left the crest, settle once more on their crude nests, hissing peevishly and jabbing sharp blue bills at their near neighbors. The few gulls, mewing aimlessly, circle in, alighting. One banks, checks its flight, bends swiftly down upon the ledge, where the last, pathetic generation of great auks gleams raw and unborn on the rock. A second follows and, squalling, they yank at the loose embryo, scattering the black, brown, and green shell segments. After a time they return to the crest, and the ledge is still. The shell remnants lie at the edge of tideline, and the last sea of the flood, perhaps, or a rain days later, washes the last piece into the water. Slowly it drifts down across the sea-curled weeds, the anchored life of the marine world. A rock minnow, drawn to the strange scent, snaps at a minute shred of auk albumen; the shell fragment spins upward, descends once more.

Farther down, it settles briefly near a *littorina*, and surrounding molluscs stir dully toward the stimulus. The periwinkle scours it, spits the calcified bits away. The current takes the particles, so small as to be all but invisible, and they are borne outward, drifting down at last to the deeps of the sea out of which, across slow eons of the Cenozoic era, the species first evolved.

For most of us, its passing is unimportant. The auk, from a practical point of view, was doubtless a dim-witted inhabitant of Godforsaken places, a primitive and freakish thing, ill-favored and ungainly. From a second and a more enlightened viewpoint, the great auk was the mightiest of its family, a highly evolved fisherman and swimmer, an ornament to the monotony of northern seas, and for centuries a crucial food source for the natives of the Atlantic coasts. More important, it was a living creature which died needlessly, the first species native to North America to become extinct by the hand of man. It was to be followed into oblivion by other creatures, many of them of an aesthetic and economic significance apparent to us all. Even today, despite protection, the scattered individuals of species too long persecuted are hovering at the abyss of extinction, and will vanish in our lifetimes.

The slaughter, for want of fodder, has subsided in this century, but the fishes, amphibians, reptiles, birds, and mammals—the vertebrate animals as a group—are obscured by man's dark shadow. Such protection as is extended them too rarely includes the natural habitats they require, and their remnants skulk in a lean and shrinking wilderness. The true wilderness—the great woods and clear rivers, the wild swamps and grassy plains which once were the wonder of the world—has been largely despoiled, and today's voyager, approaching our shores through the oiled waters of the coast, is greeted by smoke and the glint of industry on our fouled seaboard, and an inland prospect of second growth, scarred landscapes, and sterile, often stinking, rivers of pollution and raw mud, the whole bedecked with billboards, neon lights, and other decorative evidence of mankind's triumph over chaos. In many regions the greenwood not converted to black stumps no longer breathes with sound and movement, but is become a cathedral of still trees; the plains are plowed under and the prairies ravaged by overgrazing and the winds of drought. Where great, wild creatures ranged, the vermin prosper.

The concept of conservation is a far truer sign of civilization than that spoliation of a continent which we once confused with progress. Today, very late, we are coming to accept the fact that the harvest of renewable resources must be controlled. Forests, soil, water, and wildlife are mutually interdependent, and the ruin of one element will mean, in the end, the ruin of them all. Not surprisingly, land management which benefits mankind will benefit the lesser beasts as well. Creatures like quail and the white-tailed deer, adjusting to man, have already shown recovery. For others, like the whooping crane, it is probably much too late, and the grizzly bear and golden eagle die slowly with the wilderness.

This book is a history of North American wildlife, of the great auk and other creatures present and missing, of how they vanished, where, and why; and of what is presently being done that North America may not become a wasteland of man's creation, in which no wild thing can live.

"Everybody knows," one naturalist has written, "that the autumn landscape in the north woods is the land, plus a red maple, plus a ruffed grouse. In terms of conventional physics, the grouse represents only a millionth of either the mass or the energy of an acre. Yet subtract the grouse and the whole thing is dead."[1]*

The finality of extinction is awesome, and not unrelated to the finality of eternity. Man, striving to imagine what might lie beyond the long light years of stars, beyond the universe, beyond the void, feels lost in space; confronted with the death of species, enacted on earth so many times before he came, and certain to continue when his own breed is gone, he is forced to face another void, and feels alone in time. Species appear and, left behind by a changing earth, they disappear forever, and there is a certain solace in the inexorable. But until man, the highest predator, evolved, the process of extinction was a slow one. No species but man, so far as is known, unaided by circumstance or climatic change, has ever extinguished another, and certainly no species has ever devoured itself, an accomplishment of which man appears quite capable. There is some comfort in the notion that, however *Homo sapiens* contrives his own destruction, a few creatures will survive in that ultimate wilderness he will leave behind, going on about their ancient business in the mindless confidence that their own much older and more tolerant species will prevail.

The *Terra Incognita*, as cartographers of the Renaissance referred to North America, had been known to less educated Eurasians for more than ten thousand years. Charred animal bones found here and there in the

* Reference Notes begin on page 285.

West, and submitted to the radiocarbon test, have been ascribed to human campfires laid at least twenty-five thousand years ago. Thus one might say that the effect of man on the fauna of North America commenced with the waning of the glaciers, when bands of wild Mongoloid peoples migrated eastward across a land bridge now submerged by the shoal seas of the Bering Strait. In this period—the time of transition between the Pleistocene and Recent epochs—the mastodons, mammoths, saber-toothed tigers, dire wolves, and other huge beasts which had flourished in the Ice Age disappeared forever from the face of the earth, and the genera which compose our modern wildlife gained ascendancy.

Man was perhaps the last of the large mammals to find the way from Asia to North America. In any case, many species had preceded him. The members of the deer family—the deer, elk, moose, and caribou—had made the journey long before, as had the bison, or buffalo, and the mountain sheep. Among all modern North American hoofed mammals, in fact, only the pronghorn antelope emerged originally on this continent. The gray wolf, lynx, beaver, and many other animals also have close relations in the Old World, so close that even today a number of them—the wolverine and the Eurasian glutton, for example, and the grizzly and Siberian brown bear—are widely considered to be identical species. Similarly, many bird species are common to both continents, including the herring gull, golden plover, mallard, and peregrine falcon. The larger groupings—the genera and families which contain those species and many others—are widespread throughout the Northern Hemisphere. Even among the songbirds, which are quite dissimilar on the two continents in terms of individual species, the only large American family which has no counterpart in Eurasia is that of the colorful wood warblers, *Parulidae*.

Since the American continents are connected overland, it seems rather strange that the faunas of North America and Eurasia are more closely allied than the faunas of North and South America. One must remember, however, that the Americas were separated for fifty million years or more in the course of the present geologic era, and during this time their creatures had evolved quite differently. It is only in recent times, in geological terms —two million years ago, perhaps—that the formation of the huge icecaps, lowering the oceans of the world, permitted the reappearance of the Panama bridge between Americas.

The animals moved north and south across this land bridge, just as they had moved east and west across the dry strait in the Arctic. But the

GREAT AUK

South American forms, become senile and over-specialized in their long period of isolation, were unable to compete with the younger species which were flourishing throughout the Northern Hemisphere. Many archaic monkeys, marsupials, and other forms were rapidly exterminated by the invaders. Though a certain interchange took place across the land bridge, the northern mammalian genera came to dominate both continents, and their descendants comprise virtually all the large South American animals of today, including the cougar, jaguar, deer, peccaries, and guanacos.

The armadillo, opossum, and porcupine, on the other hand, are among the primitive creatures which arrived safely from the opposite direction and are still extending their range. A large relation of the armadillo, *Boreostracon*, and a mighty ground sloth, *Megatherium*, also made their way to North America. These slow-witted beasts penetrated the continent as far as Pennsylvania, only to succumb to the changes in climate which accompanied the passing of the Ice Age.

The mass extermination of great mammals at this time occurred everywhere except in Africa and southern Asia. Alteration of environment brought about by climatic change is usually held accountable, but the precise reasons are as mysterious as those offered for the mass extinction of the dinosaurs some seventy million years before. Even among large animals the extinctions were by no means uniform: in North America

the moose and bison were able to make the necessary adaptations, while
the camel and horse were not. The camel family survived in South America in the wild guanaco and vicuña, but the horse was absent from the
Eastern Hemisphere until recent centuries, when it returned with the
Spaniards as a domestic animal.

Large creatures of the other classes were apparently less affected than
the mammals. Great Pleistocene birds such as the whooping crane and
the California condor prevail in remnant populations to this day, and many
more primitive vertebrates, of which the sharks, sturgeons, sea turtles, and
crocodilians are only the most spectacular examples, have persisted in their
present form over many millions of years. For these, the slow wax and wane
of the glacial epoch, which witnessed the emergence of mankind, was no
more than a short season in the long history of their existence on the earth.

The last mastodons and mammoths were presumably hunted by man,
who may have been hunted in his turn by *Smilodon*, the unsmiling
saber-toothed tiger. It is very doubtful, however, whether the demise of
these creatures at the dawn of the Recent epoch was significantly hastened by nomadic hunters of the Eskimo, Athabascan, Iroquoian, Siouan,
and Algonquian races, the numerous tribes of which were wandering east
and south across the continent. The red men were always few in number
and, the Pueblo peoples of the Southwest excepted, left little sign of their
existence. They moved softly through the wilderness like woodland birds,
rarely remaining long enough in one locality to mar it.

The visits by Vikings, few records of which have come down from the
Dark Ages, were transient also, and the forest green soon covered their
crude settlements, leaving only a few much-disputed traces. These fierce
warriors, whose sea-dragon galleys were the most exotic craft ever to pierce
the North Atlantic fogs, had colonized Greenland by the tenth century
and were thus the earliest white discoverers of the Western Hemisphere.
That they also discovered North America by the year 1000 seems hardly
to be doubted, and the Norse colonists of an ill-defined stretch of northeast
coast were the first to record the resources of the new continent. In addition
to the wild grapes for which the country was called Vinland, "there was no
lack of salmon there either in the river or in the lake, and larger salmon
than they had ever seen before," according to the chronicle of Eric the
Red.[2] But they concerned themselves chiefly with the export of timber
and fur, and in their murderous dealings with the Skrellings, as they called

the red men, established a precedent firmly adhered to in later centuries by more pious invaders from France, England, Spain, and Holland. The last Vinland colony, in 1011, was beset less by Skrellings than by civil strife; in the following spring, the survivors sailed away to Greenland, and the history of Vinland, brief and bloody, came to an end.

The modern exploitation of North American wildlife, then, commenced with Breton fishermen who, piloting shallops smaller still than the very small *Santa María*, were probably appearing annually on the Grand Banks off Newfoundland before the voyage of Columbus, and certainly no later than 1497, the year that Americus Vespucius and the Cabots explored Vinland's dark, quiet coasts. "The soil is barren in some places," Sebastian Cabot wrote of Labrador or Newfoundland, "and yields little fruit, but it is full of white bears, and stags far greater than ours. It yields plenty of fish, and those very great, as seals, and those which commonly we call salmons: there are soles also above a yard in length: but especially there is great abundance of that kind of fish which the savages call baccalaos." [3] The baccalao, or cod, abounding in the cold offshore waters of the continental shelf, formed the first major commerce of what Vespucius, in a letter to Lorenzo de' Medici, would term the New World; in its incidental persecution of sea birds, this primitive fishery was to initiate the long decline of North American fauna.

Though the Breton fishermen left no records, it must be assumed that they located almost immediately the great bird colonies in the Magdalen Islands and at Funk Island, a flat rock islet thirty-odd miles off Newfoundland. Since many sea birds, and especially those of the alcid family—the auks, puffins, guillemots, and murres—are of general distribution on both sides of the North Atlantic and nest on the rock islands of Brittany even today, these sailors were quick to recognize their countrymen. A concept of the plenty they came upon may still be had at Bonaventure Island, off the Gaspé Peninsula of Quebec, where the four-hundred-foot cliffs of the seaward face form one vast hive of alcids. The birds swarm ceaselessly in spring and summer, drifting in from the ocean in flocks like long wisps of smoke and whirring upward from the water to careen clumsily along the ledges. Above, on the crest, the magnificent white gannets nest, and the kittiwakes and larger gulls patrol the face, their sad cries added to a chittering and shrieking which pierce the booming of the surf in the black sea caves below. At the base of the cliff the visitor, small in a primeval emptiness of ocean, rock, and sky, feels simultaneously exalted and diminished; the bleak bird rocks of the northern oceans will perhaps be the final outposts of the natural profusion known to early voyagers, and we moderns, used to remnant populations of creatures taught to know their place, find this wild din, this wilderness of life, bewildering.

The largest alcid, and the one easiest to kill, was the great auk. Flightless, it was forced to nest on low, accessible ledges, and with the white man's coming its colonies were soon exterminated except on remote rocks far out at sea. The size of a goose, it furnished not only edible eggs but meat, down and feathers, oil, and even codfish bait, and the Micmac Indians were said to have valued its gullet as a quiver for their arrows. The greatest colony of garefowl was probably at Funk Island, where Jacques Cartier, as early as 1534, salted down five or six barrels of these hapless birds for each ship in his expedition. In 1536 an Englishman named Robert Hore improved upon old-fashioned ways by spreading a sail bridge from ship to shore and marching a complement of auks into his hold. Later voyagers, sailing in increasing numbers to the new continent, learned quickly to augment their wretched stores in similar fashion, not only at Funk Island but at Bird Rocks in the Magdalens and elsewhere. The great auk is thought to have nested as far south as the coast of Maine, with a wintering population in Massachusetts Bay, but the southern colonies were probably destroyed quite early.

As a group, the alcids have always been extraordinarily plentiful—the Brünnich's murre and the dovekie, which may be the most numerous of northern sea birds, each boast colonies in Greenland of two million individuals or more—and the great auk was no exception. The relative inaccessibility of its North Atlantic rookeries deferred its extinction for three centuries, but by 1785, when the frenzy of colonization had subsided, George Cartwright of Labrador, describing the Funks, was obliged to take note of the bird's decline: ". . . it has been customary of late years, for several crews of men to live all summer on that island, for the sole purpose of killing birds for the sake of their feathers, the destruction which they have made is incredible. If a stop is not soon put to that practice, the whole breed will be diminished to almost nothing, particularly the penguins: for this is now the only island they have left to breed upon. . . ." [4] Cartwright does not mention the complementary industry of boiling the birds in huge try-pots for their oil, an enterprise made feasible on the treeless Funks by the use of still more auks as fuel.

The naturalists of the period, unhappily, did not share Cartwright's alarm. Thomas Pennant, writing in the previous year, makes no mention of auk scarcity, and Thomas Nuttall, as late as 1834, is more concerned with the bird's demeanor than with its destruction. "Deprived of the use of wings," he mourns, "degraded as it were from the feathered ranks, and almost numbered with the amphibious monsters of the deep, the Auk seems condemned to dwell alone in those desolate and forsaken regions of the earth. . . . In the Ferröe isles, Iceland, Greenland and Newfoundland, they dwell and breed in great numbers. . . ." [5] Though Nuttall pointed out, somewhat paradoxically, that recent navigators had failed to observe them, his contemporary, Mr. Audubon, was persuaded of their abundance off Newfoundland and of their continued use as a source of fish bait. In 1840, the year after Audubon's account, the auk is thought to have become extinct off Newfoundland, and two decades later Dr. Spencer F. Baird was of the opinion that, as a species, the bird was rather rare. His remark may well have been the first of a long series of troubled observations by American naturalists in regard to the scarcity of a creature which was, in fact, already extinct.

"All night," wrote Columbus, in his journal for October 9, 1492, "they heard birds passing." [6] He was already wandering the eastern reaches of the Caribbean, seeking in every sign of life a harbinger of land. The night flyers mentioned were probably hosts of migratory birds, traversing the Caribbean from North to South America, rather than native species of the Greater Antilles or Hispaniola. Columbus could not have known this, of course, nor did he suspect that the birds seen by day which raised false hopes throughout the crossing were not even coastal species, but shearwaters and petrels, which visit land but once a year to breed.

Certain shearwaters, storm petrels, and alcids are still very common in season off the Atlantic coasts, but it is no coincidence that the great auk and two species of petrel were the first North American creatures to suffer a drastic decline. The Atlantic islands, rising out of the endless fetch of the wide, westward horizon, were much frequented by ships, and often provided new ship's stores for the last leg of the voyage. Fresh meat was usually supplied by sea birds, incredibly plentiful on their crowded island nesting grounds; in temperate seas, the shearwaters and petrels, like the great auks farther north, were conscripted commonly as a supplementary diet.

In spite of local plenty, the bird communities of islands around the world are often early victims of extermination. The breeding range of island species is small and therefore vulnerable, and the species themselves may

GUADALUPE PETREL

be quite primitive. Some are relict populations of forms which, on the mainland, have long since succumbed in the struggle for survival. Other species, freed from competition and mammalian predation, grow over-specialized, diminished in vitality, and thus are ill equipped to deal with new factors in their environment.

Man is invariably a new factor of the most dangerous potential. The fiercest animal of all, he is especially destructive when he introduces, in addition to himself, such rapacious mammal relatives as the rat, the mongoose, and the cat, all of them beasts superbly equipped to make short work of birds, eggs, and other edible life escaping the attention of their large ally.

The ship rat may have explored Bermuda as early as 1603. That year a Spanish crew under Diego Ramírez, frightened at first by the unearthly gabblings of myriad nocturnal spirits, discovered upon closer inspection that these evil things were birds, and highly palatable birds at that. The good impression of the Spaniards was confirmed six years later by a Mr. W. Strachey, shipwrecked in those parts with Sir George Somers on the *Sea Venture*,* who wrote as follows:

A kind of webbe-footed Fowle there is, of the bigness of an English greene Plover, or Sea-Meawe, which all the Summer we saw not, and in the darkest nights of November and December . . . they would come forth, but not flye farre from home, and hovering in the ayre, and over the Sea, made

* The accounts of this shipwreck are said to have inspired Shakespeare's *The Tempest*.

SHORT-TAILED ALBATROSS

a strange hollow and harsh howling. They call it of the cry which it maketh, a cohow. . . . There are thousands of these Birds, and two or three Islands full of their Burrows, whether at any time . . . we could send our Cock-boat and bring home as many as would serve the whole Company.[7]

Strachey's implication that the nesting burrows were confined to a few islands—or more properly, islets—is significant, for the cahow, or Bermuda petrel, was the first New World example of a creature endangered by its narrow habitat. The cahow's original nesting range throughout the islands was doubtless restricted to the offshore rocks not long after the first sail broke the ocean horizons. In addition to man and his faithful rats, a number of hogs were turned loose in the Bermudas very early, and these are thought to have rooted out the colonies on the larger islands. Nevertheless, the cahow and the "pimlico," known today as Audubon's shearwater, remained abundant on the islets of Castle Roads and elsewhere, and it may have been the famine in the winter of 1614–1615 which brought about the final decline of the former. The following year, a proc-lamation was issued "against the spoyle and havock of the Cahowes, and other birds, which already wer almost all of them killed and scared away very improvidently by fire, diggeing, stoneing, and all kinds of murtherings." A law protecting the nesting birds was passed in 1621 which, to judge

BERMUDA PETREL, or CAHOW

from its results, was unavailing. About 1629, scarcely a quarter-century after the first accounts of it, the cahow disappeared entirely.

In the ordinary course of events, the cahow would have thus become the first North American species to die by the hand of man. (Bermuda is here considered an extension of North America, since it cannot be geographically allied to any other land mass and since, in this period, it was part of the Virginia Colony. For the purposes of this book, North America may be taken to include the continent north of the Mexican border, with its off-shore islands and the oceanic islands of Bermuda, although the border is not a continental line, and is somewhat north of the vague faunal "boundary" which roughly separates the representative animals of the two Americas.) But the species was marvelously resurrected in 1906, when an unknown petrel was discovered in a Castle Island crevice. The bird at first was considered a new species, but three other specimens located in subsequent years closely fitted a description of the historic cahow constructed from antique remains. In 1951, some nesting burrows, occupied, were found on islets near Castle Roads. Carefully guarded, these burrows are nonetheless subject to the whims of rats as well as to confiscation by the yellow-billed tropic birds, and there is small hope that the cahow's stamina can maintain it another century. Less than one hundred individuals are now thought to exist, but the fact remains that the species managed to survive nearly three hundred years of supposed extinction. Its status as a "living fossil" cannot compare with that of the coelacanth which, first captured

BLACK-CAPPED PETREL

off South Africa in 1938, is a five-foot specimen of an order of fossil fishes thought to have vanished from the earth, not three hundred but three hundred million years ago. Nevertheless, the cahow's story is remarkable, and one must admire the persistence of the survivors. Scattered out across the great Atlantic, they have homed to their rock islets every autumn, year after year after year, to perpetuate their kind beneath the very shadows of the planes which fly man in and out of Bermuda's airfield.

Though remains have been found in the Bahamas, the former occurrence of the cahow off the coasts of the Atlantic States can only be presumed. Similarly, the Guadalupe petrel, first noted on Guadalupe Island off Baja California in 1887, has never been recorded elsewhere, though probably it ranged to California before cats left behind by transient fishermen apparently overpowered it. Little is known of its original distribution, and it is not likely that we will learn much more, the species having disappeared after 1912. The short-tailed albatross of the western Pacific, on the other hand, was sighted offshore commonly, from Alaska to California, until an Oriental market for its feathers all but finished it, and is therefore a member *in absentia* of our fauna.

The diablotin, or black-capped petrel, not only has visited our coasts but has journeyed far inland. This oceanic wanderer makes its nest in West Indian mountain burrows, and has turned up, usually after storms, in such unlikely haunts as Kentucky, Ohio, New Hampshire, Ontario, and Central Park, in New York City. As a significant food source for mankind, however, it has a history almost as dark and brief as that of its near-relative, the cahow. An account dating from 1696 refers probably to the diablotin in observing that "The difficulty of hunting these birds preserves the species, which would have been entirely exterminated years ago, according to the bad custom of the French, did they not retire to localities which are not accessible to everyone." [8] Localities inaccessible to man, however, were readily accessible to mongooses and opossums imported to its islands, and as a consequence the species has all but disappeared. Its last nesting grounds are unknown, and the few sightings of this large black-and-white petrel in recent decades are largely of random individuals glimpsed on Columbus's western ocean. Columbus himself may well have seen it, and the ultimate record will doubtless be made from aboard ship. One imagines with a sense of foreboding this strange, solitary bird passing astern, its dark, sharp wing rising and vanishing like a fin as it banks stiffly among the crests until, scarcely discernible, it fades into eternities of sea.

The sight . . . is a pleasure not able to be expressed with tonge . . . full of herons, corleux, bitters, mallardes, egertes, woodcockes, and of all other kinde of smale birdes, with hartes, hyndes, buckes, wild swyne, and sondery other wild beastes as we perceved well both then by there foteing there and also afterwardes in other places by ther crye and brayeng which we herde in the night tyme. . . .   —JEAN RIBAUT (1563).

2 : The Tropical Border

THE SPANIARDS who extended the explorations of Columbus to the mainland were greeted by a variety of wildlife which will not be seen on this continent again. In addition to the animals of temperate America, they found an array of tropical species which had established in south Florida and along the Mexican border the northern outposts of their distribution. The latter were the first mainland species to give way to the white man's extension of his own range to the New World, and it may be that southern creatures now thought of as rare vagrants were once native, and that others have come and died away, entirely unrecorded.

Unhappily we know little of what the Spaniards saw, so intent were they on gold. Ponce de León, an adventurer of advancing years, was anxious as well to locate a fountain of youth, and his impatience allowed him little time to reflect on the natural scene. The accounts of the conquistadors who came after him were likewise few and imprecise. During three centuries of Spanish reign, the world was none the wiser for the existence in Florida of numerous animals not remarked upon until after 1819, when the Spanish left. An almost immediate discovery was the American crocodile, attaining an impressive length of no less than twenty-three feet; since it formerly ranged far up the east coast of Florida, as well as on the southwest coast and in the Keys, one wonders how so noteworthy a beast could have gone for so long undetected.

Three possibilities seem likely, the most obvious being that the American crocodile was never prosperous in Florida. Also, it is an unsociable inhabitant of mangrove archipelagos and other salt wastes of limited attraction to the Spanish then and to Americans now. Finally, there is every likelihood that the animal was confused with its more common kin, the freshwater alligator, which is smaller, browner, and broader through the nose, and does not expose an evil-looking tooth, a habit of the crocodile even when its capacious mouth is closed. The alligator, though pursued for its hide and much reduced in numbers, is not in present danger of extinction. Current laws for its protection do not always deter small boys and other assailants (in one part of Florida, not long ago, the alligators were virtually extirpated by an outraged citizenry when the badly chewed body of one small boy was discovered in the local swamp; as it happened, the child was naked, and it apparently occurred to no one to inquire by what unholy devices these man-eaters first removed his clothes). Nonetheless it has

ALLIGATOR   CROCODILE

reproduced itself sparingly from Texas to the Carolinas. The crocodile, which is thought to have come to Florida by way of the Gulf of Mexico—an Asian relative is known to have completed an ocean journey of over five hundred miles, from Java or Sumatra to the Cocos Islands—has withdrawn to the keys and mudbanks of the wild Cape Sable area.

The verb "withdraw" is used advisedly here. We are apt to think of wild animals as retreating from civilization in the same way that they might flee before a forest fire or flood. Actually, such retreat is ordinarily impossible, since any suitable habitat they might withdraw to is filled to capacity already by the same species. In other words, when one speaks of a species "withdrawing" or "retreating," one really means that it has been exterminated in certain units of its range, or that the habitats of the species within these units have been destroyed. It is the limits of the range which have retreated, for the affected animals themselves are dead.

The reptiles and amphibians of the world began a general withdrawal from existence many millions of years ago. The amphibians—newts, salamanders, caecilians, frogs, and toads—no longer play a significant role in the animal kingdom, serving chiefly as incidental food for other creatures, including man. In their great days, certain forms attained a size of fifteen feet or more, and might be said to have ruled the earth. Similarly, the huge reptiles which dominated the land, sea, and even the air of the Cretaceous are all gone. Of their numerous orders only four survive today, and one of these may vanish in our time, since its sole living representative, the lizard-like tuatara of New Zealand, is said to be on the threshold of extinction. The remaining reptilian orders—the turtles and tortoises, the crocodilians, and the snakes and lizards—are widespread in temperate and tropical regions, but their species are for the most part small, and a number of these, losing the use of limbs and sight as they seek shelter underground, become more and more degenerate as the centuries pass. Certain species are still prospering, but as a class the reptiles are slowly trailing the amphibians into obscurity.

In North America, only a few reptiles are large or impressive enough to attract man's attention. The poisonous snakes invite a certain deference, and the rattlesnake is even canned occasionally for human consumption. Small turtles and lizards are conscripted commonly as pets—the baby red-eared turtle, the green anole or "chameleon," and the horned lizard or "horned toad" are perhaps the most in demand. The diamond-back terrapin of Atlantic and Gulf Coast estuaries and salt marshes was at one time a popular delicacy, although the New York *Morning-Telegraph*, for May 7, 1912, was of the opinion that the terrapin "was never intended for vulgar palates." Nevertheless, the terrapin catch in the Chesapeake Bay area alone amounted to nearly 90,000 pounds in profitable years, and it was only a waning of interest in this expensive little animal which saved the species from extinction.

Since the alligator is generally protected, the last North American reptiles of economic significance are the sea turtles. The hawksbill turtle furnishes the "tortoise shell" of commerce, now largely replaced by plastics, but it is the green turtle, named for the hue of its edible fat, which has been referred to as the most valuable reptile in the world.

As early as 1620, "in regard that such waste and abuse hath been offered and yet is by sundrye lewd and impvident psons inhabitinge within these Islands who . . . snatch & catch up indifferentlye all kinds of Tortoyses both yonge and old . . . to the much decay of the breed of so excellent a fishe . . . ," the Bermuda Assembly passed "An Act Agaynst The Killinge Of Ouer Yonge Tortoyses," which protected any green turtle, as this fishe is now known, less than eighteen inches in breadth, within a fifteen-mile radius of the islands. Offenders were fined fifteen pounds of tobacco, half of which was put to public use and half presented to the informer.

These measures were finally in vain. The green turtle no longer breeds in Bermuda, nor anywhere in North America. So abundant in colonial times, from Massachusetts to Florida, that a man might catch one hundred off Cape Hatteras in a single day, it declined with the addition of the white man to its long list of predators. On the Florida coast, according to Audubon, both adults and egg nests were preyed upon by turtlers, bears, cougars, and bobcats, and, if the latter two enemies seem implausible, the fact remains that no nest has been found in Florida for over fifty years. Reaching a weight of five hundred pounds or more, the green turtle frequents the algae beds of shallow waters and buries its eggs in the sand of open beaches, two habits which, increasing its vulnerability, have helped to reduce it to its present low estate. A market is still operative at Key West for green turtles taken anywhere in the Caribbean, and a point may be reached where individuals become so scattered along the countless tropic coasts as to fail to form an effective breeding population. The last green turtle, one of the few large species to survive the Age of Reptiles, will probably live its life out undetected. Seeking a mate, it may glide for many years over remote lagoon bottoms, its heavy shell crusting with marine creatures, until it comes to rest on some final sand, too ancient to stir ever again.

GREEN TURTLE

The land Ponce de León named Florida in 1513 contains today the last true wilderness in the nation. The Everglades, a trackless waste of swamp and hammock, sawgrass and palmetto, of orchids and strangler figs and poisonous manchineel, rolls south a hundred miles from Lake Okeechobee to the mangrove estuaries and shallow flats of Cape Sable, Florida Bay, and the inner Keys. The Cape Sable area is also vast and virtually uninhabited, and Okeechobee itself is twenty miles across. To the north of the lake lies a different wilderness, broad distances of long-grass prairie, the Kissimmee, some wild birds of which are not again encountered anywhere east of the coastal plains of Texas. Cypress swamps and limestone springs provide other distinct habitats, and far out in the Gulf the Dry Tortugas, named for the green turtles that once abounded there, support tropical sea birds seen nowhere else in North America.

A good deal of Florida's flora and fauna is peculiar to this four-hundred-mile peninsula, a fact not surprising when one considers that much of it is tropic, remote biologically from the temperate land mass to the north and remote geographically from other areas in the same latitudes. Its waters, fresh and salt, still swarm with fish, and its wildernesses, resistant to man, shelter a variety of life unmatched elsewhere on the continent. Florida can claim today almost all its original land mammals, including significant populations of the bobcat, river otter, black bear, and cougar, or mountain lion.

WEST INDIAN MONK SEAL

Though a number of its species are uncommon, comparatively few are presently in danger. Among wild creatures rarity is a relative condition, not always determined on the basis of actual numbers. Creatures uncommon in Florida are often abundant in the lands and islands to the south; similarly, what might be an endangered population for a widespread, gregarious, and economically significant species would be very healthy indeed for one by nature localized or solitary. In point of fact, the only endangered Florida creatures not found elsewhere in the tropics—the miniature key deer and the greenish Cape Sable sparrow—are probably no more than isolated races of the white-tailed deer and seaside sparrow, two very widespread forms.

The species which most concern us, therefore, are those which were once common on the southern boundaries but are now in various stages of disappearance, as well as those which, everywhere scarce, include this continent among their last retreats. They are not many, but as a group they are unusually interesting and picturesque, and their loss, in a few cases already consummated, will be a serious one to North American wildlife.

The obscure West Indian monk seal was once widespread in the Caribbean, but vanished first as early as 1835. A small herd discovered in the Triangle Islands, off Yucatán, a half-century later, was promptly set upon by zoo collectors and other enthusiasts, with the result that, over the years, at least four became residents of the New York Aquarium. A second result, compounded by West Indian natives who pursue the species for food and oil, was the virtual certainty of its eventual extinction: the last seal seen in Florida appeared at Key West in 1922, and though a few persist in the Yucatán islands, they are vulnerable to passing fishermen, and will probably disappear in the near future.

Ponce de León, who landed first north of St. Augustine, then rounded Florida to the west coast, and touched at the Dry Tortugas, very likely came upon this animal; coursing the coastal waterways, he must also have seen the manatee. A Spaniard named Hernández was subsequently impressed by the manatee's mental acumen, but actually the species could not even be called alert. A large, phlegmatic browser of submerged herbage, it is best known for its breasts, rude appendages which formed the apparent basis of the mermaid legends, since the manatee, cleft-faced, wrinkled, and bristled, qualifies in no other respect. Once common enough on the coasts of the Gulf States, the West Indies, and northern South America, with a few individuals summering as far north as Virginia, the hapless manatee continues to be shot, not only as incidental food by local people but by nautical tourists seeking target practice. Others are killed by recurrent cold waves, by boat propellers, and infrequently by crocodiles and sharks. A few persist in southern Florida, where, literally and figuratively, they appear to be treading water.

The Spanish may never have consumed this beast, for history shows that, even in emergencies, they were slow to take advantage of natural provender. Their early attempts to colonize southern coasts were marked by chronic famine, and the transient French colonists in Florida in 1564

MANATEE

fared no better. Soldiers and gentlemen, the European adventurers disdained agriculture, and when their supplies were gone they made bread from old fish bones, and begged food of the same red men for whom they had shown contempt.

By this time, the "Christians," as the Indians knew them, were renowned for brutality in all the native villages of the Southeast. Unlike Columbus, who was touched by the simplicity of the aborigines and forbade unfair trade with them, these ungentle men had their hearts set on plunder. Ponce de León, the victim of an arrow, perished for his pains, as did Vázquez de Ayllón, five years later in Carolina, and Pánfilo de Narváez, who once appeased his frustrated zeal with the slaughter of two thousand peaceful savages. (Though the latter incident should assure Narváez's place in history, his fame stems chiefly from the fact that Cabeza de Vaca, whose fantastic wanderings on foot from the Gulf Coast through Texas and New Mexico became one of the great sagas of early America, was a survivor of the Narváez expedition.) Not surprisingly, the Indians were hostile when the redoubtable de Soto, between 1539 and 1542, struggled north and west from the swamps of Florida to the Carolinas, Arkansas, and Texas, leading a full complement of armored cavalry and foot soldiers and, more remarkable still, one thousand-odd balky swine.

The few contributions to American natural history made by these strong men were largely inadvertent. The American wild mustang and burro are Spanish fugitives, and de Soto's swine, which escaped in numbers, are said to be ancestors of the modern wild razorback hogs of southern swamplands; his expedition also discovered the Mississippi paddlefish, a primitive spade-snouted relative of the sturgeons found in large inland waters. Coronado, journeying north out of Mexico in the same period and wandering as far as Kansas in search of the elusive gold, returned with the first full reports of prairie dogs and bison. "During May," he remarked of the latter, "they shed the hair on the rear half of their body and look exactly like lions." [1]

More important, Coronado saw, somewhere in New Mexico, a predator which once prowled north to central California and east to Louisiana. The jaguar is the greatest cat of the Americas, resembling a very large, heavy-set leopard. Like the much smaller ocelot (and unlike the margay and jaguarundi cats, which, in company with the coati, some tropical bats, and smaller mammals, wander infrequently as far north as extreme south Texas and southeast Arizona), "el tigre" was formerly an established species north to the Red River in Arkansas, and a number of debatable early

OCELOT

records place it as far east as the Appalachians. An account of the coastal Carolinas in 1711 notes that "Tygers . . . are more to the Westward. . . . I once saw one that was larger than a Panther [i.e. cougar], and seemed to be a very bold Creature. . . . It seems to differ from the Tyger of Asia and Africa." [2] Another writer subsequently stated that they were found in the mountains of North Carolina as late as 1737. Audubon's contemporary, Richard Harlan, claimed the jaguar was still seen east of the Mississippi in the beginning of the nineteenth century, though this seems quite unlikely. The short, explosive roar of this fierce creature was silenced early, at least partly as a consequence of bounties imposed by early Spanish authorities in the Southwest. It was last recorded in California in 1860, and in New Mexico about 1903, and although an occasional animal still prowls the Texas and Arizona border the jaguar must now be considered extirpated from North America. The ocelot, though it frequents three counties in south Texas, will probably follow close behind.

The most frequent southern visitors are, of course, the birds, and species new to North America are still recorded periodically. These include a scattering of West Indian wanderers as well as the parrots, trogons, chachalacas, and other jungle criers which cross the lower Rio Grande and the border of southeast Arizona. Such strong-winged birds as pigeons and hawks stray north in considerable variety, and some of these remain to nest. But most tropic species are transient, however numerous, and seldom become truly established; the brilliant scarlet ibis and the flamingo, for example, while considered quite common until a century ago, were never shown to have bred on our southern coasts, and probably were always more noticeable than abundant.

The species which remain established in North America over a significant range are usually members of three orders: the wading birds, the pigeons,

JAGUAR

and the hawks. Some waders—herons and egrets, ibises, and the roseate spoonbill—are here in numbers, and their bright, noisy rookeries are a striking facet of the southern coasts and swamps; though not all of them are common, their peril as a group came about through special circumstance (see Chapter 8), and is largely past. Most southern doves and pigeons are so local in their distribution here as to be of small importance; three exceptions of wider range—the band-tailed pigeon, and the ground and white-winged doves—are, like the waders, in no present danger of extirpation. The southern hawks, solitary symbols of the passing wilderness in the dead trees of defeated landscapes, are, on the other hand, vanishing one by one.

The birds of prey peculiar to the South include kites, buteos, a falcon, and a curious falcon relative of vulturish appetites, the caracara, which is found locally in south Texas and Arizona, and on the Kissimmee Prairie of central Florida.

Of these, the best known is the Everglade kite, which escaped attention even longer than the crocodile. Though it once bred commonly all through the southern Everglades, it has never occurred north of Tallahassee Bay, and its first nest was not located until 1896. The white man has since made vain attempts to domesticate the Everglades through drainage, a project which, in company with drought, has largely eradicated the only known food of this black, red-beaked, and sadly over-specialized hawk, the fresh-water moon snail, *Pomacea caliginosus*. The Everglade kite, confined in recent years to remote corners of Okeechobee, is shot at consistently by restless duck hunters—as many as five have been found floating in front of a

CARACARA

single blind—and, as of this moment, is the rarest bird in North America. It is also increasingly scarce in Cuba, though a southern race occurs quite commonly from Veracruz and Campeche in Mexico south through the Americas. As a species, indeed, it may be in less danger than three other kites which also occur on this continent.

The kites are among the most graceful of hawks, and the swallow-tailed kite, which resembles a great black and white swallow, is perhaps the most striking of all North American birds. It once turned and slipped through the air of two continents, from Canada to the Argentine, and has been glimpsed as far east as New Hampshire, as far west as Colorado. One bird even engineered the difficult west-east crossing of the North Atlantic, and appeared in the British Isles. Sharing the tameness of all kites, however, it has remained innocent in the ways of man, and his firearms have reduced it to a pitiful remnant in the remote swamps of Florida, South Carolina, and Louisiana.

The white-tailed kite, in turn, has withdrawn westward, and, though once native to Florida and the Gulf States, is now rarely seen east of California, where by 1927 there were thought to be less than one hundred remaining. Its abundance appears to be controlled by the plenitude of field mice, to which these birds are addicted to the point of specialization, and its chief peril lies in the destruction of mice pasture by modern farm machinery and overgrazing. It is uncommon throughout its range, which extends to Guatemala, and may be the rarest of the kites. Sometimes it nests in orange groves, and the spectacle of this delicate gray-mantled bird, head and tail a vivid white against the bright green and orange of a sunny orchard, is not easily forgotten.

The Mississippi kite, blue-gray and black-tailed, has perhaps fared better, though it, too, has withdrawn southward from a range which once included

MISSISSIPPI KITE
WHITE-TAILED KITE
SWALLOW-TAILED KITE
EVERGLADE KITE (female)   EVERGLADE KITE (male)

SHORT-TAILED HAWK

the Central States; unlike its relatives, it is not native to the tropics, and it drifts south of the border only in winter.

The buteos or buzzard hawks include those familiar to most of us, the ones that circle to black pinpoints on blue seas of summer sky. They are also known, quite inaccurately, as "chicken hawks," and are severely persecuted for the depredations of foxes, raccoons, and the great horned owl. Nevertheless, though much reduced, the northern buteos have managed to maintain safe numbers: it is the southern visitors, never firmly established, that will be the first to go.

The small short-tailed hawk, which maintains an uneasy foothold in the Cape Sable jungles, is one that might be mentioned here since, unlike the tropical buteos frequenting the Mexican border country, it is rare throughout its Central and South American range. Among its relatives in the Southwest, three barely penetrate the United States, and a fourth, the handsome Harris's hawk, is still readily seen in the southern parts of all the border states. However, the white-tailed hawk, a pale soarer once widespread in the Great Plains country of south Texas, is dying out with the invasion of this grassland by mesquite and brush, which make its open-country hunting difficult.

The Great Plains, extending to the Texas coast, have traditionally been a mighty sea of grass. Over the years, however, the country has been fenced and broken, while its cattle ranching has grown ever more intensive. One result, by no means inevitable, has been overgrazing, which stamps out the food grasses, encourages flash floods and erosion, and, followed by drought,

WHITE-TAILED HAWK

can turn the land at last to sand and gravel. The bare land cannot carry prairie fires, which formerly served to kill back or eradicate the stubborn brush, and the thrifty mesquite and opuntia cactus invade quickly. Meanwhile, the draining of the small rivers for irrigation has lowered the water table in the region. The shallow ponds and oxbow swales dry out and crack, and valley woodlands of mulberry, huge live oak, and the raspy-leafed anacua—dense groves which sheltered jaguar and the small red wolf—shrink and wither away. Great areas of grass and woodland thus give way to mesquite desert, at an awesome economic loss to man. In the case of the white-tailed hawk and other forms of wildlife, this destruction of suitable habitat may prove fatal.

Though man is the usual catalyst, the causes of scarcity are rarely identical for any two species, and the hawks are no exception. All hawks, however, have been heavily reduced by that body of American gunners which regards the passing bird of prey as a fair target, and the danger is particularly grave when the species in question, like the beautiful, black-bellied Aplomado falcon, has never been a common bird. This swift, sharp-winged hawk flew north formerly to the deserts and dry canyons of the Southwest, and remained in certain areas to nest. Because of its rarity it also fell victim to oölogists, and especially to that avid breed of amateurs which, in its curious need to possess an uncommon egg, has too often presided at the extinction of a species. The Aplomado falcon is no longer a breeding bird of the United States, and is not often seen even in Mexico.

Though somewhat foreshortened, the Florida wilderness has so far survived man's best efforts to destroy it, if not to deface it, and to a lesser degree the same might be said of much of the swamp-tangled Gulf Coast. Increasing populations and industrialization in these regions, with accompanying development and drainage of marshes by omnivorous earth-moving equipment like the drag line, now present a serious threat to the coastal lowlands and their wildlife, the wading birds in particular, but it is in south Texas that the destruction of habitat has been most alarming. Not only are the grassland environments deteriorating, but the north bank of the lower Rio Grande, an area unique in the United States, is succumbing swiftly to development and drought. This small wedge of valley between the border and Rio Hondo, extending upriver a scant sixty-five miles, supports the last virgin red elm, hackberry, huisache, and ebony jungle in the nation, and an array of tropical birds and other creatures found nowhere else above the border.

The Rio Grande road, north and west, crosses a parched arroyo, Tigre Grande, named in memory of some historic jaguar. Beyond Laredo, the traveler encounters a mesquite-and-gravel badland which may well be the most oppressive landscape in the country, and it is only at the junction of the Rio Grande with the Pecos that a certain monumental quality offsets the desolation. The western mountains appear in the form of brown foothills, and the plateaus, high-flowered with yucca and prickly pear, take on a pale, fierce beauty. Seen across the desert washes from the north, the canyons and dark, cluttered peaks of the Big Bend are especially stirring. From here the Rio Grande, narrow and slow, curls north into New Mexico, and Old Mexico, a dust-misted world ever visible to the southward, suggests a limitless extension of brown barren.

The mountains of southeast Arizona rise from the desert floor like islands

APLOMADO FALCON, with Gambel's quail

MASKED BOBWHITE

from the sea, and here one finds an odd oasis. High desert valleys, like deep river beds among the mountain masses, climb to sage foothills and painted canyons, chaparral slopes and sharp-shadowed, grassy ravines; higher still, cool deciduous woods turn to northern evergreen—ponderosa pine and Douglas fir and Engelmann spruce—and finally to snow peaks. The wide range of habitats to be found within a few thousand perpendicular feet shelter everything from cactus wrens to chickadees, including such rare visitors as the rose-throated becard, but here, too, overgrazing of the spare grassland has encouraged blight and a serious decline of the game birds of the border region. The first to suffer, predictably, were those more at home below the border.

The masked bobwhite, a speckled, rich-hued race of the common quail, was native in the nineteenth century to this part of the country, and was even abundant in the Altar Valley foothills. With the introduction of cattle, its narrow grassland habitat was devoured, and the last United States bird was reported killed in the Baboquivari Mountains in 1912. Within a few years it was also presumed extinct in Mexico, but in the late twenties it returned from the dead in a most dramatic fashion. An American tourist familiar with birds stopped for dinner at a Mexican inn, and ordered quail. Since the order was to take a little while, he walked around outside, and, happening into the back yard, discovered forty-odd masked bobwhite in a cage, including the bird intended for his dinner. He purchased the entire flock and carried them over the border, and these birds became the nucleus for the captive stock now found in the United States. Though a few wild birds are still thought to exist in remote areas of the state of Sonora, the survival of the breed may yet depend on the fact that an informed traveler ordered quail at a certain wayside *cantina*.

The bobwhite's relative, the harlequin-faced "fool quail," earned its common name as a consequence of its trusting nature, which has contributed importantly to its decline. The harlequin quail, in recent years, has become uncommon to very rare throughout its American range, from west Texas to southern Arizona, and though it has been called "one of Arizona's rarer vanishing birds," [3] it has not yet gotten its proper share of attention. The other desert quails and the Merriam's turkey, a western race once in serious peril, are of interest to sportsmen and therefore receive a good deal more encouragement.

The border westward from southeastern Arizona, across the Sonoran and Colorado Deserts to the green slopes of coastal California, traverses an arid, stony land on which man has had little effect. The region attracts few tropical vagrants, since that part of Sonora lying south of this stretch of boundary is largely the *Gran Desierto*, an awesome waste of black volcanic rock and blinding sand which spreads to the sterile salt shores of the Gulf of California; the north part of the Baja California peninsula, cut off by salt water and desert from the Mexican mainland, shelters a fauna related closely to that of adjoining areas in the United States.

As a group, then, the tropical species have withdrawn southward, but it should be noted that a few of them have reversed the process and continue to extend their northern range. The bizarre, armor-plated armadillo, an obscure border mammal only a quarter-century ago, has burrowed its way north to Oklahoma and Arkansas and east to Louisiana and west Florida, and in its near-sighted fashion gives every indication of intending to push onward. A much more extravagant example is that of the cattle egret, long an inhabitant of Africa and southern Asia, which apparently crossed the

ARMADILLO

HARLEQUIN QUAIL

South Atlantic to South America some thirty years ago, and first appeared in Florida in 1948, the same year it traveled to Australia. In the past decade, far from behaving in the reticent manner of the usual exotic, it has established itself in several states and has visited widely on this continent. The first Canadian specimen alighted on a Grand Banks trawler in 1952, and three of these enterprising birds have since contrived, by some incredible hook or crook, to find Bermuda in the open ocean.

Ornithologists were startled by this explosion of egrets, for which no satisfactory explanation has been found, but they agree that the main reason for the bird's success, once it arrived, was the lack of native competition. Feeding chiefly on insects disturbed by browsing cattle, they fill an unoccupied "ecological niche"; no native species had yet learned to adjust its habits so precisely to the white man's livestock.

The concept of ecology—the relationships of living things to their environments—is important to an understanding of wildlife abundance. In nature, each creature has a niche or environment in which it finds the conditions necessary for survival and reproduction. The dimensions of this niche vary considerably with the range of conditions which the species in question can tolerate: certain salamanders, for example, cannot exist outside of subterranean caves, while the sperm whale finds matters to its liking throughout the oceans of the world.

In addition, a creature is more or less "adaptable" according to its ability to adjust to alterations in its environment. As a general rule, the younger genera still evolving, less specialized than more ancient forms, can adapt more readily and therefore tend to be more abundant throughout a wider

CATTLE EGRET

range. The range of a specialized creature may be extensive, but it is usually controlled by one or more precise factors. The Everglade kite, as we have seen, is restricted to certain types of marsh. Amphibians, which cannot tolerate salt water, never spread to oceanic islands, as reptiles, birds, and even small mammals, drifting on floating trees, have been known to do. Both amphibians and reptiles are paralyzed by cold, and are therefore confined to the temperate zones and tropics. Crows, bears, and man, on the other hand, not only are omnivorous but are able to adjust to wide limits of temperature and climate. Adaptable or not, however, no animal can survive the destruction of its environment. A poisoning of the earth's atmosphere, for example, would prove fatal even to that most adaptable of all creatures, man.

Man the predator, as a sudden and violent new factor in the animal ecologies of North America, was to overwhelm the great auk and other species. But his indirect effects, and primarily the mutilation of his surroundings which accompanied his settlement, would prove most harmful to wildlife at large. In the course of his invasion of the New World, the forests and rivers, plains and prairies suffered changes more drastic than those undergone in all the hundred centuries since the last glacier, and even creatures never preyed upon directly declined rapidly in his wake.

The course of man's march across the continent has generally been north and west. In the time of Coronado, the Spanish were already probing northward on the new ocean discovered by Balboa. Though they settled Santa Fe by 1610, they were not to colonize California for two centuries, despite the fact that one Juan Cabrillo may have sailed as far as Oregon as early as 1542. Nor were the English far behind him. In 1579 Sir Francis

Drake, the distinguished gentleman pirate, ventured north through the "vile, thick, and stinking fogs",[4] of this verdant coast, seeking the western exit of a Northwest Passage to India. Across the silent continent, the vastness of which had yet to be imagined, other Europeans sought an eastern entrance, touching at Baffin Land and Hudson Strait. Their countrymen, in the next decades, would settle the east coast, where the first explorers at Roanoke had "found such plenty, as well there as in all places else, both on the sand and on the green soil of the hills, as in the plains, as well as on every little shrub . . . that . . . in all the world the like abundance is not to be found. . . ."[5]

Besides, what could they see but a hideous and desolate wilderness, full of wild beasts and wild men? And what multitudes there might be of them they knew not.   —WILLIAM BRADFORD (c. 1620)

3 : The Eastern Slope

EARLY IMPRESSIONS of the riches, fine climate, and gentle denizens of the New World were recorded almost entirely by adventurers who arrived at benevolent seasons, observed from a distance, and, having exploited their simple hosts, withdrew. The people who came after, bent on settling this paradise, had a contrary reaction. With the departure of their ships for Europe, they felt homeless, cast away, and the wild animals and dark forests dismayed them. They had not been prepared for the fierce extremes of climate, or for the hostile reception of the natives. The French and Spanish in Florida, after 1562, paid dearly for the ill will engendered by the conquistadors; and the very same people whom Captain Barlowe described, on the first voyage to Roanoke, in 1584, as "most gentle, loving, and faithful, void of all guile and treason, and such as live after the manner of the golden age" [1] almost certainly contrived the total disappearance of that colony a few years later for reasons which, considering the treatment of the red men then in fashion, must have seemed to them excellent. The James-town Settlement, in 1607, managed to survive this cumulative hatred, but it was cruelly beset by savages "creeping on all fours from the hills like bears, with their bows in their mouths." [2] To the wretched colonists, al-ready plagued with famine and disease, the Indian betrayed small evidence of the golden age; as Bradford would discover at Plymouth, the natives seemed far "readier to fill their sides full of arrows than otherwise." [3]

The Jamestown and Plymouth colonies prevailed because, unlike pre-vious settlements, they managed to live off the land. When the *Mayflower* rounded Cape Cod in 1620, tobacco had already been grown and exported from Jamestown, and a Virginia price list of 1621 indicates an extensive fur trade. Mink, marten, otter, and wildcat brought up to ten shillings apiece, and prime beaver were worth seven. Sturgeon and caviar were also commodities; as Captain John Smith noted, "We had more Sturgeon, than could be devoured by Dog and Man," [4] and over a century and a half later, the sea sturgeons still ascended the Virginia rivers in multitudes.

At Plymouth, despite an inauspicious start, a fine first spring had im-proved the Pilgrim spirits. The Indians, weakened by disease, were at pains to be obliging, and by September, Edward Winslow, for one, was very optimistic:

> I never in my life remember a more seasonable year than we have here enjoyed; and if we have once but kine, horses, and sheep, I make no question but that men might live as contented here as any part of the world. For fish and fowl, we have great abundance. Fresh cod in the summer is but coarse meat with us. Our bay is full of lobsters all the summer, and affords a variety of other fish. . . . The country wants only industrious men to employ; for it would grieve your hearts if, as I, you had seen so many miles together by goodly rivers uninhabited. . . .[5]

Thomas Morton, whose dexterity at bartering with the Indians and unseemly appetite for diversion so upset the Pilgrims that Miles Standish was sent to lay hands on him and pack him off to England, left apparently without ill will, for this happy man confirmed Winslow's good report in his own *New English Canaan*, one of the first books to give significant attention to the animal life of North America. (Previously, John White, gentleman, of the ill-fated Roanoke colony, had done watercolors of the loggerhead turtle, alligator, frigate bird, pelican, and other creatures, and John Smith described some twenty birds in his *Map of Virginia*; minor references had also been made elsewhere.) Morton's discovery of "pide Ducks, gray Ducks, and black Ducks in great abundance," and "Millions of Turtledoves one the greene boughes . . . whose fruitfull loade did cause the armes to bend . . ." [6] can only have enticed further innocents from abroad.

"Of birds diversely colored there are infinite," the Calverts wrote from Maryland in 1633. "Eagles, bitterns, swans, geese, partridge, ducks, red, blue, partly-colored birds, and the like. By all which it appears, the country abounds not only with profit but with pleasure. And to say truth, there wants nothing for perfecting of this hopeful plantation; but greater numbers of our countrymen to enjoy it." [7] One must keep in mind that the glad reports of this period were motivated in part by the colonists' desire to share with others an existence made miserable as much by their own religious strictures as by hardship. Winslow, Morton, and the Calverts notwithstanding, the prevailing view for a century to come would be closer to that of the poet Michael Wigglesworth, who, concluding that the Almighty nursed a grudge against New England, called it "a waste and howling wilderness." [8] According to the Reverend Cotton Mather, the Devil himself had placed the Indians in this North American limbo, presumably to cheat them of God's tender mercies, including those visited upon them by His European henchmen in their program of conversion-by-the-sword. Though best known as a defender of the faith against the perfidies of witches, this holy man was also an early commentator on the natural scene, and was of the firm opinion that the wild pigeons, in their annual departure from his domain, repaired to "some undiscovered Satellite, accompanying the Earth at a near Distance." [9] This view of their disappearance, as it turned out, was little more preposterous than others to be advanced two centuries later.

The wild pigeon, wood pigeon, or turtledove had been from the very beginning a symbol of the huge resources of the new continent. Cartier had been struck by its abundance, and Champlain slaughtered quantities on the coastal islands on his early trips to New France. But the passenger pigeon, as we now know this bird, was a mixed blessing for the Pilgrims. In 1643, it descended on the Plymouth crops with such violence as to cause a serious threat of famine. Five years later, however, an epidemic of pigeons when crops were poor staved off a famine, and their effect was generally beneficial. Indeed, they were slaughtered with such enthusiasm that by 1672 John Josselyn could observe, "But of late they are much diminished, the English taking them with Nets." [10] Though the birds sold in Boston as late as 1736 at six for a penny, the great flocks were already disappearing from the East.

The pigeon, like all wildlife of the period, was treated according to Mather's edict that "what is not useful is vicious," for, except in Bermuda, the earliest game laws in the colonies were negative in tone, promoting destruction rather than protection. In 1629, three years after the settlement of New Amsterdam, the Dutch West India Company, like the Plymouth Colony before it, encouraged the prosecution of its fur trade by granting hunting privileges to persons settling the New Netherlands. The following year, the Massachusetts Bay Company established the first New World bounty system with the payment of one penny per wolf, a hint as to wolf numbers—assuming a wolfer could make an honest shilling at his trade—which staggers the mind. Undoubtedly the gray wolf was incredibly numerous, and its depredations were prodigious. As Morton's contemporary, William Wood, observed in his *New England's Prospect*, "there is little hope of their utter destruction, the Countrey being so spacious, and they so numerous, travelling in the Swamps by Kennels: sometimes ten to twelve are of a company. Late at night, and early in the morning, they set up their howlings and call their companies together, at night to hunt, at morning to sleepe; in a word, they may be the greatest inconvenience the Countrey hath, both for matter of dammage to private men in particular, and the whole Countrey in generall." In 1717, nearly a century later,

GRAY WOLF

wolves were still so prevalent that a project to build a fence clear across Cape Cod, from Sandwich to Wareham, was seriously considered. The idea was to make a livestock sanctuary of the outer Cape, but people living on the wrong side of the proposed fence, imagining that they would have even more of these "ravening rangers" to deal with, malingered, and the enterprise was defeated.

Meanwhile, the other colonies had bountied the wolf, and by 1800 its "utter destruction" in New England and in eastern Canada had been largely effected. Connecticut had already withdrawn its bounty, and the last wolf in New England was killed in Maine in 1860, though the animal prevailed in Pennsylvania and upper New York State until the turn of the twentieth century; New York paid out six bounties on the wolf in 1897.

Farther south, New Jersey established bounties on the wolf in 1697, allowing ten shillings to Negroes and Indians and twice that sum to "Christian" killers. In fact, the animal was very common south to Florida, and John Lawson, surveyor-general of North Carolina, remarked in 1711 that "they go in great Droves by night." His *History of North Carolina*, which devotes considerable space to wildlife, antedates by two decades the better-known work by Mark Catesby which is generally considered to be the first American natural history. Lawson's observations on the abundance of wolves, cougars, beaver, wild pigeons, parakeets, trumpeter swans, turkeys, and sturgeon, among others, are accurate and, in the light of subsequent events, illuminating. To a certain extent, Lawson deprecates the wolf legend: "They are not Man-slayers, neither is any Creature in Carolina unless wounded." (If Lawson shared the opinion then prevalent that the Indian was one of the native "Creatures," he was mistaken in this latter observation, for he himself was slain by red men whose wounds, presumably, were only spiritual.) It is the cougar, or mountain lion, rather than the wolf, which he calls "the greatest Enemy to the Planter of any Varmine in Carolina." Of the bison, he says, "He seldom appears amongst the English inhabitants, his chief Haunt being in the Land of Massiasippi."

Catesby, in 1731, agrees that "this awful creature" was rarely seen among the Carolina settlements, and that the wolves "go in droves by night, and hunt deer like hounds with dismal, yelling cries." He confirms the "incredible numbers" of pigeons, which he claims were commonly shot from rooftops in Philadelphia and New York. In regard to the "hooping Crane," an Indian informed him "that early in the Spring, great multitudes of them frequent the lower parts of the Rivers near the Sea"; of the elk he says, "they usually accompany bufaloes, with whom they range in droves in the upper and remote parts of *Carolina*." He mentions the consumption of songbirds—the "rice-birds [i.e. bobolinks] are esteemed in Carolina the greatest delicacy of all other Birds"—and was one of the first to refer to the "Largest White-bill Woodpecker," or ivory-bill, suggesting that its destruction was already in vogue at the time of the first settlements: "The bills of these birds are much valued by the Canada Indians, who make coronets of them for their Princes and great warriors, by fixing them round a wreath, with their points outward. The Northern *Indians*, having none of these birds in their cold country, purchase them of the Southern people at the price of two, and sometimes three buckskins a bill."

Catesby also refers in a significant manner to the fatal habits of the sole North American parrot: "The orchards in autumn are visited by numerous flights of them; where they make great destruction for their kernels only: for the same purpose they frequent Virginia; which is the furthest North I ever heard they had been seen. Their guts are certain and speedy poison to Cats." This latter observation is but one of a number of vivid mistakes, but Catesby for his time was a scientific observer, working in the main with first-hand evidence; though the eminent French writers Buffon and Brisson were his near-contemporaries in Europe, their material on American forms lacks his authority. His notations on the beneficial habits of snakes in regard to rodents, on the bald eagle's habit of pirating the osprey, and so on, are precocious and do him credit; as the minutes of the Royal Society for December 21, 1732, attest, he was "a gentleman well skilled in Botany and Natural History, who travelled for several years in various parts of America." [11] His "curious and magnificent work," to give it its full name, was *The Natural History of Carolina, Florida, and the Bahama Islands, containing the figures of Birds, Beasts, Fishes, Ser-*

pents, Insects, and Plants. To which are added, Observations on the Air, Soil and Waters: with Remarks upon Agriculture, Grain, Pulse, Roots, Etc. It is dedicated to Queen Caroline—"I hope your Majesty will not think a few Minutes disagreeably spent, in casting an Eye on these Glorious Works of the Creator, displayed in the New World; and hitherto lain concealed from the View of Your Majesty. . . ." and its illustrations, as Catesby makes bold to suggest, are by no means contemptible. His birds are presented against a floral background (an innovation which Audubon was to develop to better advantage), and a few of them, though stiff with the heraldic air common to wildlife portraits of the time, are striking. American natural history owes much to Mark Catesby, who has been everlastingly commemorated in the Latin name of no less a species than the common bullfrog.

The name *Rana catesbiana*, as this imposing amphibian is known to science, represents a system of nomenclature which saw its inception in the *Systema Naturae* of Linnaeus, a few years after Catesby's death. An erudite Swede, Carl von Linné, with his assistant Gmelin, established the binomial system, by which the world's flora and fauna are quickly identified and related according to genus and species, rather than in vague, general terms (Catesby called the bullfrog *Rana maxima Americana Aquatica*); the genus *Homo*, to cite a familiar example, is composed of several species, among which *sapiens* alone has lived to tell the tale. The Linnaean system, though dispelling much early confusion and redundancy and rendering obsolete Mark Catesby and his predecessors, encouraged a minor evil which plagues the natural sciences to this day. Since its consequences will be referred to increasingly later on, it may as well be dealt with promptly.

In the nineteenth century the number of undiscovered bird and mammal species fell far behind the number of would-be discoverers, and partly, at least, as an outlet for frustrated zeal, many species were discovered all over again, by the simple expedient of dividing them into geographic races, or subspecies. These new forms were alleged to exhibit evolutionary departures from the forms originally described, and were immortalized by the prompt attachment of a subspecific name to the original two, in what became known as the trinomial system; the song sparrow, to name one ubiquitous bird, is represented in the 1957 edition of the American Ornithologists' Union checklist by no less than thirty-one varieties.

In the course of time, one or more pairs of an active species may become

WHITE-CROWNED SPARROW

NUTTALL'S
WHITE-CROWNED SPARROW

separated from the ancestral population, establishing themselves on the far side of a mountain range, perhaps, or on an offshore island, though the geographic barrier is not always so well defined. If the food, climate, competition, and other conditioning factors in the new range differ appreciably from those in the original home of the species, certain changes or mutations may appear in the superficial characters of the animal; should these become sufficiently marked, the population is then recognized as a subspecies.

Thus, a traveler on the Pacific coast in spring and summer, journeying from Santa Barbara, say, to the Olympic Peninsula, and flying on to South Alaska, will encounter three distinct subspecies of the white-crowned sparrow, *Zonotrichia leucophrys*. Nuttall's white-crowned sparrow, *Z. l. nuttalli*, of coastal California is replaced on the Oregon and Washington coasts by *Z. l. pugetensis*, which is noticeably darker. From southern British Columbia northward, the Puget Sound sparrow is replaced in turn by Gambel's white-crowned sparrow, *Z. l. gambeli*, which differs from the preceding subspecies in possessing a pinkish rather than yellowish bill. At the limits of their ranges, the subspecies intergrade, producing intermediate races chiefly distinguishable to the amateur by their variations on the slow, wistful song peculiar to this bird.

If its isolation is complete and its separate evolution is continued long enough, a subspecies may undergo mutations of its reproductive organs. Should this bring about the loss of mutual fertility with its ancestral form, it is then considered a new and distinct species, though in certain instances distinct species are recognized which have not lost the capacity to inter-breed, e.g., the wolf and the domestic dog. Nevertheless, the inability to breed successfully with any other form of life is the usual criterion of a species; subspecies are essentially identical, and can interbreed. Some authorities maintain that the absence of intermediate races between differing populations is sufficient evidence for naming a new species, but there is no general agreement on this point, and decisions in the matter are often arbitrary. The American Ornithologists' Union, for example, considers the

CAPE SABLE SPARROW

Cape Sable sparrow and the Ipswich sparrow valid species, but many noted
field men regard these rare forms as well-defined subspecies of the common
seaside and savanna sparrows, respectively. The sparrows, perhaps the
youngest of the bird families, are still in an active state of evolution, and
the complex and continuing differentiations among their members continue to be a source of controversy.

For most of us, in any case, it is less important that the turkey, prairie
chicken, wolf, cougar, bison, elk, and other creatures now extirpated from
the East were subspecies than that such creatures ever existed there
at all. One is apt to think of them as southern or western forms, as indeed
they were, for all practical purposes, by the nineteenth century. By that
time the settlers, having discouraged the native peoples in such early
battles as the Pequot and King Philip's Wars in the North and the Tusca-
rora War in the South, were able to move quite freely through the country
east of the Appalachians, and the large animals in their path died out.
The wolf of the southeast disappeared with its northern kin, though a
last one was reported in North Carolina in 1905. The cougar prevailed a
little longer, though its bounty in Connecticut was last paid in 1769. It
occurred in Vermont and New Hampshire as late as 1880, and New York
bountied one hundred and seven animals in 1890. The last record for the
Northeast was 1903, in the Adirondacks, but it held on until recently in
the more remote terrains of the Appalachians, and a few have managed to
persist in the Florida Everglades until the present. In the past few years
there have been reports of a small remnant population in New Brunswick.
    The elk and, more surprisingly, the bison, ranged east in the woodlands
to Pennsylvania and New York, and possibly to western New England,

IPSWICH SPARROW

and their range extended south through the Atlantic States at least as far as Georgia; probably both species once strayed to the coastal savannas, but had commenced their retreat at the time of the first white settlements. East of the Appalachians, the last bison was killed in 1801, at Buffalo Cross Roads, near Lewisburg, Pennsylvania, and a cow and her calf killed at Valley Head, West Virginia, in 1825, were the last east of the Mississippi. The elk held on in Pennsylvania until 1867, when the last one is said to have been killed by an Indian named Jim Jacobs. It has since been re-stocked here and there in the Appalachians and in New Hampshire. Farther north, the larger fur animals, as well as the moose and wood-land caribou, retreated into Canada; the moose, which tramped Long Island until the Civil War, still occurs in northern Maine and elsewhere along the boundary—a few years ago, one errant individual made its way south into Connecticut—but the caribou was last seen there in significant numbers in the nineties, and was last recorded in Maine in 1905.

These eastern animals were exterminated as quickly and efficiently as expedience permitted, and today it seems a little sad that the one large species afforded significant protection in early times was the one that, in the end, least needed it; the white-tailed deer is more numerous today than it was when North America was wilderness, and is by far the most abundant larger mammal in the country.

To give man credit where precious little is due, it should be pointed out here that certain creatures, almost in spite of him, thrive with the advance of civilization. The city species—largely hard-bitten Old World sophisticates such as the house sparrow, starling, pigeon, Norway rat, and the redoutable house mouse, *Mus musculus*—accompanied the white man to the New World and require no description, but certain native species also fare very well. The majority of these are songbirds—the orioles are a cheerful example—of which the preferred habitat is wood edge, orchard, and cultivated land, rather than that unbroken wilderness forest which once, it is said, would have enabled an ambitious gray squirrel to travel from the Atlantic to the Mississippi without setting paw to the ground. The gray squirrel, like the deer, skunk, raccoon, red fox, and cottontail rabbit, nonetheless prospers at the edges of civilization, and where not unduly persecuted these species have increased. Of the deer it might almost be said that, in direct opposition to the history of most large species, which fled before the ax, it was in most dire need of protection while the virgin forests stood.

The fall of this forest, in the East, was extensive and very rapid, for what could not be put to use was easily exported, and farm clearing was indiscriminate and wasteful. The dense sylva of varied hardwoods furnished the implements of survival—gun stocks of black walnut, boat ribs of oak, ax handles, singletrees, and wagon hubs of hickory and black gum, birch canoes, briar pipes fashioned of laurel and rhododendron, black ash fish baskets and chair bottoms, flexible spade handles and oars of the white ash. But the finest tree was an evergreen, the great white pine, which, two hundred feet and higher, soared over the northeast wilderness and stretched south in the Appalachians as far the Carolinas; the white pine was the light, strong stuff of houses, of boat planking and ship masts, and, in company with fish and fur, was the leading resource of the colonies.

In one short century of settlement, this wilderness was broken. William Penn was an early defender of the trees, and parts of Pennsylvania, not long after his death, already suffered the long-lived effects of ruthless cutting—erosion, flood, parched summers, and poor crops. The clearing, indeed, was feverish, for the settlers dreaded the dark monotone of trees, the wild beasts and savages they concealed, the wind-borne, whispered reminder of a wilderness unconquered. For every tree that was put to use, countless others knew only the manic ring of axes, and, prostrated in their prime, were left to rot in the tangles of second growth.

This new growth, tender, low, and variegated, proved a blessing to the deer, which supplied the Indian tribes with food and clothing, and were also in demand throughout the settlements. In early years their numbers had been so reduced that in Massachusetts a closed season was enforced by 1696, and by 1718 a closed term of three full years became necessary; two decades later, a system of wardens or "deer reeves" was initiated. Though Massachusetts was the pioneer in all these measures, a closed season on deer was established, by the time of the Revolution, in every colony but Georgia. (Delaware, a quarter-century after Massachusetts, set up the same closed season—January 1 to July 1—and adhered to it firmly for almost two hundred years until, in 1910, the deer having been exterminated from the state, its closed season became academic. The flat, open coastal plain of Delaware is ill-suited to deer, of course, and even in 1941, when the animal had attained near-epidemic populations elsewhere, a state census for the Fish and Wildlife Service could locate but nineteen, as opposed to an estimated six hundred in heavily populated Rhode Island, and seven hundred and fifty thousand in Pennsylvania.) With protection, the deer has kept pace with a sprawling civilization, and allows heavy annual hunting; in places, its abundance has constituted such a menace that the removal of protection from does and fawns proved a blessing not only to agriculture but to the starved animals themselves.

The key deer, a dwarf race of the white-tailed deer confined entirely to the pine keys of Florida, does not share the current deer prosperity. Hurricane, fire, and the persistence of meat hunters using dogs and jack lights have reduced the range of this miniature animal to the area of Big Pine Key, where a totally inadequate refuge area of about fifteen acres was set aside by Congress in 1958. A fondness for cigarette butts, which tempt it onto the Key West Highway, has also contributed to its decline, and since the hurricane of 1937, and despite full protection, its numbers have remained below one hundred and fifty.

Bird protection in colonial days was deemed unimportant at best, although Massachusetts, in 1710, prohibited the use of boats, sailing canoes, and camouflaged canoes in the pursuit of waterfowl, a precocious and commendable measure enacted less than a century after William Brad-

ford first warned of waterfowl decline. A more significant law, as things turned out, was passed two years earlier in New York, when a closed season was established in certain counties for the upland game birds—the ruffed grouse, quail, turkey, and heath hen. Of these four species, only the grouse and, on Long Island, the quail, still afford limited hunting in the state.

John Josselyn, who noted the pigeon's decline, spoke wistfully also of the turkey, "the English and the Indians having now destroyed the breed, so that 'tis very rare to meet with a wild turkie in the woods." [12] The eastern turkey was once common from Maine, Ontario, and Minnesota to the Gulf States, but with the destruction of the virgin forests its disappearance from New England was swift. It remained common from Kentucky southward into the nineteenth century, but since then, restocked flocks excepted, it has been all but extirpated from its northern range, and is now rare outside of remote southern forests.

The so-called gallinaceous birds are no more renowned for their intelligence than are their relatives, the domestic chickens, though the wild turkey and the ruffed grouse have grown relatively wary. The imported pheasant is much less so, and others, like the northern ptarmigans, the harlequin quail, and some of the western grouse, are celebrated for their foolishness far and wide. As game birds, fit for dog and pot, these species receive considerable assistance from the hunters, and in the East this assistance arrived in time to spare all but one.

Like the key deer, the heath hen is a subspecies, but, unlike the key deer, it is virtually identical with its parent form, the prairie chicken—though darker underparts and a lesser number of the prominent neck feathers characteristic of the prairie chickens have been noted. This bird is significant not only because its demise removed an important segment of the total population of the species but because the dramatic circumstances of its dying years did much to advance the cause of conservation.

Of the three recognized races of the prairie chicken, one, the heath hen, is extinct and a second, the Attwater's prairie chicken, confined to a few small areas of coastal prairie in Texas, is in immediate danger. The range of the latter form, which once extended into Louisiana, has been decimated by agriculture and overgrazing, and the population, which once must have neared a million, is now a scattered remnant. The common prairie chicken, farther north, though its range has extended in recent years into the prairie provinces of Canada, has continued to decrease in actual numbers, so that the species as a whole must be regarded as threat-

KEY DEER, with mourning doves

ened. (A related species, the lesser prairie chicken of western Kansas, western Oklahoma, and north Texas, has suffered a parallel decrease and finds itself in the same parlous state.)

In its several forms, the prairie chicken once occupied a large area of the United States, including the Atlantic States from Maine to Virginia, the Central and North Central States, the western Gulf States, and the Great Plains area of the Southwest. It has largely declined with the destruction of the prairie and grassland which it prefers, but it is also true that, unlike more successful game birds, it is easily discouraged from renesting after failure; it has been given, as well, to disappearances which are not readily explained and, last but by no means least, it is apparently one of the least suspecting of an unusually innocent family. The glum history of the heath hen gives reason to fear that these related forms may follow it into oblivion.

The heath hen inhabited the scattered grasslands, pine plains, and blueberry barrens of the East, and was once an exceedingly abundant bird from New England to Virginia, as well as on the larger offshore islands. Its obliging nature made it a staple item for the pots of the first colonists, and according to one source it was "so common on the ancient busky site of the city of Boston, that laboring people or servants stipulated with their employers, not to have the Heath-Hen brought to table oftener than a few times in a week." [13] So industriously was it pursued on Long Island that a New York statute of 1791 declared that "the person who shall kill any Heath-Hen within the counties of Suffolk or Queens, between the 1st day of April and the 5th day of October, shall, for every such offense, forfeit and pay the sum of two dollars and a half." (This section of the statute was quoted in a letter to the ornithologist Alexander Wilson in 1810 by Dr. Samuel Mitchill of New York; Wilson appends an amused footnote which, though it may or may not entertain us still, supplies an uneasy insight into the sociological concepts of the day: "The doctor has probably forgotten a circumstance of rather a ludicrous kind, that occurred at the passing of this law. . . . The bill was entitled, 'An Act for the preservation of Heath-Hen, and other game!' The honest Chairman of the Assembly—no sportsman, I suppose—read the title, 'An Act for the preservation of *Heathen*, and other game!' which seemed to astonish the northern members, who could not see the propriety of preserving *Indians*, or any other heathen." [14]) Forty years later, Audubon remarked on the rarity of the species, and it was last recorded on the mainland in 1869. A few lingered on in the Elizabeth Islands of Buzzards Bay until 1876, after which it was entirely restricted to the island of Martha's Vineyard. By the turn of the century, less than one hundred remained alive.

WHITE-TAILED DEER

WILD TURKEY

In 1907—these were the violent, early years of conservation—a reservation for the heath hens' protection was established on the island, in the sandy scrub-oak plains to the north of the Edgartown–West Tisbury Road, and a thorough control of their predators was instituted. (Prominent among these, it should be noted, was the feral house cat, a beast given to immense destruction wherever it is deserted by feckless owners.) The population had risen to eight hundred or more when, in 1916, a spring fire destroyed the greater part of their habitat and the majority of their nests. This is somehow ironic, for it may have been the control of natural fires in the eastern states which prevented the recurrent burning back of the pine plains and barrens; without fire, much of the bird's open-country habitat became overgrown, and it was thus reduced to isolated and vulnerable bands.

The following winter, the remnants were besieged by a wave of goshawks, descending from the north, and their numbers were reduced once more to less than one hundred. Despite complete protection, including the extension of predator control beyond the boundaries of their reservation, the heath hens never recovered. Beset by sterility, an excess of males, and other problems mysterious to their well-wishers, the population proved inadequate for the regeneration of the race, or even for self-maintenance. But thirty remained in 1927, and the last bird, an old male which frequented the James Green farm near West Tisbury, was seen a final time on March 11, 1932.

Though the heath hen persisted until recently, its disappearance as an important food source in the colonies had occurred nearly two centuries before, and was accompanied at the time by the decline of the black bear, deer, wild turkey, and, to a lesser extent, of the waterfowl and wild pigeons, the former abundance of which had made survival possible for the nomadic red men. In consequence, the vanquished and scattered tribes of the eastern Algonquins, incidental victims of the white man's war of attrition against the land, were slowly dying. On the 14th of May, in the year 1789, the once fierce Mohegans presented a petition to the "Most Honourable Assembly of the State of Connecticut Conv'd at Hartford," which read as follows:

> Your Good old Steady Friends and Brethern the Mohegan Tribe of Indians Sendeth Greeting:
> We beg Leave to lay our Concerns and Burdens at Your Excellencies Feet. The Times are Exceedingly Alter'd, Yea the Times have turn'd everything upside down, or rather we have Chang'd the good Times, Chiefly by the help of the White People, for in Times past, our Fore-Fathers lived in Peace, Love and great harmony, and had everything in Great plenty. When they Wanted meat they would just run into the Bush a little ways with their Weapons and would Soon bring home good venison, Raccoon, Bear, and Fowl. If they choose to have Fish, they wo'd only go to the River or along the Sea Shore and . . . presently fill their Cannoons With Variety of Fish, Both Scaled and shell Fish, and they had abundance of Nuts, Wild Fruit, Ground Nuts and Ground Beans, and they planted but little corn and Beans and they kept no Cattle or Horses for they needed none—And they had no Contention about their lands, it lay in Common to them all, and they

HEATH HEN

had but one large dish and they Cou'd all eat together in Peace and Love—But alas, it is not so now, all our Fishing, Hunting and Fowling is entirely gone. . . .

And so we are now Come to our Good Bretheren of the Assembly With Hearts full of Sorrow and Grief for Immediate help. . . .

Your Excellencies Compliance and Assistance at this Time will make our poor hearts very Glad and thankful.

This is the most humble Request and Petition of Your True Friend & Brethern Mohegan Indians,

By the Hands of our Brothers

> Harry x Quaduaquid, his mark
>
> Robert Ashpo

ATTWATER'S PRAIRIE CHICKEN

PRAIRIE CHICKEN

A plain, rich in woods and savannas, swarming with Bisons or buffaloes, Stags, and Virginian Deer, with Bears, and great variety of game, occupies an amazing tract, from the great lakes of Canada, as low as the gulph of Mexico; and eastward to the other great chain of mountains, the Apalachian. . . .   —THOMAS PENNANT (1785)

4 : Fur Countries and Forest Lakes

IN THE CENTURY and a half after the settlement of Jamestown, the English colonists concerned themselves chiefly with the ouster of the Dutch from New York, as well as with the suppression of the Algonquin and Cherokee nations; they consolidated the eastern slope of the continent, and not until late in the eighteenth century, just prior to the Revolution, was there any serious attempt to cross the great Appalachian barrier.

From New France, however, the St. Lawrence led west to the inland seas and thence to the Mississippi, and French exploration commenced quickly. Tadoussac, a Quebec village still extant at the mouth of the Saguenay River, was established a quarter-century before Jamestown, and Port Royal (now Annapolis Royal, Nova Scotia) was permanently settled by 1610. The French outposts, originally shore stations for the cod fisheries, ex-

LAKE STURGEON, with walleyed pike

panded with the development of the fur trade, a commerce conducted
through barter with the Montaignais, Hurons, and northern Algonquins.
These tribes were informal French allies against the Iroquois, who would
later join forces with the English; the latter, after early failure to gain
control of the St. Lawrence fur trade, were no more than sporadically
troublesome to the French until the end of the seventeenth century, when
the fine fur supply available to the New England colonies began to dwindle.

In New York, however, the Dutch West India Company, alarmed by
the decline of their beaver, armed the Five Nations of the Iroquois against
the French and Hurons in an attempt to gain access to the northern trade.
Though the Iroquois vanquished the Hurons, the British, by 1664, had
vanquished the Dutch; the French, meanwhile, had penetrated as far west
as Lake Superior and Wisconsin and were fortifying their supply route.
La Salle reached Ohio by 1670, seeing "more wild cattle than anyone can
say" [1]—a companion, Father Louis Hennepin, discovered Niagara Falls on
forays from this expedition, and later St. Anthony's Falls, the present
site of Minneapolis—and Père Marquette, three years later, descended
Lake Michigan, the Wisconsin River, and the Mississippi as far as Arkansas.
He returned to describe "buffaloes in great numbers," the Mississippi
paddlefish, and the great red, green, and black cliff drawing near Alton,
Illinois, known as the Piasaw monster. He also mentions "monstrous fish,
which struck so violently against our canoes, that at first we took them to
be large trees, which threatened to upset us." [2]

This description can have referred only to the lake sturgeon, a great
primitive species which still attains a length of eight feet and a weight of
over three hundred pounds. Our largest fresh-water fish was then abundant

in the Ohio River, the Mississippi River drainage, the Great Lakes, Lake of the Woods, the St. Lawrence, and in a number of large Canadian lakes. Probably it is now extinct in the United States river systems and is extremely scarce in all its former waters, almost entirely as a result of overfishing.

The redoubtable La Salle, venturing forth again in 1680, continued Marquette's exploration to the mouth of the Mississippi, taking possession for the French of a vast region he named Louisiana. Meanwhile, the British, ever restless, reconnoitered the French fur countries from the north. In an effort to lure the Indian trappers away from the St. Lawrence trading posts, they set up, in 1670, a syndicate known as the Governor and Company of Adventurers into Hudson's Bay, with posts on both James and Hudson Bay. Most of these posts were seized promptly by the French, and held until the conclusion of King William's War in 1697, when the British regained control of the area. Sixteen years later, at the Treaty of Utrecht, they acquired not only Hudson Bay but Newfoundland, Nova Scotia, and New Brunswick as well; at the Treaty of Paris, in 1763, a wholesale redistribution of territories awarded the British the great bulk of North America east of the Mississippi.

The Governor and Company of Adventurers into Hudson's Bay is known today as the Hudson's Bay Company, and its significance in the history of North American wildlife has been considerable. While it can scarcely be said that in the course of its long tenure the Company has proved a blessing to American wildlife, its policies have been far more constructive, in the main, than those of the lumber, mining, and other concerns which join it these days in a shrill effort to deny their part in the pillage of the continent's resources. In fact, the Hudson's Bay Company has made definite contributions, even from the beginning. Its field personnel has included men genuinely concerned with wildlife, and its comprehensive records have been most useful to naturalists for well over two centuries.

A typical contribution was the discovery, in 1861, of a rare new species of American goose by the company's chief factor, Bernard Ross. The Ross's goose winters in the Sacramento Valley region of California, with occasional individuals straying as far south as Bustilles Lake, Chihuahua, and its total numbers, more or less stable, have been estimated as low as two thousand, though five times that figure is probably more accurate. The birds are consistently shot as snow geese, which they closely resemble in miniature, and, though protected, are chronically imperiled. Confusion as to their actual number has been compounded by the fact that their breeding

ROSS'S GOOSE   TRUMPETER SWAN

grounds, on the remote Perry River south of King William Sound, were not located until 1940, and research there is presently incomplete. The Perry River colony was found, fittingly enough, by Hudson's Bay Company personnel.

The Company's role in the history of another bird, while considerable, is less auspicious. Between 1853 and 1877 it handled 17,671 swan skins, a number which, while not staggering, represented an unhealthy proportion of the population of North America's largest waterfowl. The majority of these skins, then much in demand as items of female apparel, belonged originally to the trumpeter swan; the whistling swan, a smaller and more wary bird, had the added advantage of nesting farther north, out of harm's way.

The trumpeter was named for its voice: "I have heard them," wrote Samuel Hearne, a pioneer naturalist in Canada, "in serene evenings after sunset, make a noise not very unlike that of a French horn, but entirely divested of every note that constituted melody, and have often been sorry that it did not forebode their death." [3] This statuesque bird, which attains a weight of thirty pounds and a wingspread of ten feet, bred formerly from western Alaska south to Indiana, and wintered from Chesapeake Bay and the Mississippi Valley west along the Gulf Coast, as well as in the lower Columbia River, and in the Sacramento Valley. It is now confined, in the United States, to the Red Rock Lakes district of Montana and to Yellowstone Park, with a few birds wintering on the Snake River in Idaho. There are also small breeding populations on the Copper River and on the wet spruce muskeg of the Kenai Peninsula in Alaska, which are presumed to winter with a resident population in southeast Alaska and British Columbia.

As civilization decreased their range, the swans became increasingly vulnerable to hunters, Indians, and trappers, who usually took them on their breeding grounds. In the 1920s, an estimated four hundred and fifty individuals remained of the flocks which had once carved the skies of a continent, and by 1935 only seventy-three remained in the United States. With complete protection, the bird has recovered very slowly, and its entire population now approximates fifteen hundred.

The varied and splendid waterfowl of North America have been decimated since early times, and, though we can attribute the original losses to such practices as market gunning and spring shooting, the fact is that bad land management, drought, and excessive drainage, in combination with the usual ravages of civilization, have since destroyed most of the waterfowl breeding and wintering habitat in the nation; in other words, the ducks, geese, and swans would be far reduced in number today even if never besieged by shot and shell. Protection has spared not the multitudes but the stragglers.

Curiously, however, the species imperiled have not been those most persecuted; only the redhead, of the popular market ducks, could ever be said to have approached the danger point. The Ross's goose and trumpeter swan were no more than incidental victims of the carnage, and the beautiful wood duck, which required full protection in the United States and Canada from 1918 to 1941, is a solitary woodland form. It declined by slow attrition, rather than on the grand scale of its swarming marshland relatives.

One obscure species, however, may well have succumbed to an earlier form of persecution. The Labrador duck is said to have been a strong and hardy bird, and the full reasons for its disappearance will probably remain mysterious. Nevertheless, though its nesting grounds were never discovered, it is assumed to have bred on the Labrador coast, once the favorite grounds of eider and other sea ducks pursued for their feathers and down. Between 1750 and 1760, a great many "feather voyages" were made to Labrador from the New England colonies, and, though these were abandoned shortly thereafter for want of victims, the native Indians and fishermen maintained a steady pressure on the remnant nests and eggs; it is possible, indeed likely, that the Labrador duck never recovered from this early onslaught.

In any case, this small, pretty black and white species flew south in winter at least as far as the Chesapeake Bay. The idea that the Labrador duck was "probably a mere straggler on the coast of the whole Atlantic, and chiefly inhabits the western side of the continent," [4] was of course only

LABRADOR DUCK

wishful thinking. According to Audubon, "It also at times enters the Delaware River, in Pennsylvania, and ascends that stream at least as far as Philadelphia." [5] The so-called "pied" or "sand-shoal" duck was already uncommon then, for Audubon himself never saw it alive; he based his description, as did other writers who came after, on a pair now owned by the Smithsonian Institution, shot originally off Martha's Vineyard by Daniel Webster. In 1872, the bird was called "extremely rare now, and apparently in a fair way to becoming extinct," [6] a prophecy confirmed but three years later when, on the 12th of December, the last authenticated specimen was shot down by a gunner on Long Island.

Today, off Long Island's beaches on a still day of winter, the great rafts of black and white pied sea ducks are a fine sight—the trim old-squaw and neat bufflehead, the mergansers and goldeneye and dark, heavy-bodied scoters. The sharp air is clean, virtually odorless, and only the strange gabble of the old-squaws breaks the vague murmur of the tide along the shore. Alone on the beach, one can readily imagine that, momentarily, the loveliest pied duck of them all might surface, startled, near a sand spit, the white of it bright in the cold January sun, as it did winter after winter long ago.

The fur trade fast became the chief business of the colonies, exceeding in importance the commerce in timber and fish. The "fur countries," as they were called, were roughly that wilderness of forest lakes, of loons and geese, moose and bear, which we think of today, rather romantically, as the Great North Woods. In colonial times the term embraced the hard-wood and evergreen backwoods of the Northeast as well as the spruce muskeg of eastern Canada, which stretches north from Quebec and the Great Lakes to Labrador and Hudson Bay; the western limits of the fur countries were then unknown. The region was bitter cold in winter and was composed largely of woodland tracts veined heavily with water. The cold encouraged a rich coat of fur, the wet habitat increased its luster, and the woodland shade protected the dark sheen from the bleaching effects of sunlight. These conditions were met to a certain extent quite far southward in the Appalachians and later in the Rockies, but furs taken elsewhere were generally inferior.

The most precious fur bearers were the various members of the weasel family—the winter short-tailed weasel in its white or "ermine" phase, as well as the otter, mink, pine marten, fisher, and wolverine. (Another weasel, the striped skunk, achieved a belated popularity with the decline of its less musky brethren.) Of these, only the aquatic mink and otter and the ubiquitous weasels remain widespread, at least in the United States, and the first two have been seriously reduced throughout their range. The marten, fisher, and wolverine, fierce, solitary carnivores dependent on deep, unbroken tracts of virgin forest, declined quickly. Probably the wolverine was never common south of Canada. A quick, powerful animal the size of a bear cub—and considered to be a bear, in fact, until the nineteenth century —it occurred formerly throughout the northern states from Maine to Washington, and south sparingly in the Adirondacks, the Rockies, and the Coast Range. Though an occasional wanderer is reported along the north-west border, the wolverine is now confined, in the United States, to remnant populations in the Rockies and in the Yosemite region of California.

The marten and fisher, however, were more widespread. Both species were found, in the Appalachians, as far south as Virginia, and the arboreal marten is still locally abundant in northern Maine and the Adirondacks, the wilder mountain areas of the Northwest, in Canada, and in Alaska. The fisher, a larger animal and individually, except for the rare strains of the red fox, the most valuable fur bearer among all North American land species, brought $345 in some years for an exceptional pelt. The price on its head contributed to its decline, but, like the marten, it has been most seriously diminished by lumbering, forest fires, and the elimination of pregnant females in winter trapping. It was disappearing in New York and

FISHER

New England by the nineteenth century, and has been called "alarmingly scarce" in the United States, although recently it has made a good recovery in New Hampshire, Maine, and the Adirondacks. In Canada it decreased after 1870, and an estimated 10,500 are thought to remain in the Dominion. Unlike the wolverine and marten, the fisher is not a widespread Alaskan species, though it occurs in extreme southeast Alaska; it is still trapped wherever found, but its chief peril may lie in the destruction by lumbermen of the bark-eating porcupine, which is an important source of the fisher's food.

In the other families, the black bear and gray wolf were also taken whenever the chance presented itself (the muskrat, like the skunk, was a prize of a later, less glorious era), but the leading fur bearer, the creature of destiny the pursuit of which inspired much of the early exploration of North America, was not a wild carnivore at all but a sedentary, civic-minded rodent.

The beaver was once extremely abundant throughout the continent, the deserts of the Southwest and the tundra of the Arctic excepted. Exploited for its rich, dense fur from the outset, this largest of the American rodents commenced its decline as early as 1638, when to its misfortune the compulsory use of it in the manufacture of hats was decreed by King Charles II.

By this time the American beaver was already renowned in Europe—not surprisingly, since its virtues and attainments, as recorded by admirers well into the nineteenth century, have rarely been equaled by any animal before or since. The forepart of the beaver of yore, for example, was composed of meat, and the hindquarters, owing apparently to constant submersion, of fish, a circumstance of some comfort to religious Europeans, since it permitted the consumption of beaver even on fast days. The equipment of this marvelous creature included the forefeet of a dog and the hind feet of a swan, hooked teeth capable of capturing fish, and a tail of awe-inspiring versatility. Its mansion was an imposing edifice, several compartmented stories of notched logs, the floors of which were carpeted with boughs of softest evergreen; "the window which looks out upon the water," observed the eighteenth-century naturalist Buffon, "serves them as a balcony for the enjoyment of the air, or to bathe during the greater part of the day."

Its physical endowments, however, were puny by comparison with the advanced evolution of its social mores, a vivid account of which was transcribed in 1825:

> The beavers are divided into tribes, and sometimes into small bands only, of which each has its chief, and order and discipline reign there, much more, perhaps, than among the Indians, or even among civilized nations. . . .
>
> Each tribe has its territory. If any stranger is caught trespassing, he is brought before the chief, who for the first offense punishes him *ad correctionem*, and for the second deprives him of his tail, which is the greatest misfortune that can happen to a beaver, for their tail is their cart, upon which they transport, wherever it is desired, mortar, stones, provisions, &c. and it is also the trowel, which it exactly resembles in shape, used by them in building. This infraction of the laws of nations is considered among them as so great an outrage, that the whole tribe of the mutilated beaver side with him, and set off immediately to take vengeance for it. . . .
>
> The Indians have related to me in a positive manner another trait of these animals, but it is so extraordinary that I leave you at liberty to believe or reject it. They assert, and there are some who profess to have been ocular witnesses, that the two chiefs of two belligerent tribes sometimes terminate the quarrel by single combat, in the presence of the two hostile armies, like the people of *Medieve*, or three against three, like the Horatii and Curiatii of antiquity. Beavers marry, and death alone separates them. They punish infidelity in the females severely, even with death. . . .
>
> The Great Hare at Red Lake wished to make me believe that, having come to the spot where two tribes of beaver had just been engaged in battle, he found about fifteen dead or dying on the field; and other Indians, Sioux and Chippeways, have also assured me that they have obtained valuable booty in similar circumstances. It is a fact that they sometimes take them without tails. I have seen such myself. In fine, these animals are so extraordinary, even in the eyes of the Indians themselves, that they sup-

pose them men, become beavers by transmigration, and they think in killing them to do them a great service, for they say they restore them to their original state. . . .[7]

Whatever one's opinion of this service to the beaver, the high regard in which it was held in no way impeded its destruction, and since the animal is, in fact, rather stupid and defenseless, the progress of civilization was everywhere accompanied by its extirpation. The beaver hat went out of fashion in the beginning of the nineteenth century, but the beaver was virtually extinct east of the Mississippi shortly thereafter. John Godman, an early and articulate spokesman for animal protection, remarked in his *American Natural History*, published in 1831:

It is a subject of regret that an animal so valuable and prolific should be hunted in a manner tending so evidently to the extermination of the species, when a little care and management on the part of those interested might prevent unnecessary destruction, and increase the sources of their revenue. . . . In a few years, comparatively speaking, the beaver has been exterminated in all the Atlantic and in the western states . . . and the race will eventually be extinguished throughout the whole continent. A few individuals may, for a time, elude the immediate violence of persecution, and like the degraded descendants of the aboriginals of our soil, be occasionally exhibited as melancholy mementos of tribes long previously whelmed in the fathomless gulf of avarice.

Godman's warning, while in advance of its time, was also tardy. A Hudson's Bay Company sale, in November 1743, disposed of 26,750 beaver pelts, as well as 14,730 martens and 1850 wolves; that these were by no means the only victims, even among their own kind, is indicated by the fact that 127,080 beaver, 30,325 martens, and 1267 wolves, as well as 12,428 otters and fishers, 110,000 raccoons, and a startling aggregation of 16,512 bears were received in the French port of Rochelle in the same year. People today who have no reasonable expectation of seeing even one of these creatures in the wild without considerable effort to do so might well look carefully at these figures. In the same year, too, for reasons which such harvests make all too evident, a French soldier and trader named Vérendrye was seeking new sources farther west, where Cree Indians had informed him that the beaver were very numerous. Vérendrye extended the canoe routes of the Great Lakes past Lake of the Woods and north to Lake Winnipeg, where he turned south into the prairies of the Dakotas and the Mandan country on the upper Missouri; probably he reached Montana

BEAVER

and Wyoming, thus achieving the first recorded expedition to the virgin terrains of the American Northwest.

Meanwhile, English expansion westward had scarcely begun. Conrad Weiser's journey from William Penn's colony at Philadelphia to the Iroquois stronghold at Onondaga, near Lake Erie, 1729–1733, was a considerable undertaking, and Washington's expedition to the Ohio River country of western Pennsylvania, then contested by the French, was truly an expedition, even in 1753; the northern Alleghenies remained a barrier. Farther south, sporadic attempts to breach the Blue Ridge and the Appalachians were inconclusive until the era of the intrepid Daniel Boone. "It was on the first of May, in the year 1769," he recounted some years later, "that I resigned my domestic happiness for a time, and left my family and peaceable habitation on the Yadkin River, in North Carolina, to wander through the wilderness of America. . . ." In Kentucky he "found everywhere abundance of wild beasts of all sorts, through the vast forest. The buffalo were more frequent than I have seen cattle in the settlements . . . fearless, because ignorant of the violence of man." An Indian was to tell him, "We have given you a fine land, but I believe you will have much trouble in settling it." [8] Settle it Boone did, losing a brother and two sons to the savages in the process. In 1776 he laid out for once and for all the Wilderness Road across the Cumberland Gap into Kentucky; the western horizon came in view across the rich heartland of the central continent in the same year American independence was declared.

"Notwithstanding America has withdrawn itself from us," Thomas Pennant wrote, just after the Revolution, "it is charity to point out the benefits they may enjoy, from the gifts of nature they possess." This sensible attitude was typical of Pennant, an Englishman whose *Arctic Zoology* is one of the foremost of all contributions to North American natural history. He was sensible, as well, in his observation that the Great Plains were once beneath the sea, that the red men had reached this continent by way of the Bering Strait, and that a sort of epilepsy was an affliction not uncommon

among moose. In almost every respect, his text was superior to anything which appeared in the half-century after Catesby, including significant works by George Edwards (1743), John R. Forster (1771), and John Latham (1781).

Edwards, who never visited America, depended largely on Catesby and on the Hudson's Bay Company for his material, and was given to imprecise descriptions: the "quick hatch" or "wolverene," he reports, "was of the size of some wolves I have seen brought from Germany." [10] Forster compiled what might be called the first American check list of wild creatures, including a list of 302 bird species, distinguished chiefly by its inaccuracy. Latham, like Edwards, was derivative and vague. It may well be that the most important publication of the period was the *Travels* (1753) of Peter Kalm, a Swedish correspondent of Linnaeus who devoted considerable attention to American flora and fauna. Another work of at least historic interest was the *Notes on the State of Virginia,* first printed in Paris in 1781, by no less a person than Thomas Jefferson, then a member of the United States Peace Commission seeking settlement of the war. The first of the few United States Presidents to concern themselves with nature, Jefferson included in his treatise some accurate if not very interesting information on wild species, and mentions the Carolina parrot, passenger pigeon, and "white-billed woodpecker" among Virginian birds.

The *Arctic Zoology,* then, could be called an epochal work, but it was compromised by Pennant's failure to adopt the binomial system, then coming into general use, and a number of redundancies and outright errors mar the three-volume work. He perpetuated Buffon's beaver legends, as well as the notions that parrot guts were fatal to cats, that wolverines drop moss from tree limbs to lure deer into ambush, and that wolves, when famished, dine on mud. For the most part, however, he made the best of contemporary information. His remarks on the growing scarcity of certain species were accurate, and it seems fitting, in this regard, that a portrait of the ill-fated Labrador duck should have been selected as his frontispiece. Of the elk, he reports a decrease in the face of civilization, and says of the bison, "The Indians, by a very bad policy, prefer the flesh of the Cows; which in time will destroy the species." (The idea that the Indian was the sole culprit in the destruction of the bison was to gain in popularity as its slaughter by white men increased.) The ivory-billed woodpecker he calls scarce, and though he refers to the "most amazing numbers" of the passenger pigeon, he also quotes a letter had from a Mr. Ashton Blackburne, in 1770: "Sir William Johnson told me that he killed at one shot with a blunderbuss, a hundred and twenty or thirty. Some years past they

SEA MINK, with black duck

"Reconstruction: There are no drawings in existence (except this one). B.H."

have not been in such plenty as they used to be. This spring I saw them fly one morning, as I thought in great abundance; but everybody was amazed how few there were; and wondered at the reason."

Pennant refers also to a "strange animal seen by Mr. Phipps and others in Newfoundland, of a shining black: bigger than a Fox; shaped like an *Italian* grehound; legs long; tail long and taper. One gentleman saw five sitting on a rock with their young, at the mouth of a river; often leapt in and dived, and brought up trouts, which they gave to their young. When he shewed himself, they all leapt into the water and looked at him. An old furrier said, he remembered a skin of one sold for five guineas. The *French* often see them in *Hare Bay*." Since the otter was then a familiar animal and since Hare Bay is a coastal habitat, the rest of the description leads one to suspect that the range of the now extinct sea mink may have been wider than is generally imagined. Little is known about this animal, which was first scientifically described in 1903 from bones discovered in Indian shell heaps near Brookline, Maine, but it has been called "fully twice as large as the mink from inland." "These sea mink," the same account says elsewhere, "used to bring considerably more than others on account of their great size." [10] The usual range given for the sea mink is the coast of Maine, New Brunswick, and Nova Scotia; it is represented on earth by two poor skins and a number of bones.

Since Pennant was writing at the time of the Revolution, it must be assumed that such information as he had in regard to the western fur countries was derived largely from French accounts. Actually, he made free use of many sources, including the journals of Steller, the description of Greenland's fauna by "Mr. Otto Fabricius," and the findings of his friend, the eminent Russian zoologist Dr. Peter Pallas. Thus he was able to discuss such animals as the grizzly bear, the "argali" or mountain sheep, and the musk ox when the English-speaking world hardly knew they existed.

This was soon to change, however. The forests westward, after the Revolution, were claimed promptly by the thirteen states—Connecticut, its size and location notwithstanding, proclaimed itself king of a territory stretching from Pennsylvania to Lake Michigan and the upper Mississippi—but in the next decades these new lands were ceded to the Union. The states had small idea of what they had claimed, few Americans having crossed the mountains or journeyed the Ohio. It was not until the Louisiana Purchase, in 1803, acquiring from Napoleon Bonaparte 828,000 square miles of southern lowlands and northern Great Plains, from the Mississippi to the Rockies, that the great movements toward the West began. That same year, President Jefferson dispatched Lewis and Clark to extend United States commerce westward, and to establish friendly relations with the plains Indians. They followed the Ohio, then ascended the muddy Missouri into North Dakota, passing the winter of 1804–1805 with Mandans of the Sioux nation. In the spring they approached and crossed the Rockies, and continued on across the Columbia Plateau and the Cascades to the Western Sea. An overland route was now established, and only nomadic plains tribes such as the Blackfoot, Pawnee, and Sioux remained to contest the way.

The Lewis and Clark Expedition, which opened two decades of feverish western exploration, expansion, and consolidation, brought back awed accounts of the great grizzly bear. "These bear being so hard to die rather intimeadates us all," Captain Lewis remarked. "I must confess that I do not like the gentlemen and had reather fight two Indians than one bear." [12] Two years later Zebulon Pike was sent to investigate the sources of the Mississippi; he journeyed subsequently to New Mexico and Colorado, where he came upon Pike's Peak, and returned from the latter foray with a pair of grizzly cubs. These were kept alive at Peale's Museum in Philadelphia until, their ill nature worsening, they were executed in the name of the public weal. Though Pike wrote Charles Willson Peale that grizzlies "seldom or never attack a man unprovoked, but defend themselves courageously," his opinion was in advance of his time and was generally discredited. The animal was already legendary by the time Thomas Say, in 1823, published its first description. (In scientific parlance, an animal is considered to be "described" upon the first publication of its precise physical description, including skeletal and other anatomical measurements as well as superficial characters. At the same time it is usually given a Latin name which classifies it in the animal world according to genus and species, though the classification is often an arbitrary one on the part of its describer and may later be contested. Until introduced to science by virtue of its description, a species is not formally considered to exist, a technicality of small consequence to the creature itself, which may have been getting along quite nicely without a name for more than a million years.)

Say, with Titian Peale, accompanied Major Stephen Long on his 1819 expedition to the Rocky Mountains; the two were the first of numerous naturalists to accompany government exploring surveys during the cen-

GRIZZLY BEAR

tury. Titian Peale, like his brothers Rembrandt and Raphael, became one of the outstanding painters of the period, and some of his wildlife portraits are striking. Long's expedition represented activity resumed after the War of 1812, which was brought about partly by British sponsorship of Shawnee warriors under Tecumseh. The Shawnees, abetted by southern Creeks, were seeking to stem the surge of expansion into their hinterlands. Their defeat, in 1814, began the permanent decline of both of these great Indian nations: two-thirds of the Creek lands were ceded to the United States, and the Shawnees, with the Senecas, Delawares, and other tribes, were forced to declare war on the British. In 1818 Andrew Jackson, whose long career of disservice to the Indians had begun in the Creek War four years earlier, crushed an uprising of Florida Seminoles, and his seizure of the area was followed a year later by Spanish cession of that territory. Great Britain had already ceded the northern part of the Dakotas in the establishment of a permanent boundary extending from Lake of the Woods to the Rockies; the new republic was assuming its final shape.

In regard to the mammals, the scientific knowledge born of this period was exploited first by Richard Harlan and, more importantly, by the aforementioned John Godman, whose *American Natural History* was the finest treatise on this subject since the time of Pennant. Dr. Godman, a professor at the Franklin Institute of Pennsylvania, was a very learned man, and his scientific turn of mind may be seen in the fact that the first North American mammal he comes to grips with is the "American, or red variety" of the species *Homo sapiens*. This placement of the Indian among the North American mammals makes us rather uneasy today, but it should be said, to Godman's credit, that he speaks highly of the red man in his original state, undebased by the white man, and treats him with considerably more respect than did Witmer Stone who, as late as 1902, remarked of the arctic fox that "in its family life it is certainly the equal, if not indeed the superior, of many of the native Eskimo tribes inhabiting the same region, at least in matters of forethought, cleverness, and morality." [13]

From the Indians, Godman proceeds systematically to the bats, shrews, and moles. He speaks also of the decline in the East of the moose, elk, wolf, and cougar, and follows the lead of Pennant in blaming the red men for the bison's decline, castigating with spirit the barbarous practice of stampeding the animals over cliffs. "It is extremely fortunate," he concludes, "that this sanguinary and wasteful method . . . is not very frequently resorted to by the savages, or we might expect these animals in a few years to go entirely extinct." He dismisses peremptorily the legends of the beaver, perpetuated in part "by the impassioned eloquence of BUFFON, to which nothing is wanting but truth in order to render it sublime." And he summarizes the latest information on the grizzly, his opinion of which remains the popular one even today:

> This bear, justly considered as the most dreadful and dangerous of North American quadrupeds, is the despotic and sanguinary monarch of the wilds over which he ranges. Gigantic in size and terrific in aspect, he unites to a ferociously blood-thirsty disposition a surpassing strength of limb, which gives him undisputed supremacy over every other quadruped tenant of the wilderness, and causes man himself to tremble at his approach, though possessed of defensive weapons unknown to any but the human race. To the Indians the very name of the Grizzly Bear is dreadful, and the killing of one is esteemed equal to a great victory:—the white hunters are almost always willing to avoid an encounter with so powerful an adversary, and seldom or never wantonly provoke his anger.

The grizzly, at this time, had already been awarded its scientific name, *Ursus horribilis*.

The white man's caution in regard to the "horrible bear" was lessened considerably by the advent of the repeating rifle, and the grizzly, alone of the three species of North American bears, is today endangered. The smaller black bear, of forests, swamps, and mountains, has adapted somewhat to the presence of man, and has maintained fair numbers in much of its original range, from Florida and Mexico to Alaska; only the glacier bear, a small blue-gray race native to Alaskan glaciers between Lynn Canal and Cape St. Elias, has been seriously threatened, because of its provocative color. Now protected, its numbers do not exceed five hundred. The polar bear, whose wide range on the tundras and ice packs from Alaska to Labrador and Greenland comprises one of the least hospitable areas of the earth, has escaped undue attention from mankind, though hunting pressure implemented by the ski plane may shortly overpower it. But the grizzly, in all its forms, is waning everywhere, and its natural domain, which once extended from the eastern edge of the Great Plains to the Pacific, and from the mountains of Mexico to the Northwest Territories and Alaska, has shrunk to a few scattered wilderness provinces.

The Great Plains grizzlies were probably declining before the appearance of the white man. The plains tribes killed this bear whenever practicable, and their interest in its destruction, prideful as well as material, was assisted by horses inherited from the Spaniards. The bears were also lassoed in fun by the *vaqueros* of Spanish California, and were pitted against large, vicious bulls, which they destroyed with monotonous regularity. Though common enough in Godman's time, the California grizzlies scarcely survived the settlement of the state, and became extinct there in the 1920s. Today they are limited, in the United States, to remote regions of the Rocky Mountains, though a few may persist in the state of Washington. A 1949 census by the Fish and Wildlife Service estimated a total national population of seven hundred and fifty animals, none of them truly protected except in the national parks. Theoretically, they enjoy a season closed to hunting, but numbers are killed out of season, from Wyoming to Alaska, as allegedly dangerous predators. While they are still not uncommon in the fastnesses of western Canada and Alaska, the last band of these impressive creatures in the United States will probably be the one which now makes nocturnal visits to the lonely, smoldering garbage dumps off the main roads of Yellowstone Park.

The so-called Alaska brown bears—the Kodiak bear and the Alaska Peninsula bear—differ from the typical grizzlies in degree only. They tend to be larger (they are said to be the largest terrestrial carnivores in existence), with more massive heads and shorter claws. These enormous animals have measured as much as nine feet two inches, with weights as high as 1656 pounds, and consequently are favored targets for big-game hunters from all over the world. They are disliked by commercial salmon fishermen, who tend to attribute the results of their own wastefulness to the limited predations of the bears, and by the small cattle interests of Kodiak Island, where ranching at best would be a marginal enterprise even without the presence of large carnivores. Because for most people the expense of hunting them is prohibitive, the small populations of Alaskan "brown" bears have to date survived the pressures of commercial interests and over-shooting.

These days, unless one knows just where to search in the Rocky Mountain hinterlands, the only place on the continent where the grizzly may be readily observed is from the road which traverses the high, wild terrains east of Mount McKinley, in Alaska. Solitary, huge, the bears bring to life the barren, alpine tundra, the dwarf birch and willow thickets, and the gravel bars of the swift, gray glacier rivers.

The notorious silvertip, provoked, can be a fearsome animal. Human fatalities, while infrequent, are still regular, and clearly there is no place for it in settled country, even if it could scratch out an existence. But grizzlies are still killed needlessly—self-defense, like sport, is a term which lends itself to wide interpretation—and the time is not far off when Godman's "monarch of the wild" will disappear. No one who has ever seen a grizzly will dispute its title; shambling, rooting, or frozen against a hillside, fur roughened by the wind, it stirs the heart. For many of us, the great grizzly will always represent a wild, legendary America somewhere to the north and west which we were born too late ever to see.

ALASKA PENINSULA BEAR, with dog salmon, short-billed gulls

New Plymouth Colony have great profit by whale killing. I believe it will
be one of our best returns, now beaver and peltry fale us. . . .
—EDWARD RANDOLPH (1688)

Now small fowls flew screaming over the yet yawning gulf; a sullen white
surf beat against its steep sides; then all collapsed, and the great shroud of
the sea rolled on as it rolled five thousand years ago.
—HERMAN MELVILLE (1851)

5 : Ocean Coasts and the High Seas

THE FUR TRADE in North America was of such immediate importance that
it tends to obscure that older commerce of the colonies, the marine fisheries. These fisheries, still significant today, bred a redoubtable race of
Yankee mariners, and some of these enterprising men quickly turned their
hand to sources of swifter profit.

The feather trade in great auks, eider, and other sea birds has been mentioned earlier. The great, warty Atlantic walrus, like the auk, is thought to
have strayed in winter as far south as Massachusetts Bay, and it boasted a
large breeding colony at Sable Island, east of Nova Scotia. Beginning in
1633, a number of expeditions from Massachusetts Bay visited the island

for the express purpose of butchering "sea-horses," and the voyage of 1641 produced over four hundred pairs of ivory tusks, valued at the considerable contemporary sum of three hundred English pounds. By mid-century the Sable Island colony was no more, and a single specimen reported from Massachusetts in 1734 was the last ever recorded in this country. Today it rarely ventures south of Labrador. The walrus was pursued for its skin, oil, and ivory, commodities now reserved for the spare Eskimo economy; the joys of execution are still permitted the white hunter, however, and the few thousand of these sluggish creatures remaining on the bleak coasts and ice packs from Nome to Greenland are intermittently assaulted by sports-men not overly particular about a sporting target. The carcasses, where possible, are turned over to the natives, whose interest in the walrus as an item of diet was recorded most vividly in the journals of an early explorer of the Arctic, Captain G. F. Lyon:

. . . the party which had been adrift killed two large walruses, which they had carried home during the early part of the night. No one therefore came to the ships, all remaining in the huts to gourmandize. We found the men lying under their deer-skins, and clouds of steam rising from their naked bodies. From Kooilittuk I learnt a new Eskimaux luxury; he had eaten until he was drunk, and every moment fell asleep with a flushed and burning face and his mouth open. By his side sat Arnalooa, who was attending her cooking-pot, and at short intervals awakened her spouse, in order to cram as much as was possible of a large piece of half boiled flesh into his mouth with the assistance of her fore finger, and having filled it quite full, cut off the morsel close to his lips. This he slowly chewed, and as soon as a small vacancy became perceptible, this was filled by a lump of raw blubber. During this operation the happy man moved no part of him but his jaws, not even opening his eyes; but his extreme satisfaction was occasionally shown by a most expressive grunt whenever he enjoyed sufficient room for the passage of sound.[1]

The walrus was once circumpolar in its distribution, and its slaughter has not been confined to North America. Few marine animals, in fact, are found only in the waters of a single continent since, by comparison with the land, the ocean is relatively stable and continuous in its climate and conditions and offers few barriers to the dispersal of species. The reptiles and mammals which invaded the sea, finding no competition on their own evolutionary level, have thrived across the ages, while their terrestrial rela-tives, exposed constantly to the competition of younger forms and to

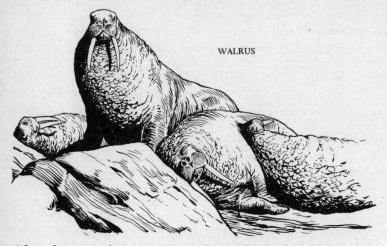

WALRUS

violent changes in their environments, have suffered a long history of extinction. The greater need to adapt has encouraged the evolution of many more land than marine species, but the latter, as a group, have endured longer. Most marine reptiles and mammals have retained their terrestrial breeding habits, but the colorful and poisonous sea snakes, the whales, porpoises, and dolphins, and the sirenians—manatees and dugongs—are exclusively marine. The worldwide distribution of species like the sperm whale and the killer whale or orca, which is actually a large porpoise, have made them unique among the mammals.

Shore whaling—the pursuit and capture of such shoal water species as the humpback whale and the pilot whale or blackfish from small boats put to sea directly from the open coast—was a very early practice in North America, especially on the east end of Long Island, where East Hampton and Southampton were extensively settled by the middle of the seventeenth century. The methods were adapted from those of the coastal Indians, who were expert boatmen and who, as described by a Captain George Waymouth in 1605, "go in company of their king with a multitude of their boats; and strike him with a bone made in fashion of a harping iron fastened to a rope . . . which they veer out after him; then all their boats come about him as he riseth above the water, with their arrows they shoot him to death; when they have killed him and dragged him to shore, they call all their chief lords together and sing a song of joy. . . ." [2]

As the market for whale oil expanded, the whales alongshore became scarce, and attention was turned to the larger species of the open ocean. Combining Indian techniques with ancient European methods, the American whalemen learned their lessons quickly, moving farther and farther from the beach as the surf boat gave way to the sloop, until at last, by the end of the century, their sails dropped out of sight of land. Harpooning the leviathans from whaleboats dispatched from a mother ship became the colorful and dangerous practice, and the era of the "Nantucket sleigh ride" had begun.

Nantucket was the logical source of American ocean whaling, not only because it was situated on the early whale grounds but because its poor soil compelled its settlers to gain their living from the sea. "In the year 1690," as Obed Macy wrote in his history of the island, "some persons were on a high hill observing the whales spouting and sporting with each other, when one observed: there—pointing to the sea—is a green pasture where our children's grand-children will go for bread." [3] Sag Harbor and New Bedford were among the towns engaging extensively in whaling, but the industry remains most closely associated with the stark sea island lying south of Cape Cod on the Nantucket Shoals.

In the early years, the whales most sought were the bowhead or Greenland whale and its near-relative, the right whale—so called because, a valuable oil-and-baleen species which shared with the bowhead the crucial characteristic of floating on the surface when killed, it was the "right" whale to pursue. The baleen, known commercially as whalebone, is fixed in the huge mouths of these species in a series of triangular strips sometimes thirteen feet in length; a hairy fringe on the inner edges of the strip serves to strain from the sea the quantities of plankton or "brit" required to feed the baleen species.

In the seventeenth century the sperm whale or cachalot was little known, and was thought to be very rare. But in 1712 Captain Christopher Hussey, blown far out to sea in a storm, discovered that the sperm whale was extremely abundant far offshore, and was furthermore a "floater"; the high quality of its blubber oil and the case of pure spermaceti enclosed in its huge head gained prompt attention, and the pursuit of it was to lead the Yankee whalemen around the world.

The sperm whale differs from the baleen whales in possessing free, toothed jaws, and it feeds largely on squid and cuttlefish, often thousands of feet below the surface. (Its apparent inability to digest properly the hard

SPERM WHALE

beaks and cuttlebones of these creatures produces in its stomach a hard, waxy residue called ambergris, found sometimes in defunct specimens but more often vomited out by the afflicted animal, to be washed up eventually ashore. An excellent fixative for fine perfumes, ambergris is valued at more than one hundred dollars a pound.) The saga of American whaling is based largely on this species, which is considerably less docile than the baleen whales. A Nantucketer named Peleg Folger, of the sloop *Phebe*, gave this account in 1754: "We struck a large spermaceti & got in three irons and one tow-iron. . . . As soon as the tow-iron went into the whale, she gave a flank and went down & coming up again she bolted her head out of the water almost if not quite as far as her fins. And then pitched the whole weight of her head on the Boat—stove ye boat & ruined her and killed the midshipman (an Indian named Sam Lamson) outwright a Sad & Awful Providence." [4] It was a sperm whale that, in 1820, twice attacked and finally sank the Nantucket whaler *Essex* in the open ocean some twelve hundred miles northeast of the nearest land at the Marquesas, an incident which, related by a survivor, First Mate Owen Chace, was a source of Herman Melville's *Moby Dick*.

The whaling towns flourished in the late eighteenth century, the period of the Revolution excepted, but it is the first half of the nineteenth century that has been called "the Golden Age of Whaling"; in 1846, seven hundred and forty-odd whalers were sailing from American ports alone. Shortly thereafter the sperm whale, which, as the bulwark of the new nation's economy in the years after the Revolution, may have rivaled the beaver as the most significant wild creature in the history of North America, began an inevitable decline. Whale oil was gradually displaced by kerosene, and the whalemen turned again upon the baleen whales. Baleen, used in quantity now for the stays and hoops of nineteenth-century fashions,

BLUE WHALE
GRAY WHALE
BOWHEAD WHALE

was bringing outlandish prices, and the Norwegian development of the harpoon cannon, in combination with the steamship and motor winch, made the exploitation of the remaining right and bowhead whales an efficient business. These animals, indeed, were often killed for the sake of their baleen alone. The British attacked them in the North Atlantic, while an American fleet sailing out of San Francisco wreaked havoc among the North Pacific whales, pursuing them into the Arctic Ocean. The Pacific right whale vanished from the California coast after 1885, and the right whales of both hemispheres were nearing extinction when the International Whaling Convention of 1937, awarding these species complete protection, came tardily to their rescue. The Convention also prescribed whaling seasons and grounds, set up a minimum legal size for each species, outlawed the killing of cows accompanied by calves, and so forth.

Modern whaling, conducted largely in the Antarctic by Norway, Great Britain, Russia, Holland, and South Africa, is supported by the finner or rorqual whales, the "wrong" baleen whales of former times; their tendency to sink when killed is now corrected by inflating them with air. The sperm whale, which has recovered somewhat, is also taken in controlled numbers, and its spermaceti is still the finest lubricant for watches and other precision instruments. But some of the rorquals are declining, including the blue or sulphur-bottom whale, which has almost disappeared from Arctic and temperate seas and is still hunted on a regulated basis in the Antarctic. In considering huge animals, we are apt to think of the great prehistoric reptiles such as the brachiosaurus, which was several times the size of today's elephant; we are apt to forget that the blue whale, at birth, is larger than the elephant, and that the adult, which attains a length of over one hundred feet and an avoirdupois of three hundred thousand pounds, is far and away the greatest creature that ever existed on earth. Its extinction, should this be permitted to occur, would be tragic and unnecessary.

Most of the commercial whales are cosmopolitan, and are found, or were found formerly, in all the oceans of the world. An exception is the gray whale, which some authorities believe was the so-called "scrag" whale referred to in early accounts of shore whaling. If so, the species was entirely exterminated in the Atlantic, and is now limited to both coasts of the North Pacific, from Korea and Baja California to the Arctic. A small inshore whale which bred formerly in San Diego and Mission Bays, it was presumed extinct, or nearly so, in two separate periods within the past century, and not until 1911 did the existence of the western Pacific population become known to American naturalists. The protection it was granted in 1937 was considered a futile gesture, but in the last two decades it has made a good recovery, and an estimated population of four thousand (1957) has already encouraged talk of renewed slaughter. The gray whale's breeding lagoons in Baja California are no longer remote, however, and the species may decline in the face of civilization without active assistance on the part of man.

Some species of small "beaked" whales, an ancient group which may be passing slowly from existence, appear rarely in North American waters. There are only a few scattered records, on the Atlantic coast, of the Sowerby and Gervais whales, and of the Stejneger's whale in the Pacific, and the habits of these mysterious creatures are virtually unknown.

For more than a century American whaling was confined to the Atlantic Ocean. The first whale taken by an American in the Pacific was a cachalot ironed in 1788 by a Nantucketer, Archaelus Hammon, of the English ship

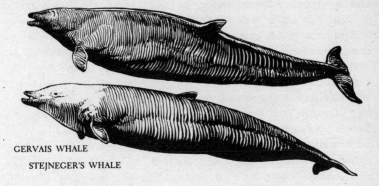

GERVAIS WHALE
STEJNEGER'S WHALE

Emelia; finding few whales in the Falkland Islands region of the South Atlantic, the *Emelia* had rounded the Horn, and had sighted the distinctive forward spout of the sperm whales off the Chile coast. But other marine mammals of the Pacific had already been exploited, for at this time Pacific North America was the object of new interest on the part of both Spain and Russia. In 1769, when Gaspar de Portolá came north out of Mexico to establish the first California settlements at Monterey, he feared he might have to defend the territory "from the atrocities of the Russians, who were about to invade us." [5]

Actually, the Russian activity was little more than an extension of their fur trade, which had spread to the Western Hemisphere as early as 1741. That year Admiral Vitus Bering, dispatched by Peter the Great to chart the unknown reaches of the Siberian coast and of the American continent, and to determine whether the two were joined, discovered the Aleutian Islands and the Alaskan mainland, apparently at what is now Cape St. Elias. He was accompanied by an industrious German, Georg Wilhelm Steller, for whom nine North American plant and animal species and three geographical locations have since been named, and whose contributions included the sole scientific descriptions ever recorded of two species now extinct; though some remains have been located, Steller was the only naturalist ever to see the sea cow and the Pallas cormorant alive.

The Pallas cormorant was known only from Bering Island—"a special kind of large sea raven," according to Steller, "with a callow white ring about the eyes and red skin about the beak, which is never seen in Kamchatka, occurs there. . . ." [6] Therefore it is not technically a North American bird, but the following account by L. M. Turner in 1886 suggests that its range included the western islands of the Aleutians: ". . . the natives of Attu speak of a large cormorant, which from the description given by them, could have been none other than the greatly desired Pallas's cormorant (*Phalacrocorax perspicillatus* Pall). This bird is now not to be found, where but twenty years ago (when no fire-arms were used) it was quite abundant at Attu and among the other Nearer islands." Elsewhere he says, "The natives of Attu . . . describe it as being fully twice as large as the red-faced cormorant and of different plumage." [7] In any case, as Elliott Coues had observed in 1872, "none of the ornithologists who have lately visited Alaskan shores have found the bird," [8] and probably it had disappeared twenty years earlier, the victim of foraging fishermen. There are but four skins in existence.

The Steller's sea cow, or rhytina, enjoys an uncertain position in the North American fauna, though Dall included it in his list of Alaskan mammals, and though there is some indication that it frequented St. Lawrence Island, where the Eskimos speak of a "real walrus," without tusks, occurring there long ago. This huge relative of the manatee may have weighed three tons, and was also a native of Bering Island, where, like the cormorant, it was pursued as food; it disappeared on some indefinite date prior to 1868, and possibly much earlier, for reasons which Steller illuminated in his journal:

> Along the whole shore of the island, especially where streams flow into the sea and all kinds of seaweed are most abundant, the sea cow, so called by our Russians, occurs at all seasons of the year in great numbers and in herds. . . . Signs of a wonderful intelligence . . . I could not observe, but indeed an uncommon love for one another, which even extended so far that, when one of them was hooked, all the others were intent upon saving him. . . .[9]

Two marine mammals of great economic importance—the sea otter and the northern fur seal—were also noted by the Bering Expedition, and as a consequence further exploration of the raw, gray shores was immediately set in motion. "As soon as the sea otter and other pretious furs are exhausted," Pennant observed, "Kamchatka will be deserted by the Russians, unless they should think fit to colonize the continent of America." [10] At this time the fur seals and otters of the Commander Islands and the Kamchatka Peninsula of Siberia were already declining, and the abundance

PALLAS CORMORANT

of otters on the kelp beds of Bering Island and the Aleutians encouraged the Russians to sail farther east and south in search of more; they established posts from the rain-green sounds of east Alaska to British Columbia and, eventually, to California. Native hunters were conscripted, and by 1804 the Alaskan village of Sitka alone was able to export fifteen thousand otter skins.

Another Russian explorer, Gerasim Pribilof, had located in 1786 the remote volcanic islands in the Bering Sea since named for him. The cobbled beaches swarmed with seals, and there was, as well, a fine colony of otters. Pribilof secured five thousand of the latter, and a voyage of the following year took two thousand more; no sea otter has ever been seen on the Pribilof Islands since. The supply of northern fur seals seemed inexhaustible, however, and the onslaught of this species, which was to increase in ferocity for another century, commenced in earnest.

By this time the illustrious Captain Cook had entered the northern fogs from a southerly direction, the forerunner of numerous British and American navigators who, seeking new fur sources for the China trade, were soon to stir Pacific silences with the creak of ships. The elephant seals and southern fur seals were already vanishing from the Falkland Islands and elsewhere, incidental prey of the whaling trade which was now rounding Cape Horn; the so-called whalemen-sealers were the true pioneers of the Pacific, fanning out on their bloody errand like sea birds across the vast blue water, scouring the South Seas and striking upon Antarctica. These voyages, as one Yankee, Captain Edmund Fanning, wrote, "came highly recommended . . . as an enterprise . . . promising to be, from the high value . . . the South Sea fur seal skins were held at in Canton, one of

GUADALUPE FUR SEAL

great profit, and although a new field, yet so encouraging, that in company with some friends, it was resolved upon sending out a vessel to procure a cargo suitable for the Chinese market." [11] Some of these vessels moved northward, scouring the Chile coast and quartering new whale grounds off Peru, engaging in piracy and reciprocal treacheries with the Spaniards, and falling at last upon the Indians of the evergreen shores of the Pacific Northwest, who offered lustrous otter skins in fair exchange for gewgaws. (For an otter skin worth fifty dollars in Canton the natives were delighted to receive five ermine skins or "clicks" worth thirty cents apiece in Boston.) One of these sailors, Captain Robert Gray, discovered the Columbia River in 1792, a fact which was to prove important in the later dispute between Britain and the United States over the Oregon Territory. In California they found the final outposts of the southern seals, and confronted the Russians, probing down from the north.

It is not known who began the California sealing, but the nations soon fell to side by side; the British whaler *Port-au-Prince* took 8338 Guadalupe fur seals from the San Benito Islands in 1805, and a Yankee crew slew 73,402 on the Farallon Islands, off San Francisco, between 1810 and 1812. The Russians, however, were most solidly implanted, importing Aleut hunters from their Alaskan posts to handle the labor of carnage. They ranged south as far as Guadalupe Island, off Baja California, and maintained a sealing station on the Farallons as late as 1840. Their eventual departure was motivated at least in part by the fact that the Guadalupe fur seal, and the elephant seal as well, were by that time virtually extinct.

The histories of these two species, which shared limited and accessible

ELEPHANT SEAL

breeding grounds on the temperate Pacific Coast, run parallel. The elephant seal, so named for its bizarre proboscis, ranged as far north as Point Reyes, and yielded about three barrels of oil per carcass, as well as a tongue deemed succulent. It was easily taken, perhaps because, as Fanning suggested, "The loudest noise will not awaken these animals when sleeping." [12] In any case, its oil was thought superior to that of the sperm whale, which was then disappearing, and as a consequence its most famous days occurred from 1855 until 1870, the year when it was presumed exterminated from the Northern Hemisphere. In 1892 nine specimens were located at Guadalupe, and seven of these, sad to say, were collected by excited scientists. Apparently a few remained at sea, however, for the species restored itself once more under protection, and, though occasionally poached for the male genitals, esteemed in the Orient as an aphrodisiac, it has now passed out of danger. The "sea elephants" are once again appearing regularly in the Channel Islands of southern California.

The Guadalupe fur seal, prized for its hide, has had a thinner time of it, having been regarded as extinct during five separate periods of its brief history. It disappeared the first time shortly after the Russian departure, about 1840, and was promptly persecuted again upon its reappearance at Guadalupe a quarter-century later. By 1894 it was pronounced extinct a second time. Though Mexico declared the island a sanctuary in 1922, there was no authenticated record of the fur seals until 1928 when a fisherman, one William Clover, sold two captured males to the San Diego Zoo. On the

SEA OTTER

heels of a dispute over his fee, Clover threatened to see to it that the seal went extinct a third time, a mission which, for two decades, it was thought he had accomplished; he succeeded in destroying about sixty remaining animals, the hides of which he apparently sold in Panama, where he himself perished in a saloon. Despite scattered reports, no further sighting was verified until, in 1949, an old bull was photographed in the Channel Islands. Subsequent expeditions to Guadalupe failed to locate others, and its fifth extinction was generally accepted when, in 1954, four-teen were found in the island's rocky sea caves. Since then it has increased —probably it was never quite as rare as was thought—though its numbers do not exceed five hundred.

Today Guadalupe, some seventeen miles of sun-baked rock rising sharply from the open ocean, boasts a Mexican weather station as its sole habitation, but the boulders of its beaches, smoothed by centuries of seals, attest to vast animal populations long since gone; the ruins of stone huts and slaughter pens, perhaps occupied by the enslaved Aleuts transported by the Russians, are rude reminders of a rude era, at the end of which the mineral-minded Spanish withdrew southward and the Russian sea hunters returned into the north. Once their prey had been decimated, the Russians had small reason to maintain their distant outposts on the American coast.

The northern Pacific was still Russian domain, and encompassed the most important grounds of the sea otter and northern fur seal, both of them much more valuable than the southern seals. The sea otter is a heavy, four-foot relative of the inland otter, and its dark, dense fur, tipped with silvery gold, is the most precious in the world. Apparently it hauled out commonly on the mainland and frequented the river deltas, but persecution has driven it to sea; except in severe storms, when it sometimes seeks the coastal rocks, it rests in the kelp beyond the surf, and is usually seen floating on its back, its head and tail or a webbed foot protruding among the heads of these long-stalked plants, rising and falling peacefully on the incoming seas. From the high cliff road between San Simeon and the Monterey Peninsula in California, the watchful traveler can often see them, sliding like small seals through the green surf-smoked swells below the headlands; one floats on its back, clutching a large red abalone between its paws and eating from it as if it were a bowl. Sometimes a young otter trails the white-faced adult, and is harried by a hungry gull competing for scraps of abalone. They near the rocks. A sea breaks, the gull lifts, and the otters slide beneath the surface, to rise again like black shadows in the semi-transparent water beyond the foam.

The sea otter is gentle and relatively tame; its suspicion of man came to it late. Though Pennant wrote that Bering Island swarmed with otters, he also anticipated their decline, and by 1818 Baron Ferdinand von Wrangel, manager of the Russian American Fur Company, predicted general extermination. Its disappearance in the south, from Oregon to Baja California, was accompanied by that of the Guadalupe fur seal, and encouraged the Russians to relinquish to the United States, in 1824, that part of the Oregon Territory which now comprises Vancouver and most of British Columbia. (This area was ceded to Great Britain in 1846, at the time of American annexation of present-day Oregon, Washington, Idaho, and western Montana and Wyoming.) Similarly, the reduction of the mainland fur bearers as well as the sea otters and northern fur seals promoted in part the sale of Alaska to the United States. By 1867, the year of the Alaska purchase, Russia had exported Alaskan furs worth over six times what she accepted for the vast territory itself.

The United States proceeded with the destruction of the sea otters, and the Alaska Company took 47,482 skins between 1881 and 1890. In 1900, however, only 127 skins were taken, and ten years later the season's catch of a fleet of sixteen schooners was less than two per ship. As a result, the fur traders offered no resistance when, in the following year, an international treaty was set up to protect all otters north of the Thirtieth Parallel —Baja California and southern Japan—a measure which made a sanctuary of their entire range. The sale of sea-otter fur was forbidden in the United States and Alaska, and the last legal pelt, marketed in London that year, brought nearly two thousand dollars.

Meanwhile, the sea otters of the United States had disappeared entirely, and it was not thought that the species would survive long anywhere. But in 1933 a few individuals were located off the California coast—a small Baja California herd may have been eliminated in this period by the same William Clover who revenged himself on the Guadalupe seals—and the scattered Aleutian remnants were reappearing in bands totaling about six hundred. A few years later, a small herd established itself near Monterey, and in the last two decades the California otters have increased to several hundred. The Alaska otters, an estimated five thousand strong, have spread east from the Aleutians to Kodiak Island and Prince William Sound; despite stringent protection, over one hundred are probably poached yearly in the new state. Though the sea otter is by no means out of danger, it is already regarded acquisitively by certain fur interests in California.

The state of California includes among its natural endowments an un- usual variety of valuable marine mammals. Besides the Guadalupe fur seal, which may return to the Channel Islands in the near future, the gray whale, elephant seal, and sea otter have all restored themselves with protection, and this striking coast can boast, as well, the harbor seal, the California sea lion (this is the talented animal of circuses and zoos), and the huge, yellowish Steller's sea lion. The latter creature, even where protected, is frequently executed as an unwelcome competitor by commercial fishermen, and the fishers of abalone take a correspondingly dim view of the sea otter. Both grievances are exaggerated, and the current talk of "harvesting" the otter and the gray whale should remind Californians that no less than four of their marine mammals have disappeared one or more times in the past century, and could easily vanish once again were the material interests of a few to be given priority over the aesthetic interests of the many, the best interests of the animals themselves entirely aside.

If the sea otter is individually more valuable, the most remunerative marine fur bearer in the aggregate is unquestionably the northern fur seal. Small herds occur on Robben Island, the Commander Islands, and the Kuriles, all under Russian jurisdiction, but the great majority of the fur seals frequent the Pribilof rookeries, far out in the Bering Sea. At the time of discovery, the population there was probably about five million, and some two million were slaughtered during the next half-century. By 1835 the Russians were forced to apply certain restrictions on shore killing, and these were continued by the United States after the purchase of Alaska. In the next decade, however, pelagic sealing was adapted from an Indian practice of spearing the fur seals in the ocean as they passed northward in migration. A fleet of schooners was soon sailing from Pacific ports, from San Diego to Victoria, British Columbia, and across the ocean the Russians and Japanese contributed to the carnage. The open-water hunting was extremely wasteful, since pregnant females were not spared and since many

injured animals sank to the killer whales and sharks. (The killer whale is the fur seal's natural enemy, and a specimen has been caught with as many as eighteen seals in its stomach.) By 1890 the Pribilof herd was much diminished, but American attempts to control pelagic sealing were unsuccessful. Seizure of Canadian ships in the Bering Sea brought the United States to the edge of war with Great Britain in 1890. "It cannot be unknown to Her Majesty's Government," wrote Secretary of State James Blaine to British envoy Julian Pauncefote, "that one of the most valuable sources of revenue from the Alaskan possessions is the fur-seal fisheries of the Behring Sea. . . . It has also been the recognition of a fact now held beyond denial or doubt that the taking of seals in the open sea especially leads to their extinction. . . . By what reasoning did Her Majesty's Government conclude that an act may be committed with impunity against the rights of the United States which had never been attempted against the same rights when held by the Russian Empire? . . ."[13] International tribunals were summoned as a result of the Blaine-Pauncefote negotiations, but no effective action was agreed upon until 1911, when the seal millions had been reduced to 130,000 animals. As in the case of the sea otter, the removal of financial incentive made conservationists of one and all, and the Fur Seal Treaty of that year was set up without resistance. It outlawed pelagic sealing except by aborigines and awarded jurisdiction over seals on land to the nation controlling the breeding area, the proceeds from the sealing on all breeding grounds to be pro-rated among the four countries

GRAY SEAL

concerned (the United States, Canada, Russia, and Japan). Japan abrogated this treaty just before World War II, and since then the United States and Canada have reserved the sealing at the Pribilofs for their mutual profit and that of the seal herd. Only three-year-old bulls are slaughtered, and the Pribilof population is now thought to approach two million. The international management of the fur seal has been called "the most outstanding of all accomplishments in the conservation of wildlife," [14] a statement in no way unreasonable when one considers that federal revenues from this species alone have paid several times for the purchase of all Alaska.

The fur seals are related to the sea lions, and are similarly equipped with external ears, relatively long necks, and reversible hind flippers which enable them to proceed more or less efficiently on land. The hair seals, or "true" seals, do not share these characteristics, nor are they possessed of the fine undercoat which gives the fur seals their value. Nevertheless, the demand for their oil and "leather" has supported hair-seal fisheries in many parts of the world, the most important of which is still operating out of Newfoundland.

Of the several hair seals in the North Atlantic, the most important to this fishery is the harp seal, well over one hundred thousand of which are taken annually. The hooded seal, less common, is also killed wherever possible, including the newborn animals known as "white coats," esteemed highly for their soft white pelts. The hooded seal, potentially endangered, is nonetheless much more abundant than the large, solitary gray seal of the Bay of St. Lawrence, whose preference for more temperate seas brings it perilously close to the environs of civilization.

Aside from their contribution to the sealers, the hair-seal populations are used extensively for food and clothing by the Eskimos, from Labrador to Alaska. On the Alaska coast, the ringed and bearded seals are the common species, and are readily observed next to their blowholes in the pack ice; only the ribbon seal, a yellow-ringed brown animal prized by the natives for its decorative hide, can really be called rare. In its small range, which extends from the Aleutians to Arctic Alaska, the ribbon seal seems always to have been uncommon; Pennant mentioned with gratification the receipt of a single specimen from Dr. Pallas. As late as 1874, Captain Charles M. Scammon's account of the marine mammals of the Pacific remarks of the "banded seal" that "Of this beautifully marked animal . . . there is but very little known. The Russian traders who formerly visited Cape Romanzoff, from St. Michael's, Norton Sound, frequently brought back the skins . . . which were used for covering trunks and for other ornamental purposes." [15] (The West Indian monk seal, a rare tropical hair seal, was discussed in Chapter 2.)

In the United States, only a few isolated headlands and offshore rocks on the Pacific give any indication of the sea-mammal swarms which once roiled the coastal waters of a continent. Point Lobos and the Monterey Peninsula, in California, and Hecate Head and the Three Arch Rocks, in Oregon, are sea-lion rookeries worth going far to visit; from the lovely reserve of cypress coast at Point Lobos it is also possible to see at times the largest herd of sea otter on this jagged shore, and the barnacled gray whales parting the blue swells beneath black, ragged flights of cormorants and alcids. The din of the rookeries is muffled in the ocean wash, and the random bark which rises above the groaning of the herd is whirled away quickly on the sea wind, but facing seaward with one's back to civilization, one senses the wild quality of a scene many thousands of years old.

The animals of the sea are still pursued wherever their numbers will support a fishery. Despite recent measures controlling their harvest, many species are still dangerously reduced and their last populations largely confined to Arctic and Antarctic seas and coasts. The marine mammals, turtles, and sea birds have lost their commercial significance in this country, and today the fishermen of the coastal ports must depend once again

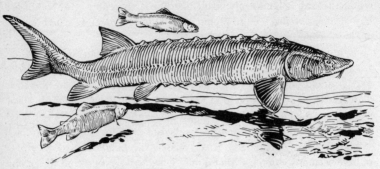

WHITE STURGEON, with king salmon

on the humble shellfish, shrimp, and lobster, the cod, hake, halibut, and other marine fishes, which have remained relatively plentiful since the Breton shallops first materialized in the fog of the offshore banks.

The marine fishes—those confined entirely in range and habitat to salt water—are rarely or never threatened with extermination by other than natural causes, since man has as yet been unable to damage the chemistry of the sea, and since the commercial fisheries cease being profitable long before a last breeding stock adequate for the repropagation of a particular species has been destroyed.

The history of the anadromous fishes—those that ascend from salt into fresh water to spawn—is somewhat similar, and, while considerable concern has been expressed for such valuable species as the shad, the sea sturgeons, the Pacific salmons, the Atlantic salmon, and, less justifiably, the striped bass, these fish have so far been endangered from a commercial and sport rather than from a natural-history point of view. The white sturgeon, a twenty-foot native of the northwest coast, from northern California to Alaska, is now rare enough to be considered an exception, however, and the Atlantic salmon has also declined seriously, as a consequence less of overfishing than of damming and pollution of streams within its range, which once extended south at least as far as the Connecticut River. Though still harvested in Canada and northern Europe, it is no longer a commercial fish in the United States. The other anadromous fishes still economically significant receive legal protection of varying degree, but the ceaseless deterioration of their native waters dims the prospects for their future.

Both marine and anadromous fishes are subject to irregular periods of scarcity, often brought about by weather conditions affecting particular spawning seasons. Rarely, their numbers are seriously reduced by volcanic eruption and other phenomena, and by such factors as a sudden increase in coastal waters of protozoans called dinoflagellates which, in great abundance, give off enough poison to render the water uninhabitable by marine animals of many kinds. The Red Tide which in 1948 killed vast quantities of fish on the southwest coast of Florida was so named because the red eye-spots of these myriad microscopic creatures gave a distinct tinge to the water. A similar, though less spectacular, mass mortality occurred in 1957.

A sudden change in water temperature can also be lethal. In 1882 a series of northerly storms and a subsequent incursion of ice into temperate seas killed incredible numbers of tilefish off the New England coast—the schooner *Navarino* traveled one hundred and fifty miles across a waste of dead and dying fish, and its captain estimated their numbers at well over a billion—and for some years afterward the tilefish, which at the time had been known to science but three years, were thought to have been utterly destroyed. At least two survived, however, for a few reappeared in 1892, and by the turn of the century the species had re-established itself. Today its face is once again familiar in New York's Fulton Fish Market.

TILEFISH

Sir, what a wonderful difference thirty years makes in the country! Why, at the time when I was caught by the Indians, you would not have walked out in any direction for more than a mile without shooting a buck or a bear. There were then thousands of buffaloes on the hills in Kentucky; the land looked as if it would never become poor; and the hunt in those days was a pleasure indeed. But when I was left to myself on the banks of the Green River, I daresay for the last time in my life, a few signs only of deer were to be seen, and, as to a deer itself, I saw none.

—Daniel Boone, conversation with Audubon (circa 1810)

6 : Hidden Worlds

In 1785, the second year of a new America, there was born in Haiti a bastard child called Jean Rabin. The previous year had witnessed the establishment by Charles Willson Peale of Peale's Museum in Philadelphia, which housed, according to one authority, "a stuffed paddlefish, an angora cat contributed by Benjamin Franklin, some mastodon bones, and some of his own paintings." [1] A decade later, there immigrated from Scotland one Alexander Wilson, aged twenty-eight, who numbered weaving, peddling, and poetry among his callings, and who chanced to establish himself near Philadelphia, the cultural seat of the republic, where Franklin and other men learned in the new sciences had already established the American Philosophical Society.

From such small seeds, during the next half-century, there flowered a series of accomplishments and events which were to establish a native American edifice of natural history. Rabin became, successively, Jean Jacques Fougère, Jean Jacques LaForest Audubon, and John James Audubon. Peale's Museum became the first in the nation devoted to natural history, and would boast Thomas Jefferson as one of its presidents. Wilson, inspired by Peale as well as by botanist John Bartram's son, William, was to construct the first American ornithology, a science of which he is now known, quite rightly, as the American father. In Wilson and Audubon, America found its first great naturalists, for until this time the natural scene had been almost entirely interpreted by Europeans; if Wilson and Audubon were not native Americans, they were nonetheless Americans when they died.

William Bartram, had he not been succeeded so closely by such giants, might well have deserved the mantle draped by tradition upon their shoulders. He published, in 1791, the first American book devoted to their common subject, and opened the eyes of his readers to the terrifying spectacle presented by an excited alligator:

> Behold him rushing forth from the flags and reeds. His enormous body swells. His plaited tail, brandished high, floats upon the lake. The waters like a cataract descend from his opening jaws. Clouds of smoke issue from his dilated nostrils. The earth trembles with his thunder.[2]

Though given to embroidery, Bartram had ample precedent and support for his mistakes. He intimates, among other things, the decline of the beaver, and makes significant mention of a popular practice of knocking wild pigeons from their roosts at night. Near Charleston, he relates, "tyger, wolf, and bear, hold yet some possession."

Another writer of the period who should be noted is Benjamin Barton, if only because his best-known publication was the first to confine itself to birds. With the development of the natural sciences, such specialization became necessary—Audubon, Spencer F. Baird, and Elliott Coues, all writing in the nineteenth century, made the last major efforts to embrace both birds and mammals—but Barton's innovation was accidental, since his original intention of covering the entire field was never realized.

Whether or not this gap in American science is tragic is problematical: Barton's view that swallows, instead of migrating, hibernated in the mud of frozen ponds reminds his rare reader that he was, after all, a product of the century past.

Wilson, a few years later, was impatient with the swallow theory, terming it "unworthy of serious refutation"; he also attacks the excesses of Buffon, whose creatures were prey to those more delicate emotions which today we reserve as peculiar to ourselves. Buffon was still very much an influence, and Wilson took irate exception to the Frenchman's "eternal reference of every animal of the New World to that of the Old . . . which would leave us in doubt whether even the Ka-te-dids of America were not originally Nightingales of the Old World, degenerated by the inferiority of the food and climate of this upstart continent." [3] Wilson's impatience, as clinical as it was peevish, represented the new scientific insistence on evidence; even so, in his quest for proof he was at times ingenuous himself. Seeking to try out Catesby's fancy concerning parrot guts and cats, he "several times carried a dose of the first description in my pocket till it became insufferable, without meeting with a suitable *patient* on whom, like other professional gentlemen, I might conveniently make a fair experiment."

Wilson's status as a professional gentleman had been a brief one. His exposure to the sciences came about quite by accident, when he settled on the Schuylkill not far from the residence of William Bartram. The older man became his friend, and Wilson was almost immediately absorbed in Bartram's own chief interest. By 1804, still largely uneducated, he had undertaken a collection of all North American birds, which he later willed to Peale's Museum. In addition to collecting, he attempted to paint every bird he could locate and to describe its habits as well, and the whole was included in an epochal nine-volume work, *The American Ornithology*, the first volume of which appeared in 1808.

Wilson's art, while authoritative and instructive, was creatively indifferent, and his astute descriptions of bird habits became his foremost contribution. A fine example is the following account of Carolina parakeets, though it lapses drastically into the very anthropomorphism for which he berated poor Buffon:

> At Big Bone Lick, thirty miles above the mouth of the Kentucky River, I saw them in great numbers. They came screaming through the woods in the morning, about an hour after sunrise, to drink the salt water, of which

they, as well as the Pigeons, are remarkably fond. When they alighted on the ground, it appeared at a distance as if covered by a carpet of richest green, orange, and yellow: they afterwards settled, in one body, on a neighboring tree, which stood detached from any other, covering almost every twig of it, and the sun, shining strongly on their gay and glossy plumage, produced a very beautiful and splendid appearance. Here I had an opportunity of observing some very particular traits of their character: Having shot down a number, some of which were only wounded, the whole flock swept repeatedly around their prostrate companions, and again settled on a low tree, within twenty yards of the spot where I stood. At each successive discharge, though showers of them fell, yet the affection of the survivors seemed rather to increase; for, after a few circuits around the place, they again alighted near me, looking down on their slaughtered companions with such manifest symptoms of sympathy and concern, as entirely disarmed me.

Though sentimental, his account of parakeet solidarity is accurate and moving. The parakeets shared this luckless habit with a number of ill-fated species, including the Eskimo curlew, a bird which Wilson, in company with other writers before and after him, failed to distinguish from the very similar Hudsonian curlew; he also identified the sandhill crane with the brown young of the whooper, and thought the ovenbird a thrush. His mistakes, however, are understandable and few, considering his training and equipment, which did not include a telescope or glass of any description until two years before his death, and some of his more startling assertions may well have been valid at the time. For example, we could scarcely agree that "there is perhaps no bird in North America better known" than the redheaded woodpecker; but we should bear in mind that this species was once heavily persecuted, and even bountied, in several states, as an alleged scourge of the orchard, and that Audubon knew of one hundred which were shot out of one cherry tree in a single day.

Other small birds then consistently shot included the bobolink and robin, as items of diet, and the kingbird, as the bane of honeybees. Wilson, who once celebrated the kingbird in a "short, poetical epitome" of ninety-three lines, spoke out strongly in their defense, and he may have been an agent in the passage in Massachusetts, in 1818, of the first law protecting non-game birds; it came to the aid and comfort of larks and robins, which henceforth were not to be taken out of season.

Wilson also described a number of new species, three of them from specimens brought back from the West in 1806 by the Lewis and Clark expedition to the Columbia. The three were named the Louisiana (western) tanager, Clark's nutcracker, and Lewis's woodpecker. "It was the request and particular wish of Captain Lewis, made to me in person, that I should make drawings of such of the feathered tribes as had been preserved, and were new," Wilson wrote in his account of the striking bird named for "that brave soldier, that amiable and excellent man, over whose solitary grave in the wilderness I have since shed tears of affliction. . . ."

The American Ornithology was the dominant work early in the century but it inspired a number of other significant contributions. In 1819 Edward Sabine and William Leach ventured into the Arctic, with notable ornithological results. Charles Lucien Bonaparte, the nephew of Napoleon, was at work in the United States on an *American Ornithology* of his own, a volume which was later incorporated with the original. John Godman and Richard Harlan were completing ambitious works on mammals. From 1826 to 1839, John James Audubon, with important assistance from William MacGillivray, produced *The Birds of America* and the *Ornithological Biography*, published in Edinburgh. Dr. Peter Pallas, in 1831, treated Alaskan fauna in *Zoographia Rosso-Asiatica*, and in the same year the *Fauna Boreali-Americana* of William Swainson and Dr. John Richardson also offered extensive new material on northern forms. The bird volume of this latter work, which established the separate identity of the Eskimo curlew, was followed in 1832 by Thomas Nuttall's *Manual of the Ornithology of the United States and Canada*, which makes the most of current information; "the small, or Esquimaux curlew," he remarks significantly, was "very fat, plump, and well-flavored" and "sought out by epicures."

The most distinguished of these works, of course, are the text and plates of Audubon, the excellence of which represented an immediate challenge to the work of Wilson. Though *The Birds of America* did not begin to appear until thirteen years after Wilson's death, the challenge had been made in person as early as 1810, a period when Audubon, in company with one Ferdinand Rosier, operated a store in the new community of Louisville,

Kentucky. On March 19 of that year, Alexander Wilson, still innocent of Audubon's existence, entered the store with an eye to the sale of a subscription to his own work, then in progress. According to Audubon's later account, this mission was a failure, for the very good reason that the young merchant considered his own paintings superior to those laid out upon his counter, and promptly produced them for Wilson's edification. Both men sincerely admired each other's work, and passed two days together collecting specimens and observing birds, including cranes—sandhill cranes, according to Wilson's account, and whooping cranes according to Audubon. The crane discrepancy was the least serious in their accounts, for, while Audubon claimed that he procured birds for Wilson heretofore unknown to the older man, and was, in effect, all that might be wished for as an aide, it was Wilson's contention that in Louisville he "received neither one act of civility from those to whom I was recommended, one subscriber, nor one new bird. . . . Science or literature has not one friend in this place." [4] Meanwhile the two had met again, the following year in Philadelphia, when Audubon called on Wilson and was taken by him to see the paintings of Rembrandt Peale. This meeting—their last, for Wilson died in 1813—was peaceable if not heartwarming, and it was not until two decades later that the Audubon-Wilson feud, if such it was, began.

The ninth volume of *The American Ornithology*, which refers to the Louisville episode, was edited posthumously by Wilson's friend George Ord, a small man of sour impulses who is now thought to have meddled extensively with the text. He promoted, among other things, the idea that Wilson resented his august admirer, Thomas Jefferson, for presidential failure to appoint Wilson to the Pike expedition of 1806, but Wilson's subsequent references to Jefferson suggest that this alleged grudge was largely a creature of Ord's imagination. The Louisville account, as well, may have been in part Ord's handiwork, but in any case Audubon took offense, and expressed his grievance at the earliest opportunity, represented by the first volume of *The Ornithological Biography*, in 1831.

The latter work is the accompanying text to the plates of *Birds of America*, and includes, besides bird descriptions, a number of "delineations" or informal accounts of frontier life and personalities, including that of Constantine Samuel Rafinesque-Schmaltz, a naturalist "who seems to have been a genius," as Coues would observe, "but one so awry that it is difficult to do aught else than misunderstand him, unless we confess that we scarcely understand him at all." [5] Among his odd and diverse accomplishments, Rafinesque included the discovery of the American crocodile, nearly fifty years before anybody else could locate it, and an anticipation of the theory of evolution, but Audubon, unimpressed, jeered cruelly at him. This supercilious attitude toward his contemporaries earned him little sympathy in the Wilson dispute, and was probably responsible in part for Swainson's declaration, in a letter dated 1830, that "Few have enjoyed the opportunity of benefiting by the advice and assistance of a scientific friend so much as yourself, and no one, I must be allowed to say, has evinced so little inclination to profit by it." [6] Possibly the Englishman harbored no real resentment of his young colleague, but if so, he was rare among Audubon's contemporaries. The partisans of Audubon will ascribe such resentment entirely to jealousy, of which the overpowering nature of the man's accomplishment doubtless generated an unusual amount, but he was by no means above reproach.

In the *Ornithological Biography*, Audubon not only refutes the Ord-Wilson account of the Louisville sojourn but accuses Wilson of having plagiarized his drawing of the "small-headed flycatcher." Actually, the drawings of this mysterious bird by the two men are quite dissimilar. Audubon gained little but retaliatory charges against himself, in the minutes of the American Philosophical Society, September 18, 1840: " 'This attack upon the reputation of a member of the Society,' said Mr. Ord, 'one who, during the long period that he dwelt amongst us, was noted for his integrity, ought not to be suffered to pass without examination.' " Mr. Ord proceeded to examine the charges himself, and speedily dismissed them. He went on to say that Audubon's figures of the female redwing and the female Mississippi kite had been taken intact from Wilson, a charge which, if inflammatory, is unhappily confirmed by even the most superficial comparison of the plates.

Various explanations have been advanced to absolve Audubon of piracy in regard to these drawings, but Nuttall, meanwhile, had troubled to point out a curious similarity in text: Wilson once described a pigeon roost at West Shelbyville, Kentucky, as extending about forty miles by three, the same dimensions applied by Audubon to a roost seen some years later near Green River by himself. Though this might have been coincidence, the following, cited elsewhere,[7] is not: Wilson, traveling between Frankfort and the Indiana Territory in 1810, observed a flight of migrating pigeons, the numbers of which he estimated at 2,230,272,000, capable of consuming 17,424,000 bushels of mast per day. Audubon, on a journey three years later between Henderson and Louisville, witnessed a flight of 1,115,136,000 birds, which he guessed might consume daily 8,712,000 bushels; that he halved, rather than doubled, Wilson's original computation is, of course, to his credit.

In addition to the small-headed warbler, as it is now referred to, both Wilson and Audubon claimed familiarity with a bird called the Blue Mountain warbler. Wilson was the undisputed discoverer of the latter, but Audubon, nothing daunted, contributed two further species—the carbonated warbler and the Cuvier's kinglet—to the growing list of American birds so marvelously elusive as to defy detection ever afterward. Unfortunately, not one of the scarce songbirds recognized today was the find of either man, although Audubon was still very much alive when the first valid rarity, Bachman's warbler, came to light.

It is unfortunate that Audubon felt obliged to compete with Wilson, and unable to allow his own work to triumph on its merit. (As early as 1827 this tendency had driven him to dismiss Wilson's correct identification of the immature bald eagle; Audubon portrayed it as the "Bird of Washington or Great American Sea Eagle," a new species of his own discovery.) Audubon's art, which requires no eulogy here, is of course greatly superior to that of his predecessor, and his prose, if more self-conscious and less dependable, is alive with the sweep and vigor which characterized the man. His account of the Green River pigeon roost is a notable example:

It was, as is always the case, in a portion of the forest where the trees were of great magnitude, and where there was little underwood. I rode through it upwards of forty miles, and, crossing it at different parts, found its average breadth to be rather more than three miles. Few Pigeons were to be seen before sunset; but a great number of persons, with horses and wagons, guns and ammunition, had already established encampments on the borders. Two farmers from the vicinity of Russelsville, distant more than a hundred miles, had driven upwards of three hundred hogs, to be fattened on the Pigeons which were to be slaughtered. Here and there, the people employed in plucking and salting what had already been procured, were seen sitting in the midst of large piles of these birds. The dung lay several inches deep, covering the whole extent of the roosting place, like a bed of snow. Many trees, two feet in diameter, I observed, were broken off at no great distance from the ground; and the branches of many of the largest and tallest had given way, as if the forest had been swept by a tornado. Every thing proved to me, that the number of birds resorting to this part of the forest, must be immense beyond conception. As the period of their arrival approached, their foes anxiously prepared to seize them. Some were furnished with iron pots, containing sulphur, others with torches of pine-knots, many with poles, and the rest with guns. The sun was lost to our view; yet not a Pigeon had arrived. Every thing was ready, and all eyes were gazing on the clear sky, which appeared in glimpses amidst the tall trees. Suddenly, there burst forth a general cry of "Here they come!" The noise which they made, though yet distant, reminded me of a hard gale at sea, passing through the rigging of a close-reefed vessel. As the birds arrived, and passed over me, I felt a current of air that surprised me. Thousands were soon knocked down by polemen. The current of birds, however, still kept increasing. The fires were lighted, and a most magnificent, as well as a wonderful and terrifying sight, presented itself. The Pigeons, coming in by thousands, alighted everywhere, one above another, until solid masses, as large as hogsheads, were formed on every tree, in all directions. Here and there the perches gave way under the weight with a crash, and, falling to the ground, destroyed hundreds of the birds beneath, forcing down the dense groups with which every stick was loaded. It was a scene of uproar and confusion. I found it quite useless to speak, or even to shout, to those persons who were nearest me. The reports, even, of the nearest guns, were seldom heard; and I knew of the firing, only by seeing the shooters reloading. No one dared venture within the line of devastation; the hogs had been penned up in due time, the picking up of the dead and wounded being left for the next morning's employment. The Pigeons were constantly coming; and it was past midnight before I perceived a decrease in the number of those that arrived. The uproar continued, however, the whole night; and, as I was anxious to know to what distance the sound reached, I sent off a man, accustomed to perambulate the forest, who, returning two hours afterwards, informed me he had heard it distinctly when three miles from the spot. Towards the approach of day, the noise rather subsided; but long ere objects were at all distinguishable, the Pigeons began to move off, in a direction quite different from that in which they had arrived the evening before; and, at sunrise, all that were able to fly had disappeared. The howlings of the wolves now reached our ears; and the foxes, lynxes, cougars, bears, raccoons, opossums, and pole-cats, were seen sneaking off from the spot, whilst Eagles and Hawks, of different species, accompanied by a crowd of Vultures, came to supplant them, and enjoy their share of the spoil. It was then that the authors of all this devastation began their entry amongst the dead, the dying, and the mangled. The Pigeons were picked up and piled in heaps, until each had as many as he could possibly dispose of, when the hogs were let loose to feed on the remainder.

Under the circumstances, Audubon's conclusion is a curious one: "Persons unacquainted with these birds might naturally conclude that such havock would soon put an end to the species. But I have satisfied myself, by long observation, that nothing but the gradual diminution of our forests can accomplish this decrease, as they not infrequently quadruple their number yearly, and always at least double it." [8] Actually, the pigeons produced but one young a year per pair, and in any case could not long have borne the degree of persecution he describes. His reference to the diminution of the forests is interesting, however, for at the time of his writing the frenzy of land-clearing still proceeded undiminished, and it is perfectly true that the decline of the forests would have decimated the pigeons had not man gotten to them first (see Chapter 8). After 1870, with the completion of the railroads, the lumber industry moved westward, and four billion board feet were cut in 1875 in the Great Lakes states alone. Eight billion board feet were being cut by 1890, after which the shattered forests of the Central States could no longer have supported the wild pigeons, by that time all but vanished from the earth.

Audubon's abundant life—his apprenticeship in David's Paris studio, his marriage and his Kentucky years, his sojourn abroad seeking publication, his profitable association with John Bachman, and the marriages of his sons Victor and John to Bachman's daughters—has been exhaustively documented, and needs no further exposition. Suffice it to say that his life's work did not end with *Birds of America*; before its publication was completed, he had conceived a companion work on American quadrupeds.

Bachman, a Charleston minister and naturalist, had been of considerable assistance in the preparation of the bird volumes, and was to become co-author of *Viviparous Quadrupeds of North America*, the text of which is largely his. Audubon's sons also made important contributions to this work: John Woodhouse Audubon, a fine artist in his own right, was responsible for many of the plates, and Victor Audubon prepared a number of the scenic backgrounds. It might be said that Audubon himself was the guiding spirit rather than the creator of this fine work, which Louis Agassiz, the articulate Swiss whose teachings in the United States after 1846 were an inspiration to the new natural sciences, was to call unequaled in Europe or America.

The text of the *Quadrupeds* takes somber account of the decline of the large eastern animals: "There is only a narrow range in the Allegeny mountains where the Elk still exists, in small and decreasing numbers, east of the Missouri . . . we regret to be obliged to state, that the Deer are rapidly disappearing from causes that ought not to exist. . . . In former times the cougar was more abundant than at present. . . . Thus it appears that the Beaver . . . may still occur, although in greatly diminished numbers, in many localities in the wild and uncultivated portions of our countries. . . ." The work, completed in 1848, described a number of small species as well, but it was not until later in the century, with the emergence of Spencer F. Baird, that the lesser mammals received a full share of attention. Nevertheless Bachman, like William MacGillivray in the case of the *Birds*, was more of a scientist than Audubon, and emphasized technical accuracy as well as a comprehensive treatment of the less dramatic forms: "Don't flatter yourself that this book is child's play," he wrote Audubon in 1839; "the birds are a mere trifle compared with this. . . . The skulls and teeth must be studied, and color is as variable as the wind—down, down in the earth they grovel, and in digging and studying we go giddy and cross. Such works as Godman's and Harlan's could be got up in a month, but I would almost as soon stick my name to a forged bank note as to such a mess of *soup-maigre*." [9]

Bachman's qualifications seem to justify these tart remarks. In addition to his holy calling, he was an accomplished naturalist, a friend of Alexander Wilson, and a recognized authority on the fauna of the southeastern states. His career was roughly contemporaneous with the adoption of systematic studies in regard to wildlife, and the more obscure species which

TOWNSEND BUNTING

were coming to light in the early nineteenth century included two rare
warblers of his own discovery, one of which Audubon named for William
Swainson and the other for Bachman himself. (Anyone familiar with the
names of North American wildlife will notice how many do honor to
figures of this period. Virtually all the naturalists mentioned here had new
birds named for them.) A number of the "new" creatures were actually
no more than female and immature specimens of familiar species, and a
few, as we have seen, may have sprung full-fledged from the minds of their
creators.

But now and again a form appears which is not so readily explained
away, and which nevertheless disappears forever, apparently without
human assistance. One of the first, and most mysterious, among the latter
was the Townsend bunting, the description of which was supported by a
collected specimen, shot in 1833, near West Chester, Pennsylvania, by
Nuttall's collaborator, John K. Townsend. The Townsend bunting was
never seen alive again, and, while it has often been dismissed as an abnor-
mal dickcissel or a hybrid, Audubon called it a "fine specimen of a new
species," [10] and it has lately been suggested that, since its characters are not
those of a hybrid, the species may have gone extinct before a second example
could be collected. "The solitary bird having been killed," remarked the
laconic Dr. Coues, "it represents a species which died at birth." [11]

Brewster's linnet, collected in 1870 near Waltham, Massachusetts, and
the Cincinnati warbler, reported a decade later, are two more hypothetical
forms known only from solitary specimens, and both are almost certainly
hybrids. In recent years, the role of the Townsend bunting in ornithological circles has been filled by Sutton's warbler, which is mentioned here
because a good possibility exists that it is an authentic species and not, as
is generally believed, a very rare hybrid between the yellow-throated **and**

parula warblers. If it is valid, it is almost certainly the very last native bird which will ever be discovered in North America; the two specimens collected were located one day eighteen miles apart, in May 1939, in West Virginia. Supporters of the Sutton's warbler point out that the second bird, a female, had frayed brood feathers, indicating the presence of a nest. It is also significant that one of the alleged parent species, the yellow-throated warbler, has never been recorded in the state. Since 1939 a half-dozen or more sight records have been made, in West Virginia and points south, about half of which can be considered valid.

If Sutton's warbler is indeed authentic, the likelihood appears to be that it is a new species recently evolved, but possibly it is old, and was discovered as it fluttered toward the abyss. The natural death of species is very slow, and rarely are we able to record the last decline within the period of one man's lifetime. The California condor, a Pleistocene contemporary of the mammoth, first noted by Lewis and Clark on the Columbia, was already retreating from a wide range which included Florida for many years before the white man hastened it along, and the Bachman's warbler, which became known to science in the same year as the lost bunting, was rare from the day of its discovery. The reasons for its rarity are obscure, for this neat, black-throated species is neither narrowly distributed nor, so far as is known, dangerously precise in its choice of habitat, and, far from being vulnerable to any designs man might have upon it, is considered the most difficult to see of all North American birds, even when singing close at hand at the top of its small voice. Yet it has remained extremely uncommon from the beginning, disappearing for a half-century before a Charles Galbraith, in 1888, shot thirty-one in Louisiana for the millinery trade. In 1897 its nest was first discovered, in both Arkansas and Missouri, and it has since been found breeding in five other states, with wanderers occurring as far north as Indiana. A few may winter in Florida and Georgia, but the majority fly to Cuba. Its preference for inaccessible, swampy areas increases the mystery of its rarity, and since, unlike most of the scarce songbirds, it appears to be growing rarer, it may well vanish of its own accord before the present century is ended.

We are apt to think of rare animals and birds in terms of large, persecuted species, and it is true that the smaller creatures—the small fish, amphibians, reptiles, birds, and mammals—have been relatively unmolested by man. Among the perching birds (an order which includes the flycatchers, swallows, jays, and crows as well as the so-called songbirds), such

SUTTON'S WARBLER

species as the robin, bobolink, and red-winged blackbird were once slaughtered in myriads for food, but it is doubtful whether any of them actually faced extinction at the time measures were set up for their defense. The North American wood warblers, however, include several precarious species. The Swainson's and the golden-cheeked warblers are uncommon and locally distributed, respectively, and two other warblers besides the Bachman's would have to be called endangered.

The yellow-breasted, blue-backed Kirtland's warbler breeds only in groves of young jack pine, in an area comprising several counties of Michigan's Lower Peninsula; it winters in the Abaco Islands of the Bahamas. First reported from near Cleveland in 1851—the specimen was presented to Dr. Jared Kirtland by his son-in-law—it remained a mysterious species until 1903, when its small breeding range was at last located. In the half-century intervening, only a few specimens had been taken, and a single bird, shot at sea during migration in 1841, was discovered in a private collection by Spencer F. Baird. A 1952 census estimated its total numbers at less than one thousand, and it is unlikely that its population ever exceeded this figure in the past century, or will exceed it in the next. For this warbler is actually benefited by forest fires, which permit the reversion of the burned-over land to the jack-pine growth it appears to require. It will not nest, however, in any area where the pines are more than eighteen feet in height, and therefore must constantly shift its territory. Theoretically, should it fail to adapt to a less specialized habitat, and should fire be entirely controlled within its range over a period of years, the Kirtland's

COLIMA WARBLER

warbler would go extinct. Meanwhile, it remains one of the handsomest and most robust of its family; a visitor to its Michigan pine barrens, in a cool spring or summer dawn, may listen for its urgent song, sounding like nothing so much, to this ear at least, as "Felicity-has-to-wee-wee."

Like the Kirtland's, the drab Colima warbler is extremely circumscribed in its known breeding range, which consists, to date, of one small area of dry mountainside—the growth is live oak and juniper—in the immediate vicinity of Boot Springs, high in the Chisos Mountains of Texas's Big Bend. The reasons for its specialization and small numbers are still unknown, and although it has been recorded from several Mexican states, and is thought to winter in Michoacán, Sinaloa, and Colima, no breeding terrain has as yet been discovered in that country. The Chisos nests were not found until 1932, and a total of eighteen individuals were seen there during a survey in 1954. Until new breeding grounds are found, the Colima warbler should probably be considered the rarest songbird in North America.

A possible competitor for this distinction is the Cape Sable sparrow, a very scarce greenish seaside sparrow confined to the extreme southwest tip of Florida. Undiscovered until 1918, it was thought extinct after the 1937 hurricane submerged its coastal savannas, but it has subsequently reappeared. The Ipswich sparrow will also become endangered with any further erosion by the sea of its only breeding ground, the former walrus colony of Sable Island, off Nova Scotia; Sable Island seems doomed to wash away, and this pale, pretty dune sparrow will go with it.

One other small bird which might be considered is the black swift. Of

KIRTLAND'S WARBLER

scattered distribution in western Canada and the Pacific States, this swift is noted for its mysterious departures from former terrains. It is thought to follow cyclones, catching insects whirled up upon the winds, and thus may travel several hundred miles from its torpid nestlings. Though probably more numerous than records would indicate, it is nevertheless rare, and the study of its habits which might explain this rarity is complicated by the fact that the few nests ever located were discovered largely on high cliff faces and behind waterfalls.

Most small North American birds, the rare ones included, are presumably faring as well as or better than they were when the white man appeared. One good reason is that birds are seldom very localized in distribution, and those that are, like the Kirtland's, Colima, and golden-cheeked warblers, not only are widely distributed during migration but are sufficiently mobile (though perhaps not sufficiently adaptable) to seek new territory should the old deteriorate. Small creatures of the other vertebrate classes—the fishes, reptiles and amphibians, and mammals—are often, on the other hand, very localized indeed. The great majority are non-migratory, and many are further limited in their distribution by physical barriers, dependence on certain foods, the presence elsewhere of more advanced relatives, and sometimes by their own lack of "vagility," or capacity for dispersal. Such creatures are apt to be specialized—adapted precisely, that is, to a given environment. There, and there only, will they thrive. As we have seen, the immediate advantages of specialization are offset by a corresponding lack of that flexibility which would not only permit of a wider distribution but would tend to protect them against alteration of their habitats; a pond, for example, which tends to be filled by stream-borne

BLACK SWIFT

detritus or by the remains of its own vegetation, and by the subsequent invasion of the marsh plants on its edges, is generally short-lived, and a creature peculiar to it will die with it. It is not unusual for a distinct form, cut off from its parent species over a long period of time, to become entirely limited to a single spring, stream, valley, mountaintop, or islet. Since any small area is exposed to drastic attrition or change, these isolated species are the most frequently endangered.

The most striking examples of isolation are found among small western fishes and among the salamanders. The eastern fishes, including those of the Mississippi drainage, are less vulnerable than their western kin, since the river systems on the eastern half of the continent are more closely related, and the distribution of particular species therefore wider and more continuous. An exception is the Maryland saddled darter, two specimens of which were removed from Swan Creek, near Havre de Grace, Maryland, in 1912, and which has never been seen since. (It should be noted here that field research in regard to the great variety of North American fresh-water fishes is far from complete; certain rare forms may have been extin-tinguished before they were discovered, others may still swim undiscovered, and a few presently considered rare or extinct may be discovered elsewhere upon further investigation. The same is true, to a lesser extent, of the amphibians and reptiles, and even of the small mammals.) In the West, on the other hand, there has been a considerable separation and isolation

MARYLAND SADDLED DARTER

of species left behind in lakes and springs by the death of Pleistocene rivers, and here, too, severe drought, abetted by man's irrigation, pollution, and introduction of competing or predatory fishes, has brought about the extinction of a number of forms (see Appendix). Less common causes are flood and hybridization: the Big Bend gambusia, a small topminnow confined to a single cattail slough by the Rio Grande, disappeared when its habitat was washed away by river flood, and the Mohave chub will probably die out in the near future, chiefly through interbreeding with a more dominant minnow which invaded its habitat via a fisherman's bait can. Still other small fish require complete protection if they are to survive, and at least one species already enjoys it; the home of the Devil's Hole pupfish has recently been included within the protective confines of the Death Valley National Monument, though it is some miles distant from the boundary. This minnow-like species, named for its playful disposition, is found in a forty-by-fifteen-foot remnant of the Ice Age lakes, and its population, which varies from fifty to three hundred, may well have, as one admirer suggests, "the smallest range of any vertebrates in the world." [12]

Its unenviable claim might be challenged, however, by the Georgia blind salamander, a pale, pinkish, semi-transparent amphibian with grotesque external gills, the only known specimen of which was forcibly removed from a two-hundred-foot well near Albany, Georgia. Similarly, six specimens of the San Marcos salamander removed from the head of the San

DEVIL'S HOLE PUPFISH

FLATTENED MUSK TURTLE

Marcos River in Texas were the last on record; the animal may have perished, it is feared, through an excess of zeal on the part of its discoverers.

Some members of the reptile class are also quite particular. The flattened musk turtle is peculiar to the Black Warrior River system in a small area of northwest Alabama, and the Brazos water snake thrives only in a few streams in central Texas.

Both amphibians and reptiles are nocturnal and secretive as a group and, except for the commercial reptiles and the poisonous Gila monster, are not nearly so menaced by civilization as are the birds and larger mammals. Again, those animals are chiefly affected whose habitats are specialized or restricted, and thus exposed to natural deterioration or the whims of man. The same is true of the small mammals—the moles, shrews, bats, and the lesser rodents—which are also apt to be secretive and nocturnal, and are similarly oblivious of man's existence. So secretive, for example, is the desert vole that only a few specimens were collected before 1950, when it was discovered that this animal wiled its days away under dead agave plants, and was relatively abundant on these premises. The shrews and small rodents include a number of extremely localized forms among their elusive members, including the Muskeget Island beach mouse, which, as the "gray mouse" referred to by Baird in his *Mammals of North America*, (1859), was the first small, localized mammal to be described. The species is found only on a sandy spit of land off the west end of Nantucket, where

SAN MARCOS SALAMANDER

it is vulnerable to feral house cats, short-eared owls, and storms; its small world, like that of the Ipswich sparrow, may one day erode away.

A relative, the Gull Island vole, was first described in 1898 from fifteen specimens taken the previous year at Great Gull Island, a rocky islet of approximately eleven acres at the east entrance to Long Island Sound. In April of the previous year one hundred workmen of the J. W. Hoffman Company of Philadelphia invaded the island for the purpose of constructing Army fortifications there, and developed a taste for the eggs of the common terns which came to nest. This habit was decried by a Mr. J. Harris Reed, who, in an address to the Delaware Valley Ornithological Club that October, went on to say, "I am also informed by good authority that the Government intends erecting another gun on the east end of the island; if such be the case, it will consume all the earth from the remaining portions of the island, to form the breastworks, which will virtually leave nothing of Great Gull Island beyond the fortifications, and will completely destroy it as a resort for Terns." [13] Mr. Reed's concern was justified at the time, for terns were then favorite victims of the milliners, but a visitor to Gull Island today will find its grass-grown, broken concrete fortifications admirably suited to the needs of its thriving tern colony: the unheralded victim of the consumption of Gull Island was its vole, a small, dark field mouse known to science only a few months before succumbing to the military.

A striking example of a creature isolated by geological change is the white-tailed, tassel-eared Kaibab squirrel. The Kaibab squirrel is confined to the forty-by-twenty-mile plateau of the same name on the north rim of the Grand Canyon, the formation of which long since separated it from

BRAZOS WATER SNAKE

GULL ISLAND VOLE   MUSKEGET ISLAND BEACH MOUSE

its parent species, the Abert squirrel, across the chasm. The Kaibab squirrel feeds almost exclusively on the cambium layer of the yellow pine, and this specialization, in combination with its isolated range, makes it especially vulnerable to change. Unlike other squirrels, it has not learned a healthy respect for automobiles, and, in view of its scarcity, American museums limit themselves to accident victims for their small supply of specimens.

Finally, among the lesser mammals, there are two whose nocturnal and secretive habits, even in conjunction with wide range and good appearance, do not alter the possibility that they are the rarest in North America. The large, showy spotted bat has been recorded in almost as many states as there are specimens, from Montana south to southern California and Texas, and the eight individuals presently known to man were apprehended in a variety of conditions, including death. One was found hanging in broad daylight from a fence, another wallowed in a water puddle, and a third obliging individual entered a biology laboratory under its own power. Because its habits are virtually unknown—it has successfully avoided bat nets, and the supposition is that it flies high and in the dead of night— and because of its wide distribution, this creature may be more with us than we imagine.

The black-footed ferret is widespread in the Great Plains, from Texas north to the Canadian prairie provinces, but a recent survey (1954) indicated but sixty to seventy authentic records between 1946 and 1953, throughout the ten states included in its range. Of this remnant, over a third were found dead, and the rest were chronically imperiled by man's poisoning of prairie dogs (see Chapter 9), upon which and in company with which this large, elegant weasel makes its living. Though it is not easily observed, due to its covert nature, "complacency regarding the future of the

KAIBAB SQUIRREL

species," as one mammalogist remarks with admirable understatement, "is not justified." [14]

The black-footed ferret was first described by Audubon and Bachman, in 1849, from a specimen sent them from the "Plains of the Platte River, Nebraska." The animal was not seen again for nearly twenty-five years, and Audubon's uneven reputation may have inspired the skepticism of other naturalists, including Baird, who commented, a decade later, "It is a little remarkable that so conspicuous and well-marked a species should have eluded the notice of all the recent explorers of the Platte region." [15] Baird, whose presence on the field of natural history was first made known in 1844, by his list of those birds frequenting Carlisle, Pennsylvania, was then a youthful collaborator of Audubon; now he had become assistant secretary of a national museum established in 1846 by the will of a generous Briton, Mr. James Smithson, and known as the Smithsonian Institution. He was also chief editor of two ponderous works, *The Mammals of North America* (1859) and *The Birds of North America* (1860) which ushered in a modern era of group endeavor (as opposed to personal performance, à la Audubon), exactitude, and a forbidding accumulation of technical weight. The transition was inevitable: in the fifteen years previous, all the far west, from Oregon to Texas, had come under American control, and the Gadsden Purchase in 1853, which extended southward the New Mexico and Arizona territories, had completed the modern boundary of the United States. Government survey expeditions, accompanied regularly by naturalists, were bringing back all sorts of creatures only recently American, and Baird, the first man to have to deal with the fauna of the entire nation, listed some two hundred and thirty-two birds unknown, only two decades earlier, to Audubon. His volumes on mammals and birds were private editions of Volumes VIII and IX of a government publication entitled, significantly, *Reports of Explorations and Surveys to Ascertain the Most Practicable and Economical Route for a Railroad from the Mississippi River to the Pacific Ocean.*

The West was open, the railroads were expanding, and a half-century of commercial slaughter had begun.

SPOTTED BAT

The vast herds which had been grazing among the wild pastures of the prairies gradually disappeared. . . .

—JAMES FENIMORE COOPER (1827)

Wolves howling, and bulls roaring, just like the long-continued roll of a hundred drums. Saw large gangs of Buffaloes walking along the river. . . . Fresh signs of Indians, burning wood embers, etc. Abundance of bear tracks. . . .

—JOHN JAMES AUDUBON (1843)

7 : Plains, Prairies, and the Shining Mountains

IN 1843, eight years before his death, John James Audubon made a journey up the Missouri River, from St. Louis to Fort Union, on the present-day North Dakota–Montana border, in order to see, collect, and portray western animals for his volume on quadrupeds. For the most part, his journal records abundance, and his observations for August 17 included antelope, bighorn sheep, deer, wolf, swans, and elk, as well as bear tracks. In the Dakotas he fell in with a British trader named Culbertson, who was later to send him the first known specimen of the black-footed ferret, and whose spirited Blackfoot princess, much admired in Audubon's journal, was referred to by an impatient Bachman, fretting at home, as a "brain-eating, horse-straddling squaw." [1]

On June 12, where the Yellowstone River joins the Missouri in South Dakota, Audubon had sighted his first bighorn sheep, a band of twenty-two. "No one," he wrote later, "who has not seen the Mauvaises Terres, or Badlands, can form any idea of these resorts of the Rocky Mountain Rams, or the difficulty of approaching these animals." [2] In the ensuing half-century these animals were nonetheless approached, and the race described by Audubon, the so-called Audubon's or Badlands bighorn, was extinct by 1905. A quarter-century later the last band of the rimrock bighorn, a race native to the lava-bed country of the northern Great Basin, was seen near Smoke Creek in northeast California. The Sierra Nevada race is also near extinction, as is the Texas bighorn, among the southern or desert bighorns; only the northern Rocky Mountain sheep, ranging from Wyoming to Alberta and British Columbia in what the first French trappers called the Shining Mountains, is still in fair condition.

The bighorn sheep was among the first western animals to fade away before the face of man, and a century of expansion devoured it. Lewis and Clark had found sheep abundant on the upper reaches of the Columbia, and they were commonly taken by the emigrants who came after. By 1811 the fur traders of John Jacob Astor's Pacific Fur Company had settled Astoria at the mouth of the Columbia, and the following year the South Pass route across southern Idaho and Wyoming, known later as the Oregon Trail, came into use. The Missouri Fur Company was already established, and the Rocky Mountain fur trade, which would flourish for another forty years, was having its random beginnings on the upper Missouri and Yellowstone Rivers. The bighorn sheep, very good to eat, was a logical source of provender in the hill country.

At first the white men came in trickles, tentative and lost in an immensity of open space, but with the construction in this period of the Cumberland Road to Illinois the flow of pioneers increased. The West was simultaneously approached by commercial steamboats, running from New Orleans up the Mississippi, and the completion of the Erie Canal, in 1825, connected the eastern seaboard with the Great Lakes. Other canals gave access to the Central States, and by 1831 the Mohawk and Hudson Railroad, between Albany and Schenectady, was in operation. Like the canal

BLACK-FOOTED FERRET.

systems, the railroads spread rapidly, extending as far as the Mississippi just after the middle of the century.

Meanwhile the Plains Indians, including the Sauk and Fox removed westward after the Black Hawk War, were resisting white expansion, though many tribes, as Audubon noted, were already debased and apathetic. Others, however, gave an excellent account of themselves against the invaders—the fur traders, Mormon settlers, and numerous exploring parties under Wyeth, Frémont, and others, as well as the soldiers traveling to the Mexican wars (the annexation of Texas as well as the Mexican cession of the present-day Southwest took place in the 1840s) and the long, slow trains of covered wagons bound for Oregon and California, an overland migration which reached its peak after gold was discovered on John Sutter's California farm, in 1848.

> For miles, to the extent of vision, an animated mass of beings broke upon our view. Long trains of wagons with their white covers were moving slowly along, a multitude of horsemen were prancing on the road, companies of men were traveling on foot, and although the scene was not a gorgeous one, yet the display of banners from many wagons, and the multitude of armed men, looked as if a mighty army was on its march; and in a few moments we took our station in the line, a component part of the motley throng of gold seekers, who were leaving home and friends far behind, to encounter the peril of mountain and plain. . . .[3]

All these people required food, and probably there were bighorn in the foothills and even on the open plains; the sheep became restricted to the mountains only with persecution. In addition to the fur trappers scouring the Rockies for beaver, the meat hunters hired by the wagon trains killed sheep commonly during the slow, tortuous journeys through the passes; by the 1870s the sheep's habits had so changed that a gentleman hunter, Parker Gillmore, could write of them as follows: "When starlight or moon-light occurs, they avail themselves of its use to descend from their moun-tain fastnesses into the valleys beneath in search of favorite food, a per-formance which they never attempt during the daylight, except in such regions as their enemy, man, seldom or never intrudes." [4] In Gillmore's time the sheep were already scarce on their mountain outposts both east and west of the Rockies; their narrow trails on the hillside faces faded everywhere, and were overgrown.

Though become too wary and scattered to invite much attention from the meat hunters, the sheep continued to decline in the face of changing circumstances. They could not support the competition of the domestic sheep imported to their terrains, and suffered seriously from scab and other diseases contracted from these stupid, stunted cousins. In the present century, the restoration of the mule deer and elk provided further forage competition, and the bighorn, bearing on its head a pair of magnificent curled horns, was beleaguered constantly by big-game hunters. No longer a legitimate game animal in most of its shrunken range, it is still poached frequently by sheepherders, prospectors, and others, even within the con-

BIGHORN SHEEP

fines of the vast, desolate refuges established in southwestern mountains for its protection.

When Francis Parkman journeyed west, in 1846, the Black Hills of the Dakotas were still a "hunter's paradise," and the bighorns still abundant:

> I ran up to the top of the opening, which gave me a full view into the rocky gorge beyond; and here I plainly saw some fifty or sixty sheep, almost within rifleshot, clattering upwards among the rocks, and endeavoring, after their usual custom, to reach the highest point. The naked Indians bounded up lightly in pursuit . . . not more than half a dozen animals were killed. Of these only one was a full-grown male. He had a pair of horns, the dimensions of which were almost beyond belief.

Parkman was mightily impressed with the West, with its wildlife, and with the Indian tribes which were his passionate interest; a youthful but nonetheless eminent Bostonian, he disliked only the Mormons—"blind and desperate fanatics"—and the Mexicans—"The human race in this part of the world is separated into three divisions, arranged in order of their merits: white men, Indians, and Mexicans; to the latter of whom the honorable title of 'whites' is by no means conceded." His social fastidiousness nags at an otherwise open-minded and vivid account of a frontier where

> curlew flew screaming over our heads, and a host of little prairie-dogs sat yelping at us at the mouths of their burrows on the dry plain beyond. Sud-

denly an antelope leaped up from the wild-sage bushes, gazed eagerly at us, and then, erecting his white tail, stretched away like a greyhound. The two Indian boys found a white wolf, as large as a calf, in a hollow, and, giving a sharp yell, they galloped after him; but the wolf leaped into the stream and swam across. . . . A herd of some two hundred elk came out upon the meadow, their antlers clattering as they walked forward in a dense throng. . . .

The Oregon Trail, Parkman's account of his travels published in 1849, is perhaps the best known of all the early impressions of the West, and did much to extend a growing curiosity in the East in regard to the new territories.

Audubon had not been the first naturalist to describe the frontier; Thomas Say, Titian Peale, Thomas Nuttall, and John Townsend, among others, had preceded him. Nor was Parkman the first literary figure; his prominence derives not only from his narrative ability but from the fact that he wrote out of thorough experience. James Fenimore Cooper had written of the West two decades earlier on the basis of a first-hand knowledge of the eastern wilderness and eastern Indian (in Parkman's time the Deerslayer's peaceful Delawares, banished westward, had become fierce horsemen of the plains), and Washington Irving's *Tour of the Prairies* represented an excursion of but a few weeks; before Parkman, the only experienced traveler in the West whose talent had been sufficient to capture wide public attention was the wandering painter, George Catlin. To Cooper and Irving, nevertheless, can be credited much of the contemporary public interest in wildlife and the natural resources of the nation, as well as the first significant warnings that these benefits were far from inexhaustible; a romantic view of the wildwood was simultaneously indulged by such painters as Thomas Cole, Albert Bierstadt, and Karl Bodmer, and a philosophic one by Ralph Waldo Emerson and Henry David Thoreau (who had already voyaged the Concord and Merrimack and was living at Walden Pond when Parkman essayed the Oregon Trail), so that in this period the concept of nature offered something to every taste.

All these men, with a number of lesser figures, watered the seeds of what would become known as conservation, and Cooper and Thoreau were even naturalists of sorts; conservation, however, spread tentative roots, and only the long-lived Emerson survived to see its first strong shoots, the preservation for posterity of Yellowstone and Yosemite National Parks. The bloodiest and most ruinous of all periods in the saga of American wildlife was still to come, and 1882, the year of Emerson's death, was also the year of the last great buffalo slaughter in the West.

Other game animals, almost unnoticed, were beginning to falter, too. The momentous movements and events of Parkman's period meant little at first in the slow time of the prairies: the mule deer, elk, and pronghorn antelope, in company with the bison, only lifted their heads to view the pack trains and covered wagons and the strange, broad-hatted, upright figures on the horses' backs. Alert, at a little distance, they would stand stock still in the rich grasses, tails flicking, jaws working, not as yet alarmed. But soon they learned to move away, the bison heaving into their ponderous, dusty canter, the antelope scampering, tail patches flashing white, the elk and deer pausing in their dignified, neat-footed flight to stare back, round-eyed, at the intruders.

The smaller animals, especially the antelope, were taken whenever possible, as a supplement to the prairie diet of buffalo meat, and the slaughter increased as the buffalo declined. At first a welcome food source, they soon became unwelcome competition for the domestic sheep and cattle which would clot the fenced prairies by the turn of the century. In any case, they were shot down indiscriminately, and, though the mule deer was never more than locally threatened, the antelope and elk were soon in danger.

The pronghorn antelope is a white-and-chestnut animal with unique pronged horns, great speed, and the bad habit of investigating anything out of the ordinary, including a red bandanna or even a pair of boots lifted out of the sagebrush by a hunter reclining on his back; it is the sole hoofed mammal indigenous to North America, the rest having migrated to this continent in prehistoric times by way of the Bering Strait. An account of an antelope hunt by Meriwether Lewis, who with Clark discovered this animal and many others, indicates how safe the species was before the rifle appeared upon the plains:

> The chief game of the Shoshonees is the antelope, which when pursued retreats to the open plains, where the horses have full room for the chase. But such is its extraordinary fleetness and wind, that a single horse has no possible chance of outrunning it, or tiring it down; and the hunters are therefore obliged to resort to stratagem. About twenty Indians, mounted on fine horses, armed with bows and arrows, left the camp; in a short time they descried a herd of ten antelopes; they immediately separated into squads of two or three, and formed a scattered circle round the herd for

PRONGHORN ANTELOPE

five or six miles. . . . Having gained their positions, a small party rode
towards the herd, and with wonderful dexterity the huntsman preserved
his seat, and the horse his footing, as he ran at full speed over the hills and
down the steep ravines, and along the borders of the precipices. They were
soon outstripped by the antelopes, which, on gaining the other extremity
of the circle, were driven back and pursued by the fresh hunters. They
turned and flew, rather than ran, in another direction; but there too they
found new enemies. In this way they were alternately pursued backwards
and forwards, till at length, notwithstanding the skill of the hunters (who
were merely armed with bows and arrows) they all escaped; and the party,
after running for two hours, returned without having caught anything, and
their horses foaming with sweat.[5]

The antelope roamed formerly with the plains bison, and was said to be
as numerous, from Alberta south to the plateaus of northern Mexico, and
west as far as the Pacific Slope, but by 1910 its bands were small and scattered, and only emergency protection spared it from complete extinction.
The pronghorns have since recovered, and are even fairly numerous in
Wyoming and Montana, but those inhabiting the black sage sidehills and
tablelands of the northern Great Basin area have declined again quite seriously in recent years.

The elk or wapiti of North America, except for a few isolated and re-
stocked herds, are now largely confined to the Rocky Mountain region from
Wyoming to British Columbia; the greatest single herd inhabits the Jack-

son Hole–Yellowstone region of northwest Wyoming. A lesser herd—the mighty Olympic or Roosevelt race—maintains itself on the Olympic Peninsula of remote northwestern Washington, where the glacier peaks, their flanks of huge fir and Sitka spruce washed by wind and rain and rushing gray-green streams, confront the cold strait of Juan de Fuca and the blue Pacific.

Though the American elk are no longer endangered, it is disheartening to reflect that they were once the most widespread of all American hoofed animals, ranging from the Southwest into Canada, and from the Atlantic to the Pacific. Their decline was no less shameful for the fact that in their darkest days, early in this century, they were killed commonly for their "tusks" alone. An elk's tooth was considered lucky, even by the Indians, who once presented Audubon with an antelope robe decorated with fifty-six of them and for that reason worth, if we are to credit the recipient, the equivalent of thirty horses. In the winter of 1915 five hundred elk were poached in the Yellowstone area alone, to supply teeth to joiners of the benevolent order named in honor of this animal.

Two other elk, regarded presently as distinct species, have fared far worse, and one is now extinct: the Arizona or Merriam's elk, large-antlered and pale-hided, ranged formerly through the Southwest, from the Wichita

MERRIAM ELK

Mountains of Oklahoma to the Mogollons of New Mexico and the Chiricahuas of Arizona, and south into Sonora, in herds of as many as two thousand. Called "very plentiful" in Arizona's White Mountains in 1876, they became hard to find within two decades. The last band met its end in 1906, in the Chiricahuas.

The tule or valley elk, which is smaller than other wapiti, was once common in the San Joaquin and Sacramento Valleys of California, but is now extinct in the wild state; two small herds, semi-domestic, are maintained, one of these near Tupman north of Bakersfield, where by 1930 the remnant elk were penned up for their own protection against the ranchers. The small, remote Tupman reserve has become much neglected through lack of public interest, and a second herd drawn from this one and established in the Owens Valley competes for forage with domestic cattle in the area, and is cut back annually. Attempts to present the excess animals to zoos have been relatively unsuccessful, since the tule elk is too similar in appearance to the common elk to attract more than professional attention.

At one time or another the white man has substantially diminished all the hoofed mammals of North America except the mountain goat (which is not a goat at all, but an antelope related to the European chamois) of the Northwest—Montana, Idaho, and Washington north to southern Alaska—and the Dall sheep, a small, white relative of the bighorn, which inhabits the northern areas of the same range as well as the mountains of the Alaskan interior; both animals have been generally spared to date by a wild and relatively inaccessible range and habitat.

Among the species once depleted but now restored to relative abundance is the peccary or javelina, a small wild pig of the Southwest and Mexico which ranged formerly to Arkansas; though its distribution has been curtailed, it is in no present danger of extinction, or even of extirpation from the United States. Similarly, the moose has maintained fair numbers in its limited United States range and in Canada, and is said to be increasing in northern New England with the reversion of timberland and stony farms to forest; it is also increasing in Alaska, where the Kenai Peninsula moose may well be the largest antlered animal ever to exist on earth. The American elk and antelope, as indicated earlier, have been restored to comparative safety, and the mule and white-tailed deers, the key deer race of Florida excepted, are once again in fine condition. The barren-ground caribou of Alaska, the Yukon, the Northwest Territories, and Labrador, though afflicted by indiscriminate slaughter and the destruction by fire and over-

PECCARY

grazing of the slow-growing lichens it requires, is still the most abundant large animal of the north (see Chapter 11). The Dawson caribou, a small, brown race of this species peculiar to the Queen Charlotte Islands of British Columbia, is thought to have vanished from the face of the earth about 1908.

To their everlasting misfortune, the hoofed animals not only are eaten with alacrity but, in company with the bears, represent the only big-game animals of North America. As in the case of the game birds, it is this latter fact which has probably spared them, for except in the far north they are no longer economically significant as human provender; the hunters, not unparadoxically, are more than anxious to keep these animals alive in order to have something left to kill. The hoofed mammals prosper with protection—with few exceptions, they do well even in captivity—and the only species besides the bighorn which is at present still declining is the woodland caribou, which replaces its barren-ground relative south of the Canadian tree line.

The hosts of woodland caribou which moved north and south on their seasonal migrations were once almost as striking as those of the bison, and, like the bison, these animals were crucial to the survival of the Indians within their range. Early in the nineteenth century the Canadian naturalist Samuel Hearne viewed the caribou slaughters with misgiving:

> The great destruction of the deer in the month of August, for the sake of their skins, which are then fittest for use, is almost incredible; and as they are never known to have more than one fawn at a time, it is wonderful

they do not become scarce. But so far is this from being the case, that the oldest northern Indian will affirm, that the deer are as plentiful now as they ever have been. . . . The herds of deer are attended in their migrations by bands of wolves, which destroy a great many of them. . . .[6]

In the United States the former range of the woodland caribou included all the Canadian border states from Maine to Washington. It was extirpated early, however, and was last seen in New Hampshire in 1885, and in Maine just after the turn of the century. In recent decades a small, wild herd was exterminated in Washington, and the last woodland caribou in the country persisted a few years longer in a marshy region near Red Lake, Minnesota. Though still quite common in Alberta, with small populations in Labrador, Newfoundland, and the Gaspé Peninsula of Quebec, the woodland caribou is embattled throughout its range.

Only one of the hoofed mammals has never been a game animal. The curious Arctic musk ox inhabits the barrens north of the tree line from Greenland to Alaska, where, in 1930, it was reintroduced on Nunivak Island. The original Alaskan population, which became extinct near Wainwright about 1865, was one of the few North American forms for the destruction of which the natives are probably as responsible as the white man; the musk-ox herd's defensive circle, bulwarked by sharp, downswept horns and a shaggy blanket of hair extending to the ground, is effective against wolves, but invited mankind to pick off the stolid animals one by one, with rifle or even spear. In the first years of this century, an estimated six hundred musk ox were killed for food by Admiral Peary's expeditions to the Arctic alone. Aside from the Nunivak herd, which numbers about one hundred and twenty-five (1957), there is another protected band on the Thelon Game Sanctuary north of Great Slave Lake, in the Northwest Territories. The few thousand scattered elsewhere on the barren coasts and islands east to Greenland are legally protected, but their predators— bears, wolves, and occasional Eskimos—pay small attention to this privileged status.

MUSK OX

The closest North American relative of the musk ox is that other wild ox, the bison, which, like the tule elk, is now extinct in the wild state. The early and accurate predictions of the bison's end are somewhat surprising in view of the fact that well into the nineteenth century an estimated sixty million still trampled the Great Plains. Nevertheless, Audubon had taken uneasy note of the dark future of the species. "Even now," he recorded on August 5, 1843, "there is a perceptible difference in the size of the herds, and before many years the Buffalo, like the Great Auk, will have disappeared; surely this should not be permitted." [7] Parkman, like Audubon, foretold the doom of the bison, and certainly this was the western species the simultaneous abundance and diminution of which was most striking and disturbing. A systematic slaughter had commenced by mid-century, and Parkman, who was fascinated by the huge, dark beasts— at certain seasons, they quite literally turned the prairies to seas of black— well understood their role in the welfare of the Plains Indians. "With the stream of emigration to Oregon and California, the buffalo will dwindle away, and the large wandering communities who depend on them for support must be broken and scattered." He points out also that "The buffalo supplies them with the necessaries of life; with habitations, food, clothing, beds, and fuel; strings for their bows, glue, thread, cordage, trail-ropes for their horses, coverings for their saddles, vessels to hold water, boats to cross streams, and the means of purchasing all that they want from the traders. When the buffalo are extinct, they too must dwindle away."

A quarter-century later, when the desperate Sioux and other tribes were contesting white seizure of their last terrains, the truth of Parkman's conclusion was only too apparent to the settlers' representatives in Washington; legislation to temper the buffalo carnage was bitterly opposed by those who saw in it a ready means of containing the Sioux. Although a protection measure was eventually passed by Congress, President Grant never got around to signing it, and the killing was allowed to continue.

The Indians themselves, contrary to sentimental legend, had been fearfully wasteful of the bison, and whenever possible took only the heifers and cows, the meat of which was much more tender and the hides, of lighter weight, more pliable. If their winter store of dried meat was sufficient, they killed frequently for the buffalo tongues alone, leaving whole plateaus of rotting carcasses to the swarming plains wolves and coyotes, and it was said that a single Indian might consume fifteen to twenty pounds of his favorite cuts during the course of a long night's feasting. Nevertheless, the red men, addicted to inter-tribal warfare, remained few and, even after they learned to tame wild mustangs, made no serious inroad on the bovine hordes. Far more bison than they could waste fell annually in blizzard and quicksand, through the river ice, and to the jaws of the ever-attendant wolves; the harsh conditions of the habitat, rather than the red hunters, kept the great animals from overgrazing and destroying the vast pasture of rich grama grass which rolled from Canada to Texas.

Or so it was until the white man first appeared, out of the forests on the grasslands' eastern edge. Within fifty years of the journey of Lewis and Clark, no more than a long course of seasons in the Indians' unwritten time, the din of civilization had resounded from behind that forest horizon. Just after mid-century were undertaken the War Department surveys for a Pacific railroad, from which were derived the comprehensive natural histories of Spencer F. Baird; it was the completion of this railroad, with the meeting of Central Pacific and Union Pacific lines at Promontory, Utah, in 1869, that set in motion the final frenzied assault upon the bison, not only by trappers, Indians, and settlers but by professional meat hunters like Buffalo Bill Cody.

> I started in killing buffalo for the Union Pacific Railroad. I had a wagon with four mules, one driver and two butchers, all brave, well-armed men, myself riding my horse "Brigham." . . .
> I had to keep a close and careful lookout for Indians before making my run into a herd of buffalo. It was my custom in those days to pick out a herd that seemed to have the fattest cows and young heifers. I would then rush my horse into them, picking out the fattest cows and shooting them down, while my horse would be running alongside of them. . . . I have killed

from twenty-five to forty buffalo while the herd was circling, and they would all be dropped very close together; that is to say, in a space covering about five acres. . . .

I killed buffalo for the railroad company for twelve months, and during that time the number I brought into camp was kept account of, and at the end of that period I had killed 4,280 buffalo. . . .

During those twelve months I had many fights with the Indians. . . . We would make our breastwork around the wheels of the wagon by throwing out the meat, and would protect ourselves by getting behind the buffalo hams. In this manner we held off from forty to sixty Indians on one or two occasions until we received assistance. I would make my smoke signals at once, which the soldiers would instantly see and rush to our rescue. I had five men killed during my connection with the U.P.R.R., three drivers and the others butchers. . . .[8]

At the time of Cody's account, only Idaho had attempted to protect the bison and other hoofed mammals; the other states, if anything, increased the slaughter. The railroad provided transportation to the eastern markets and it cut the great remaining herd in two. Other rail lines, following quickly, fanned out across the buffalo range like cracks in glass. "To the plains they brought white hunters and rifles, Dupont powder and Galena lead, Green River knives, tobacco, and firewater. They carried tongues and hides, robes and finally bones, to eastern markets."[9]

The southern herd was the first to go. Between 1872 and 1874, well over a million animals were shot yearly, and five years later a solitary survivor met its end at Buffalo Springs, Texas, on the cattle trail to Santa Fe. The northern herd was simultaneously reduced, but part of it frequented areas inaccessible to the markets before the extension westward of the Northern Pacific, in 1880. The railroad was to traverse land previously guaranteed by treaty to the Sioux, and the treaty was far more easily circumvented than were the warriors under Sitting Bull and Crazy Horse. The Sioux were crushed in October 1876, a few months after Custer and his men had been wiped out at the Little Big Horn; the capture in Arizona of the Apache chief, Geronimo, a decade later, marked the end of effective Indian resistance in the West.

Meanwhile, defeated Indian tribes joined forces with the buffalo hunters. They worked toward their own destruction willingly and well, and in 1883 a mixed company of Crees and whites trailed the remnants of the northern bison to the Cannonball River of North Dakota. There, by cutting off access to the water, the hunters accomplished the destruction of the entire herd. By the end of the year, stray animals excepted, the buffalo was gone from North America, and a measure was passed without dissent for their protection in North Dakota. Two years earlier, in *Camp Life and the Tricks of Trapping*, W. Hamilton Gibson had assured his readers that "The Buffaloes or Bison of the Western plains . . . travel in migrating herds of thousands, and are found from Texas to British America." Scarcely twelve years before, an Indian fighter, Colonel R. I. Dodge, came upon a mighty herd in Arkansas: "From the top of Pawnee Rock I could see from six to ten miles in almost every direction. This whole vast space was covered with Buffalo, looking at a distance like a compact mass." And elsewhere in the same account, which was published in 1882, he confirms Parkman's worst fears about the future of the red men: "What was mere uncleanliness in the Indian's day of plenty, has degenerated into squalor. The Indian who only ten years ago contented himself with nothing but the very choicest portions of animal food, now, pinched by hunger, eats any and everything. Dogs, wolves, reptiles, half-decomposed horse-flesh, even carrion birds, all go to appease the gnawings of his famished stomach." [10]

The white man, who had adopted all the Indians' worst practices and was given, in addition, to shooting the bison down senselessly from passing trains and other vantage points, had wiped out an animal that, until its very last decade, had numbered in the millions. A wilderness in Alberta, an area near Lost Park, Colorado, and the upland prairies of Yellowstone

BISON

Park gave shelter to the only wild survivors, and the governments of both Canada and the United States stepped forward belatedly to protect them. The Lost Park herd was destroyed for some enterprising taxidermists in 1897, but Wyoming had established a ten-year closed season on the buffalo in 1890. The Yellowstone herd of some twenty-odd animals slowly increased, and in 1908 the National Bison Range was established in the Flathead Valley of Montana, to the west of the Mission Mountains. There, in a fine, rolling terrain of grass, with evergreen hillsides of ponderosa and yellow pine, and draws choked with hawthorn and white-flowered mock orange, a buffalo herd of several hundred animals was developed over the years. Animals have since been stocked on a number of American and Canadian reserves, and a herd has also been established in Alaska.

The bison herds were almost certainly the greatest animal congregations that ever existed on earth, and the greed and waste which accompanied their annihilation doubtless warrants some sort of superlative also. Nevertheless, their disappearance was inevitable. Once the settlers discovered the agricultural potential of the long-grass prairies, and the ranchers bred fat livestock on the short-grass plains farther west, the history of these humped, sullen beasts was over. We can take comfort, though not much pride, in the fact that two wild herds were saved, for it is quite likely that, had Yellowstone Park not been recently established at the time, the bison would now be confined on earth to Canada alone.

"No sight is more common on the plains than that of a bleached buffalo skull; and their countless numbers attest the abundance of the animal at

a time not so very long past. On those portions where the herds made their last stand, the carcasses, dried in the clear, high air, or the mouldering skeletons abound. . . . A ranchman who at the same time had made a journey of a thousand miles across northern Montana, along the Milk River, told me that, to use his own expression, during the whole distance he was never out of sight of a dead buffalo, and never in sight of a live one." [11]

So wrote Theodore Roosevelt, who, still a young man, ranched in North Dakota in the two years immediately succeeding the slaughter in that state of the last great buffalo herd. The parched remnants were, for Roosevelt, a stark object lesson in the need for animal protection. An ardent amateur biologist and naturalist ever since his days at Harvard, he saw the last herd of bison on a later trip to Yellowstone Park, and one of his numerous correspondents was Buffalo Jones, the plainsman who became, at Yellowstone, the first federal warden in the United States. Once, with an assistant, Jones roped and tied an adult grizzly, removed a tin can wedged onto its paw, untied it, and let it go, a feat few men would attempt in the present day. On another occasion Jones lassoed by the hind foot a grizzly which had been molesting human habitations, suspended it from a stout limb, and thrashed it soundly with a bean pole before releasing it.

At this time, the grizzly was an unwitting figure in a controversy among biologists which still continues. In 1886, Dr. C. Hart Merriam, adhering rather too closely to the microscope taxonomy then in vogue at Harvard, was inspired to describe eighty-six separate species of grizzly and brown bears from the National Museum specimens. Theoretically, as we have seen, a species is a form which cannot interbreed successfully with any other. Since grizzlies are unsociable and short-tempered, research into their intimacies in the wild might well prove hazardous, but further analysis of defunct individuals has determined that bears in the same family group often exhibit widely divergent physical characters, including those of tooth and skull. Dr. Merriam's myriad grizzlies, with the approval of most authorities, have since been distilled to a single species, a circumstance which would surely have warmed the heart of his contemporary, Dr. Coues. As the latter once remarked, "The 'trinomial tool' is too sharp to be made a toy; and even if we do not cut our own fingers with it, we are likely to cut the throat of the whole system of naming we have reared with such care. Better throw the instrument away than use it to slice species so

RAVEN

FRANKLIN'S GROUSE

thin that it takes a microscope to perceive them. It may be assumed, as a safe rule of procedure, that it is useless to divide and sub-divide beyond the fair average ability . . . to recognize and verify the result. Named varieties . . . that require to be 'compared with the types' by holding them in a good strong light— . . . such often exist in the cabinets or books of their describers, but seldom in the woods or fields." [12]

Roosevelt, like Coues, was opposed to laboratory biology which tended to exclude or diminish the importance of natural history and the naturalist, although Merriam, despite his preoccupation with specific status, was also a first-rate observer in the field, and a general biologist whose stature in the United States, in Roosevelt's opinion, was equaled only by Louis Agassiz and David Starr Jordan; nevertheless, Roosevelt took violent exception to his friend's subsequent division of the coyote into eleven species, and to his sudden discovery of two new species of cougar in Nevada alone. If the cougar species were indeed valid, Roosevelt wrote Henry Fairfield Osborn, then he, Roosevelt, promised to unearth fifty-seven species of red fox on Long Island.

Taxonomists are divided to this day among the "lumpers"—those who, like Coues and Joel A. Allen in Roosevelt's period, deplore the niggling subdivision of essentially identical forms—and the "splitters," who regard their opponents as scientifically inexact. The former now seem to be in the ascendancy. For many years, amateur naturalists have been confounded by identification problems too technical for their experience or equipment, and the professionals themselves are demonstrating a healthy suspicion of arbitrary laboratory Creation. Though species and subspecies continue to be "discovered," the probability is that in the future many North American forms now considered distinct will be re-evaluated, and the full species, at least, may decline rather than increase in number.

Cervus roosevelti, the Olympic elk, was a new species named by Merriam some time after the coyote fracas. Roosevelt, who was nothing if not human, accepted the honor with alacrity, and it seems rather unfortunate, considering his attitude toward the splitters, that this animal is now considered but a race of the common wapiti.

The honor paid to Roosevelt by Merriam may well have been in appreciation of his actions in regard to wildlife rather than of his amateur speculations, for Roosevelt had already accomplished much. In 1887, with the editor of *Forest and Stream*, George Bird Grinnell, he had organized the Boone and Crockett Club, for the promotion not only of gentlemanly sport but of wilderness travel and exploration, observations on the natural histories of wild animals, and measures for the preservation of large game. The club shortly included among its members Senator Henry Cabot Lodge, Merriam, Elihu Root, Judge J. D. Caton, Generals William Tecumseh Sherman and Philip Sheridan, and the aged Francis Parkman, all of whom, according to the rules of eligibility, had killed an adult male of at least three species of American big-game animals. Its imposing membership undoubtedly lent weight to the Club's aspirations, and the following year, due largely to its efforts, a National Zoological Park was created in Washington, D.C., by act of Congress. The "B. and C.," as Roosevelt called it, was also to sponsor the New York Zoological Park, known commonly today as the Bronx Zoo. More important, it brought pressure upon Congress to pass, in 1894, the so-called Park Protection Act. The latter, supported strongly by Roosevelt on the basis of his personal impressions of the region as well as on the fact that a last wild herd of bison occurred there, defended the landscape and animals of Yellowstone from further exploitation by profiteers. These men had swarmed off the newly completed Northern Pacific Railroad and were already engaged in development schemes so vulgar as to amount to vandalism.

Yellowstone, established in 1872, was the first of the national parks, but Yosemite and Sequoia were established in California four years before the Park Protection Act, and Mount Rainier and Crater Lake just after 1900; these pioneer parks were to be followed in the next half-century by two

SAGE HEN

dozen more, one of the most recent of which is the Theodore Roosevelt Memorial Park, established in a wild, grassy region of North Dakota badlands in 1947.

Actually, the idea of the national park was given articulate expression as early as 1833. That year George Catlin recommended in print that a "nation's park" be created for future generations in the Indian country of the upper Missouri, but it was not until 1864 that the concept took practical form. Such writers as Thoreau, Emerson, James Russell Lowell, and Oliver Wendell Holmes had been speaking out in defense of the forests, and in 1859 Horace Greeley honored that "most unique and majestic of nature's marvels," [13] the Yosemite Valley of California, with a personal visit. He summoned the new state of California to protect instantly the giant sequoias of the region, particularly the "Big Trees" of the Mariposa Grove. Not long after, Frederick Law Olmsted, who had laid out New York City's Central Park, took up the battle for the Yosemite, and in 1864 California received both the Valley and the Mariposa Grove by federal grant, in a bill signed by President Lincoln. Four years later John Muir, a Scotsman who had just completed a journey on foot of one thousand miles from Louisville, Kentucky, to the Florida Gulf coast, first appeared in the Yosemite. He was already an impassioned and persuasive champion of wilderness preservation, and the reversion of these monumental valleys, cataracts, forests, and high sierras to federal control is largely associated with his name. He persuaded Emerson, then sixty-seven, to come to Yosemite in 1871, and guided Theodore Roosevelt there in 1903, not long after he himself had written, "It took more than three thousand years to make some of the trees in these Western woods—trees that are still standing in perfect strength and beauty, waving and singing in the mighty forests of the Sierra. Through all the wonderful, eventful centuries since Christ's time—and long before that—God had cared for these trees, saved them from drought, disease, avalanches, and a thousand straining, leveling tempests and floods; but he cannot save them from fools. . . ." [14]

It is Yellowstone Park, however, among all the national parks established since 1872, which has been most directly beneficial to American wildlife; indeed, the first effective wildlife sanctuary in the nation was this mountainous tract of the Wyoming Rockies overlapping the Idaho and Montana borders. Even today it harbors an impressive population and variety of great animals, including mule deer, elk, antelope, moose, bison, bighorn sheep, and black and grizzly bears, and the spectacle of these creatures close at hand against a glory of mountain meadows, alpine forest, geysers, canyons, torrents, and a great blue lake pinned in by snow peaks of the Rockies gives an unreal picture of the West as it once was—unreal because the animals, after all, are no longer truly wild, and the black bears, indeed, have become insolent and parasitic beggars. Only the bison, bighorn, and grizzly take pains to avoid man's sight, and must be sought in remote retreats away from the main roads. In the quiet recesses of this vast region the bull bison stamps its wallow and the grizzly contests the trail, and here small imagination is required to understand how the plains, prairies, and the Shining Mountains must have awed those first few lost and ill-equipped wanderers of the American Northwest.

The frontier, as the white man knew it, was short-lived. Parkman, who recorded it so well, lived on to see it fade. "A time would come," as he foresaw in the preface to the 1872 edition of *The Oregon Trail*, "when those plains would be a grazing country, the buffalo give place to tame cattle, farmhouses be scattered along the water courses, and wolves, bears, and Indians be numbered among the things that were."

Strictly migratory, what an enjoyable life they [curlews] must lead! . . . If the doctrine of the transmigration of souls were true, when our earthly course in the present form was run, who would not wish to be transformed into one of these migratory darlings, especially if those he or she loved passed through the same change! But to leave dear dreamland, and return to cruel reality. A large-bore gun, say a 10, with the lightest shot, is the best weapon to use for the destruction of this family. . . .

—PARKER GILLMORE (1874)

8 : The High Air of a Continent

IN THE TIME of the great western slaughters, the game animals in the East were disappearing entirely, species after species, and the laws enacted in their behalf were largely gestures of regret occasioned by their extirpation. Guns were now turned upon the birds, the legal protection of which, while still pertinent, was little more effective; an early New York law of 1838, forbidding the use of batteries, or multiple guns, in the annihilation of waterfowl, was later repealed as ineffectual for the practical reason that the commercial gunners had taken to wearing masks and had, in addition, vowed to execute informers. This was not the first protective measure withdrawn out of deference to local or political interests, and it was not to be the last.

Nevertheless, the sentiment in favor of public continence was growing, and in 1844 the New York Association for the Protection of Game, first of its kind in the nation, was established; in the very same year the native elk and wild turkey disappeared forever from the state, a circumstance which, while scarcely auspicious, probably tended to justify the existence of what must have seemed then a cranky and quixotic organization. Rhode Island, two years later, set up a closed season on game birds, outlawing the spring shooting of wood duck, black duck, woodcock, and snipe, and in 1850 Connecticut and New Jersey took the first important steps in favor of non-game birds, with laws protecting nests and eggs. In this action they were soon supported by ten other states. Unhappily, the Rhode Island waterfowl law was shortly repealed as unpopular, and the non-game-bird statutes were generally ineffective. A consequence of a flourishing public interest in private bird collections and oölogy, inspired in great measure by Wilson and Audubon, was the quest of birds' nests by schoolboys; as often as not, the oölogy of the latter was devoted to the simple destruction of eggs, and, where circumstances permitted, the adult birds into the bargain. The famine induced in the Southern States by the aftermath of the Civil War was a further setback to the songbirds, and the widespread consumption of robins and others among the larger species was practiced among the poor well into the present century.

Nevertheless, the songbirds and waterfowl, woodcock, and snipe, were not nearly so much in need of help as was the most common of American birds, the passenger pigeon, an early law in regard to which, passed in 1848 by Massachusetts, protected from molestation on the nesting grounds not the pigeons but the netters. The eastern nestings were already sporadic, but the pigeons were still so numerous in the Central States that a measure to control the harvest in Ohio in 1857 was turned down by the state senate. According to the committee report, "The passenger pigeon needs no protection. Wonderfully prolific, having the vast forests of the North as its breeding grounds, traveling hundreds of miles in search of food, it is here to-day and elsewhere to-morrow, and no ordinary destruction can lessen them or be missed from the myriads that are yearly produced." [1] And one cannot deny that the report seemed bulwarked by the several immense nestings that occurred thereafter, including one in the sandy scrub-oak

PASSENGER PIGEON

barrens of south central Wisconsin in 1871, and another one, better known, at Petoskey, Michigan, in 1878.

The Wisconsin nesting was the largest ever described, and its awesome dimensions have been placed at seventy-five by ten to fifteen miles, an area of no less than seven hundred and fifty square miles. Assuming a minimum average of twenty-five trees per acre and five pairs per tree, this single nesting was shared by 136,000,000 birds. This is little more than one-twentieth the size of the flight described by Alexander Wilson, but it is nonetheless a prodigious number, and the predators, white, Indian, and animal, swarmed down upon the roosts from every direction. The recent invention of the telegraph had speeded the glad news into all the adjoining states, and there were literally thousands of hunters and trappers on hand, armed variously with net, fire, and shot, as well as with an assortment of homemade contrivances designed to perform the most heroic destruction in the shortest possible time.

The area was laid waste. Hundreds of thousands, indeed millions, of dead birds were shipped out at a wholesale price of fifteen to twenty-five cents a dozen, on the cars of the same railroads which, by opening the great eastern markets, were accommodating the exit of the bison. The season, commencing in April, was profitable for only a month, and by June the markets were glutted, the pigeons were scattered, and the hunters had largely departed, leaving behind a rancid wasteland of ground white with guano, of broken trees, nests, eggs, and blue-feathered, fly-blown forms too shattered to ship, of starving squabs, of maggots and silent fur-clawed and beaked prowlers.

The Petoskey nesting was the last great congregation of passenger pigeons ever beheld on earth, and their subsequent decline was swift. "The pigeon was no mere bird, he was a biological storm. He was the lightning that played between the two biotic poles of intolerable intensity: the fat of the land and his own zest for living. Yearly the feathered tempest roared up, down, and across the continent, sucking up the laden fruits of forest and prairie, burning them in a travelling blast of life. Like any other chain-reaction, the pigeon could survive no diminution of his own furious intensity. Once the pigeoners had subtracted from his numbers, and once the settlers had chopped gaps in the continuity of his fuel, his flame guttered out with hardly a sputter or a wisp of smoke." [2]

In the year of the Petoskey nesting, Pennsylvania decreed that no firearms should be discharged within one mile of a pigeon roost, a measure which would have been worthy indeed in the days before the Pennsylvania roosts had passed. Even so, Pennsylvania was precocious. As late as 1879 Mr. E. T. Martin, self-advertised as "the largest dealer in live pigeons for trap shooting in the world, also a dealer in guns, glass balls, traps, nets, etc.," gave it as his opinion, in *American Field*, that the birds of the air and beasts of the field were purely and simply a gift to man from God above, "for his benefit and profit." In 1881 twenty thousand squabs removed from the nest were later shot down in a Coney Island pigeon shoot, an event made no less tragic by the fact that the shoot was sponsored by the New York State Association for the Protection of Fish and Game. In 1882, the editor of *American Field* recommended that pigeons receive protection from March through May, but the La Crosse (Wisconsin) *Republican and Leader*, for May 13 of that year, carried the following social item: "The editor of the *Field* and other sportsmen from Chicago took the evening train. They expended a large quantity of powder and shot, and in return received all the pigeons they desired." In 1893 the Messrs. W. W. Judy & Co., of St. Louis, perhaps the largest dealers in

pigeons in the nation, received their final shipment from Siloam Springs, Arkansas; an inquiry directed to them some years later elicited "the interesting statement that the Wild Pigeons have flown to Australia." [3] The last wild pigeon in Wisconsin was taken in 1899, and though stray individuals were seen fleetingly for another five or six years, and a captive bird survived until 1914, the last wild pigeon, for scientific purposes, is thought to be a specimen killed at Sargents, Pike County, Ohio, on the fourth day of spring, in 1900. *Wuskowhan*, the wanderer, as the Narragansett Indians had called the most numerous bird ever to exist on earth, had been whirled into the vortex of extinction.

With the sudden decline of the wild pigeon in the 1880s, a huge market was ready and waiting for the highly edible American shore birds, and within two decades the vast numbers of these had been so reduced that general extinction was predicted for all but the smallest species. Prior to the era of intensive market gunning, the shore birds were usually taken in small numbers, for the titillation of wealthy sporting tastes: in addition, the aborigines on the northern breeding grounds ate them in certain quantity, and the fishermen of Labrador and Newfoundland salted them down in numbers in the fall, when the Hudsonian godwit, Eskimo curlew, and golden plover, convening on the coasts for their arduous flight south to the Argentine, were especially plump and toothsome. The shore birds provided but dubious sport, since they flew often in dense flocks, decoyed too readily to tax the hunter's guile, and were apt to circle back over those already fallen, only to receive another violent discharge into their ranks.

The fastidious nimrod Parker Gillmore, who is quoted at the head of this chapter, was one of many sportsmen who visited the West in the nineteenth century on the same sanguinary errand which propels big-game hunters toward Africa today (Gillmore's contemporary, Lord Dunraven, distinguished himself by downing one hundred and twenty woodland caribou in single combat during the course of one day's outing, and achieved a similar record at the expense of the bison, under the guidance of Buffalo Bill Cody). Gillmore was less inclined to unabashed butchery than many of his fellows and spoke feelingly of the decline of American animals and birds at the hands of "border ruffians" and other ill-born *hoi polloi*. Probably he would not have condoned the spring shoots in the upper Mississippi Valley, where a wagon load of plover and curlew, heaped higher than the sideboards, was considered a fair bag by the gentry of Omaha. If blazing away into the flocks filled the wagons up too soon, the bleeding pile was speedily dumped onto the prairie, there to rot, and the wagon loaded up all over again. Deeds such as these, which have been documented, were all the more reprehensible for being performed in the name of sport, and one vastly prefers the outlook of the commercial men, who used not dissimilar methods, disapproved of waste, and called slaughter by its proper name. Presumably, had the publicized activities of the sportsmen not dulled the public conscience, the market gunners might have been called to account much earlier than they were. As it was, they barreled their booty without undue interference from our forebears, for the gratification of whose palates the dead birds were shipped eastward by the ton.

The shore birds most prevalent in the market were probably the Eskimo curlew and the golden plover, not only because they were exceedingly numerous—Audubon in 1821, near New Orleans, witnessed a flight of "millions" of golden plover, and once compared a curlew flight with those of the passenger pigeon, though this seems scarcely credible—but because their habits permitted an efficient and handsome harvest. Both birds bred on the barren ground of the far north, and both collected at Labrador and Newfoundland prior to a southward migration which often included a nonstop flight from the Maritime Provinces to South America. In early days a small segment of the flight paused here and there along the coast, and on August 29, 1863, both curlew and plover appeared on Nantucket in such numbers as to "almost darken the sun"; seven or eight thousand were destroyed before the island's supply of powder and shot gave out. The last great flight of curlew landed on Cape Cod two decades later. Probably the birds had learned to avoid the dangers of the coast by this time, for they continued to return northward in quantity in the spring, via the Mississippi Valley and the Great Plains, where they were anxiously awaited by the gunners. It has been surmised that great flocks were lost in storm during the long passages over the open ocean, and, as in the case of the pigeon, numerous foolish theories were advanced to avoid an admission

LONG-BILLED CURLEW

GOLDEN PLOVER

UPLAND PLOVER

of bleak human guilt. But the curlews were strong, swift flyers and could land, if need be, on the water. "No, there was only one cause, slaughter by human beings, slaughter in Labrador and New England in summer and fall, slaughter in South America in winter, and slaughter, worst of all, from Texas to Canada in the spring. . . . The gentle birds ran the gantlet all along the line and no one lifted a finger to protect them until it was too late." [4]

In the 1890s the curlew faded rapidly, and a decade later sight records of it were so rare that its extinction was accepted as a foregone conclusion. In fact, however, a few stray descendants of the brown clouds which once shadowed the long beaches of the Atlantic coast have survived until recent years. The last specimen collected was taken more than a quarter-century ago, in the Argentine, where agricultural development of its wintering grounds contributed to the curlew's end, but reports still come in sporadically from Labrador and elsewhere. In all probability these late reports confuse the species with the Hudsonian curlew. The last sight record presumed authentic was of a pair, apparently mated, seen on Galveston Island, Texas, in March 1945. What became of this pair—whether or not they brought off a nesting on the tundra, or whether they perished that very same year in the attrition of their swift existence—will never be known. For many people these melodic, mournful criers of wind and open places, the shore birds, are perhaps the most stirring of American birds; one prefers to think that the last curlew fell naturally to a fox or coursing

gyrfalcon in *Keewatin*, the land of the north wind, rather than that some farm boy, in Nebraska or Saskatchewan, blew it forever from the face of the earth with a single, senseless blast of a cheap gun.

Meanwhile, the golden plover was faring badly, too, and extinction was commonly predicted for this species, as it was for the long-billed curlew, the Hudsonian godwit, the upland plover, and several of the smaller shore birds. Protective measures were set up in time to spare all but the Eskimo curlew, however; if none of the species named above has made the sort of recovery which would tend to insure its future, only the Hudsonian godwit could presently be called endangered.

Like the Eskimo curlew and the golden plover, this handsome white-rumped species undertakes a long and hazardous migration route across continents and oceans. Perhaps the rarest, originally, of the shore birds—even before the heyday of the market gunner, Coues had remarked that it was "apparently not common anywhere in the U.S." [5]—it had, like the others, suffered considerable persecution everywhere on its route. It did not recover even with protection, and by 1936 was thought to be nearly extinct. In recent springs, however, these godwits have been relatively plentiful in

ESKIMO CURLEW   HUDSONIAN GODWIT

the Mississippi Valley, and there seems reason to hope that they can be restored.

The destruction of birds of all sizes and shapes had reached the proportions of a national pastime in the last quarter of the nineteenth century, and supported a number of minor industries as well. The birds were being consumed so fast that spokesmen in their defense, heretofore shrill, solitary voices, began at last to band together and to conscript others to the cause. Plainly the laws, where they existed at all, were inefficient and unenforceable, and the founding of the American Society for the Prevention of Cruelty to Animals, in 1866, while a step in the right direction, was rather beside the point. The pioneer group devoted to birds was the Nuttall Ornithological Club, established in 1873 at Cambridge, Massachusetts, by William Brewster and others, which was significant chiefly as the parent organization of the American Ornithologists' Union. The A.O.U., as it is known, was promoted in 1883 by three notable Nuttallians, Joel A. Allen, Brewster (then curator of the Museum of Comparative Zoology at Harvard), and Elliott Coues, who at this time had already challenged the gray eminence of Spencer F. Baird with his mighty *Key to North American Birds* (1872) and other works. Dr. Baird had become the venerable secretary of the Smithsonian Institution, and was about to complete, in collaboration with Dr. Robert Ridgway and the oölogist Dr. Thomas Brewer, an epochal bird text to supplant his own *Birds of North America*. Coues and Baird, Brewer and Ridgway, for another two decades, met revised edition with revised edition, until both were antiquated by the several

PROCESSION OF GAME

Soup

Venison (Hunter Style)   Game Broth

Fish

Broiled Trout, Shrimp Sauce
Baked Black Bass, Claret Sauce

Boiled

Leg of Mountain Sheep, Ham of Bear
Venison Tongue, Buffalo Tongue

Roast

Loin of Buffalo, Mountain Sheep, Wild Goose, Quail, Red-head Duck, Jack Rabbit, Blacktail Deer, Coon, Canvasback Duck, English Hare, Bluewing Teal, Partridge, Widgeon, Brant, Saddle of Venison, Pheasants, Mallard Duck, Prairie Chicken, Wild Turkey, Spotted Grouse, Black Bear, Opossum, Leg of Elk, Wood Duck, Sandhill Crane, Ruffed Grouse, Cinnamon Bear

Broiled

Bluewing Teal, Jacksnipe, Blackbirds, Reed Birds, Partridges, Pheasants, Quails, Butterballs, Ducks, English Snipe, Rice Birds, Red-Wing Starling, Marsh Birds, Plover, Gray Squirrel, Buffalo Steak, Rabbits, Venison Steak

Entrees

Antelope Steak, Mushroom Sauce; Rabbit Braise, Cream Sauce; Fillet of Grouse with Truffles; Venison Cutlet, Jelly Sauce; Ragout of Bear, Hunter Style; Oyster Pie

Salads

Shrimp, Prairie Chicken, Celery

Ornamental Dishes

Pyramid of Game en Bellevue, Boned Duck au Naturel, Pyramid of Wild-Goose Liver in Jelly, The Coon out at Night, Boned Quail in Plumage, Red-Wing Starling on Tree, Partridge in Nest, Prairie Chicken en Socle

From 1855 to 1893 John B. Drake, a Chicago hotel proprietor, gave an annual game dinner at Thanksgiving. This was the menu on November 22, 1886

works of Frank M. Chapman, Charles Bendire, and other, lesser lights, who ushered in the present century.

The first A.O.U. meeting, in September 1883, was held at New York's American Museum of Natural History, which had been founded fourteen years earlier. The formidable Coues, apparently to Brewster's consternation, was appointed temporary chairman—Baird and Allen, who might have pre-empted the honor, were not present, though Allen was to be elected first president—and after three days of "earnest and harmonious discussion," a constitution was adopted. An A.O.U. publication, *The Auk*, Dr. J. A. Allen, editor, replaced the old *Nuttall Ornithological Bulletin* a few months later. Coues wrote in its opening number, "The outcry from all quarters excepting headquarters of American ornithological science against the name of our new journal satisfies us that the best possible name is THE AUK. . . . The editors beg to say that they have copyrighted, patented, and 'called in' the following puns and pleasantries: that THE AUK is an awkward name. . . . That the Auk is already defunct, and THE AUK likely to follow suit. . . . (Not at all . . . may THE AUK in due time be also known of men as an 'antient and honourable fowle'!)" And *The Auk* is still published today.

Among the original members of the A.O.U. was George Bird Grinnell, the naturalist editor of the outdoor magazine, *Forest and Stream*. The latter publication, like the aforementioned *American Field*, was more responsible in regard to wildlife than are its flamboyant counterparts of the present, in the pages of which the growing rarity of such species as the cougar, grizzly, and even walrus seems to inspire only articles on their increased desirability as "trophies." *Forest and Stream* was already directing a large segment of popular opinion to a reappraisal of its attitude toward animals and birds, a program in which it was supported by *Youth's Companion*, *St. Nicholas*, and other publications for the young. Their editors frequently and sometimes tearfully enjoined the vandal element among the nation's juveniles to spare "the feathered songsters of the grove," and it was largely children who, in 1886, signed a pledge sponsored by Grinnell and endorsed by such persons as Henry Ward Beecher, Oliver Wendell Holmes, and John Greenleaf Whittier, neither to kill birds nor to wear their feathers. Within three years this spontaneous group numbered over fifty thousand members, and became so troublesome to *Forest and Stream* that mention of the "Audubon Society," as Grinnell called it, had finally to be excised from the pages of the magazine. In 1896, however, Audubon Societies were chartered locally in Pennsylvania and Massachusetts, and by 1902 were so widespread that a National Association of these groups was established under the chairmanship of William Dutcher.

Dutcher, in this period, was also chairman of an A.O.U. committee created in 1884 "for the protection of North American Birds and their eggs, against wanton and indiscriminate destruction." The committee, which represented the first direct action by ornithologists on behalf of imperiled species, was formed to combat the destruction of birds for the millinery trade, and its first publication had been a bulletin on bird slaughter in 1886. Entitled "Destruction of Our Native Birds," the bulletin included the information that five million birds died yearly in America for the glorification of female headgear, and that one chic lady was cited favorably in a New York fashion note for the artful arrangement upon her head of a dead crow—beak, legs, claws, and all. (In the same year Dr. Frank M. Chapman strolled twice about the streets of New York City, polling passing hats. Five hundred and forty-two out of seven hundred hats brandished mounted birds. There were twenty-odd recognizable species, including owls, grackles, grouse, and a green heron.) The bulletin also proposed a bird-protection law to be adopted by each state, the first section of which forbade the destruction of all non-game birds, and identified the game birds as those we now think of as such—roughly, the waterfowl, rails, and gallinaceous birds—as well as the shore birds; heretofore "game birds" had been a nebulous category open to personal interpretation and including, at one time or another, such sporting quarry as flickers, meadowlarks, snow buntings, cardinals, and phoebes. The second section provided for the protection of the nest and eggs of all species, game or non-game, and other sections concerned the circumstances under which specimens might be collected for scientific purposes. One section was entirely devoted to the English sparrow, a foreign import first released in 1851, which had since, as Coues once complained, "overrun the whole country, and proved a nuisance without a redeeming quality"; [6] this "sturdy and invincible little bird," its nest, and its eggs, were exempted from any protection or consideration whatsoever.

The so-called Model Law became the prototype for bird legislation throughout the nation, and contemporary state laws show few important departures from it, though they are apt to take a less generous view toward hawks and owls. This is true despite the fact that an excellent statement in defense of the raptors was made in the same year the Model Law was propounded. Dr. C. Hart Merriam, in a report for the Department of Agriculture, directed his remarks against a Pennsylvania "scalp act" of 1885, which offered a bounty of fifty cents on hawks, owls, weasels, and minks:

> By virtue of this act about $90,000 has been paid in bounties during the year and a half that has elapsed since the law went into effect. This represents the destruction of at least 128,571 of the above-mentioned animals, most of which were hawks and owls.
>
> Granting that 5,000 chickens are killed annually in Pennsylvania by hawks and owls and that they are worth twenty-five cents each . . . the total loss would be $1,250, and the poultry killed in a year and a half would be worth $1,875. Hence it appears that during the last eighteen months the State of Pennsylvania has expended $90,000 to save its farmers a loss of $1,875. But this estimate by no means represents the actual loss to the farmers and taxpayers of the State. It is within bounds to say that every hawk and owl destroys at least a thousand mice or their equivalent in insects, and that each mouse or its equivalent so destroyed would cause the farmer a loss of two cents per annum. Therefore . . . the lowest possible estimate of the value to the farmer of each hawk, owl, and weasel would be $20 a year, or $30 in a year and a half.
>
> Hence, in addition to the $90,000 actually expended by the State in destroying 128,571 of its benefactors, it has incurred a loss to its agricultural interests of at least $3,857,120. . . . In other words, the State had thrown away $2,105 for every dollar saved! And even this does not represent fairly the full loss, for the slaughter of such a vast number of predaceous birds and mammals is almost certain to be followed by a correspondingly enormous increase in the numbers of mice and insects formerly held in check by them, and it will take many years to restore the balance thus blindly destroyed through ignorance of the economic relations of our common birds and mammals.

Conservationists today might question certain finer points of Merriam's conclusions, but most would agree that, as a general statement, it is accurate and forceful. More important, it is precocious, for it anticipates much of the balance-of-nature concept which forms the foundation of modern wildlife management and which, despite Merriam and others, was to be widely neglected in the years to come. Pennsylvania, however, repealed the disastrous "scalp act" almost immediately.

Although random persecution has continued, none of the northern hawks are yet faced with extinction (the endangered hawks of the south-

BALD EAGLE

ern borders were discussed in Chapter 2), and the fish hawk, or osprey, once a favorite of the taxidermists, has substantially recovered along American coasts and waterways. But our North American eagles—the golden of the mountainous regions, and the bald eagle of the seashores, swamps, and inland waters—have been dangerously reduced in numbers throughout their wide range, which includes, or included, suitable habitat from central Mexico north through the continent to Alaska.

"For my part," Benjamin Franklin once observed, "I wish the Bald Eagle had not been chosen as the representative of our country. He is a bird of bad moral character; he does not get his living honestly. . . . Besides, he is a rank coward. . . ." [7]

Apart from his anthropomorphism, Franklin's remarks are pertinent enough. Our national symbol, sad to say, subsists largely upon carrion; its alleged depredations on the salmon of Alaska, like its other crimes, have been grossly exaggerated. Most of the fish with which it has been apprehended, if not pirated from an osprey, were salvaged from the beach, and its effect on terrestrial creatures has been negligible. Nevertheless, it has been shot so consistently by hunters and taxidermists, fishermen and farmers, that Congress, in 1940, was finally compelled to prohibit its persecution or destruction anywhere but in Alaska. The excellent enacting clause is a reproach to us all:

> Whereas the Continental Congress in 1782 adopted the bald eagle as a national symbol; and
> Whereas the bald eagle thus became the symbolic representation of a new nation under a new government in a new world; and
> Whereas by that act of Congress and by tradition and custom during the life of this Nation, the bald eagle is no longer a mere bird of biological interest but a symbol of the American ideals of freedom; and
> Whereas the bald eagle is now threatened with extinction: Therefore
> Be it enacted . . .

Americans who have watched this fine bird in the wild will agree that it

GOLDEN EAGLE

is a species of much more than mere biological interest. White-headed and austere on a solitary tree, or flapping and sailing, stiff-winged and spread-fingered, over southern waterways or northern river deltas, inland river swamps or outer beaches, coursing the nation in summer and winter from the Columbia to the Merrimack, from the Everglades to the Yukon, the bald eagle is magnificent.

The golden eagle, a more noble bird only in the sense that it captures its own food, does occasionally take the young of domestic stock as well as those of game animals, but these kills are far too sporadic to warrant general persecution. The elimination of individual birds is probably justified when property is threatened or when, as on the San Andres bighorn sheep refuge in New Mexico, the eagles imperil the young of a species even more in danger of extinction than their own. But the organized pursuit of the golden eagle by airplane and other means, as practiced in states where extensive ranching is conducted, is absurd; like the bald eagle in Alaska, it has commonly been made the scapegoat for conditions of man's own making. Since 1952 the protection of the bald eagle has been extended to include Alaska, but the golden eagle is still persecuted in certain areas of its range. Already rare on the eastern continent, it still rules the western mountain air from Mexico to Alaska. Brooding on a cliff ledge or sliding down the shadows of a steep canyon, or alert, wings raised, astride a rabbit in the bright sunlight, it is a stirring sight. Yellow-eyed and arrogant, unwilling to give ground, the golden eagle seems almost to disdain the civilization which is sweeping it away.

The A.O.U. Model Law made allowance for the occasional elimination of individual great horned owls or accipitrine hawks (the Cooper's, sharp-shinned, and goshawk), all notorious bird killers, when these were doing specific damage; they are wary woodland species, however, and are not easily shot. Even if they were, few armed Americans are capable of distinguishing one hawk from another and fewer still trouble to make the attempt, preferring to fire indiscriminately at all of them. The state of Delaware, in deference to this mentality, authorized pole traps for hawks as late as 1948, and it was only a few years ago that an annual shotgun assault on migrating raptors, sailing south in numbers down the ridges of the Alleghenies, was a popular pastime at Hawk Mountain, Pennsylvania. Despite the words of Merriam more than seventy years ago, the beneficial habits of the raptors in controlling rodent pests are still largely over-looked, and public education in this matter is so neglected that today only three states—Connecticut, Michigan, and Indiana—protect all species of this order.

The Model Law was passed almost immediately by New York and Pennsylvania, but local pressures, especially those emanating from the millinery trade, brought about its prompt emasculation; by 1895, Dutcher noted later, "feather-wearing was as rampant as ever, the legislatures of the states of New York and Pennsylvania, where the model law had been enacted, had amended or repealed the same, and bird legislation was as defective as it was before the protection movement began." [8] The following year, however, the outlook improved with the resurrection of the Audubon Societies, and by the turn of the century the Model Law was operative in five states. In the interim, the Supreme Court had decreed that all game belonged to the states rather than to the people (Geer vs. Connecticut, 1896), and that the states could prohibit export of game; subsequently the Lacey Bill, inspired in part by the pernicious effects of the English sparrow, awarded the federal government control over the importations of foreign birds and animals, and also over interstate traffic in bodies and feathers of creatures killed in violation of state laws. This measure, a severe setback to the millinery trade, can be credited almost entirely to the A.O.U. and to the Audubon Societies.

Today it seems curious that the Model Law made no attempt to estab-lish protection for the fast-fading shore birds, and two explanations suggest

AMERICAN EGRET

LIMPKIN   REDDISH EGRET

GLOSSY IBIS

themselves. First of all, in the face of certain, organized resistance on the part of a nation of hunters, the effort might have seemed, for the moment, at least, impractical. But it is more likely that even the professional ornithologists were as lamentably uninformed as to the desperate straits of the curlew and other species as they had been in regard to the pigeon, and their inability to accept the drastic decline of birds traditionally so abundant is understandable. J. A. Allen, for one, still considered the curlew a common migrant in Massachusetts in 1879, and the otherwise hard-headed Coues, a decade later, dismissed its increasing rarity as "singular"; the 1892 edition of his book refers to the curlew as "extraordinarily abundant in some places during migration, as in Labrador, where it fairly swarms in August." [9] It was not until 1897, in reference to curlew shipments from the West, that its general extinction was predicted in *The Auk*. In the subsequent New England annals of the species, no more than three were ever seen in a single group again.

On the other hand, the plight of the songbirds and plume species, which preoccupied the ornithologists of the period, must have seemed at least as fearful as that of the shore birds. In 1876 J. A. Allen had written, "Societies should be formed whose express object should be the protection throughout the country of not only these practically innocent and pleasure-giving species, but also the totally innoxious herons, terns, and gulls, whose extirpation is progressing with needless and fearful rapidity." [10]

In the case of the millinery species, a remedy could be effected by out-lawing a relatively small group, since the victims were considered neither edible nor sporting and were therefore taken largely by participants in the traffic. This traffic, nevertheless, had become international in dimension, and the battle against it was far from won, even with the passage of the Lacey Bill. Birds had always been items of ornament, but their usefulness in this regard had not been appreciated on a grand scale until about 1870, when the dictates of fashion set in motion a hecatomb which became world wide. Within a few years the industry was such that Florida, followed swiftly by Texas, passed a law to protect plume-bird eggs and young, but these measures were as easily ignored as they were impractical: all birds achieve their finest plumage in the breeding season, and their destruction at this time was fatal to the forsaken nestlings, protection or no. W. E. D. Scott, who chronicled the plume-bird disaster in Florida, visited a rookery at John's Pass in 1880 and counted over two hundred spoonbills, abundant reddish egrets, and myriads of American and snowy egrets. Six years later the spoonbills had vanished from the area, and only a few wary egrets skirted the ravaged ground; his records for other rookeries investigated were equally desolate.

Among the egrets, the American and the snowy, two spectacular white species, have recovered fairly well, and the former has even become a summer wanderer in the Northeast. Of recent years, however, it has started to decline again, not through persecution but through the gradual loss to Florida real estate of its breeding and feeding areas. The salvation of the snowy egret was due largely to E. A. McIlhenny, of the noted tabasco family, whose extensive private refuge in the hammocks of Avery Island, Louisiana, was set aside in 1892. The refuge maintained a breeding population of these birds in the grim years before protection restored them, and remains a marvelous spectacle to this day.

ROSEATE SPOONBILL   GREAT WHITE HERON

The reddish egret, on the other hand, has never fully recovered from
the onslaught, and its scattered colonies are now confined to Florida and
Texas. Among the herons, which differ from the egrets chiefly in name,
the great white heron of Cape Sable and the Florida Keys remains rare,
though its scarcity is probably a consequence less of the plume trade than
of its own evolutionary limitations. The hurricane of 1935 reduced it to
an estimated one hundred and fifty but it has since recouped considerably,
within the limitations of its narrow habitat: it also occurs in Cuba, Jamaica,
and Yucatán, but has not been shown to breed in any of those places.
The spectacular roseate spoonbill, like the reddish egret, has never regained
its former prosperity, though the latter was never great; like the American
egret, it has suffered recently from the destruction of its shallow-water
feeding flats, and must be considered an endangered species on this continent. In summer, the numbers of the spoonbill are augmented by wanderers from the tropics, but the latter do not remain to breed.

With the decline of the plume birds, the terns and gulls came into
general use, and the least tern, especially, was shot down by the thousands

LEAST TERN

on Cape Cod, Long Island, Cobb's Island, Virginia, and wherever else it congregated to nest on the outer beaches. Even the herring gull, so common today, was reduced in the East to a single colony on the Atlantic coast. The least tern survived the carnage, however, due largely to the early establishment of small guarded sanctuaries, and, with the other terns and gulls, has since been restored to abundance. Other birds killed commonly for their plumage were the warblers and buntings, among the more colorful songbirds, as well as a motley array of other species, including those detected on the sidewalks of New York by Frank M. Chapman. For a time, no bird, not even the turkey vulture, was so unprepossessing as to earn the disdain of the milliners. Only the egrets, spoonbill, and least tern, however, faced actual extinction before help arrived.

As has been noted, the Lacey Bill, in 1900, was by no means a complete solution to the problem, since it applied only to those states which protected non-game birds—in effect, those states which had adopted the Model Law. The southern and western states, to date, had been generally uncooperative, and though the laws in Canada more or less paralleled those in the eastern United States their lapses were well evidenced by the fact that as late as 1901 the province of Quebec did not include the passenger pigeon among its protected species. In Alaska, where the population was increasing swiftly, the solitary bird law in the Civil Code was concerned with the sanctity of eggs, which were not to be molested or exported.

Meanwhile, the A.O.U., returning into its scientific closet, had relegated most of its conservation effort to the burgeoning Audubon Societies—the A.O.U. Model Law, in fact, was soon known as the Audubon Law—which were attempting to set up, through the efforts of Dutcher and others, the first organized bird sanctuaries in the country. Heretofore, wildlife preserves had been random and incidental: Judge J. D. Caton had constructed a private deer park near Ottawa, Illinois, in 1858, and California, twelve years later, made a state waterfowl refuge of Merritt Lake which, though still operative, is now entirely surrounded by the business district of Oakland; after 1894, the first federal protection of wild creatures was afforded indirectly by the national parks.

The Audubon operations on behalf of the millinery species were to develop into a complex system of federal, state, and private refuges, but for a number of years their crusade enjoyed limited success, even where the law was on their side. The young director of the North Carolina Audubon Society was unaffectionately referred to in the local press as the "Honorable T. Gilbert Pearson and his legion of women and children backers," and his cause was greeted with such cynical legislation as an act "to allow N. W. Craft to collect birds on his premises at any time of year." A man haled into court in 1903 for killing a turkey hen out of season was fined one penny and costs; in the same year, Pearson ruefully recalled, the North Carolina Audubon Society had sponsored four arrests for bird-law violations "and had not lost one of our cases in the courts. The fines collected had totaled $4.01. Our efforts were succeeding." [11]

Actually, success was close at hand. The simultaneous disappearance of the bison and the passenger pigeon, not fully comprehended until this time, were only the most lurid vindications of the warnings which had been accumulating in the newspapers and magazines. Probably the most outspoken of the doom-criers was G. O. Shields, editor of *Recreation Magazine*, who once demanded public explanation of his gluttony from a Colorado hunter photographed with a monstrous pile of game. "I did write the big hog and asked him if the report was correct," Shields assured his readers, "but he evidently smelled something besides his own filth and declined to answer." The term "game-hog," still in general use, was one of Shields' happier fancies.

The outrage expressed by *Recreation* and other magazines was borne out by a growing body of natural-history texts, in which increasing pleas for conservation pierced the dry, technical prose of science. General interest was further excited by volumes of outdoor adventure, the most famous of which was *Wild Animals I Have Known*, by Ernest Thompson Seton. This book, in company with the works of Jack London and other less celebrated but no less imaginative interpreters of unusual animal accomplishments, was violently rejected by naturalists and biologists of the period, including C. Hart Merriam, William T. Hornaday, E. W. Nelson, President Theodore Roosevelt, and John Burroughs, the latter of whom referred to it in *The Atlantic Monthly* as *Wild Animals I Alone Have Known*. Seton was later to become a responsible naturalist himself, and it is unfortunate that his mighty *Lives of Game Animals* never found the popular appeal of the earlier work. There was also a variety of inspirational volumes in the guise of gentle bird lore for children and the fair sex, by Olive Thorne Miller (*Little Brothers of the Air*), Florence Merriam (*A-Birding on a Bronco*), Mabel Osgood Wright (*Tommy-Anne and the Three Hearts*), Neltje Blanchan (*Bird Neighbors*), and other talented gentlewomen. Finally, responsible opinion among educators and others was being shaped by serious, semi-philosophical essays and books. John Burroughs, Bradford Torrey, and John Muir, all three more or less in the tradition of Emerson and Thoreau, were perhaps the best known of these authors, who contributed widely to the national magazines. "Go to the sea," Burroughs cajoled his readers, "or climb the mountains, and with the ruggedest and the savagest you will find likewise the fairest and the most delicate. The greatness and minuteness of nature pass all understanding."

More and more Americans were climbing the mountains and going to the sea, and those who resisted did not long do so for want of upstanding example. President Roosevelt himself was a strenuous partisan of the outdoor life, a wilderness companion of Muir and Burroughs, among others ("I can not now recall that I have ever met a man with a keener and a more comprehensive interest in the wildlife about us," Burroughs wrote of him, "an interest that is at once scientific and thoroughly human . . ." [12]), and an accomplished sportsman in the best sense; his appearance in the White House in 1901 was one of the most auspicious and timely events in the history of American wildlife. Even before becoming President, he had written Frank M. Chapman, "I need hardly say how heartily I sympathize with the purposes of the Audubon Society. I would like to see all harmless wild things . . . protected in every way." [13] Among his early presidential acts was the implementation, on a federal basis, of the Audubon concept of sanctuaries.

The Audubon Societies were expanding rapidly. Incorporated in 1905 as the National Association of Audubon Societies for the Protection of Wild Birds and Animals, they were already combating the plume trade in other nations, and were partly responsible, in the year of their incorporation, for the Wild Birds Protection Act, in the Bahamas, aimed specifically at sparing the flamingo. At home a number of small sanctuaries had been successfully established, and the Audubon Law was now effective in thirty-three states. But it was also in 1905 that Audubon Warden Guy Bradley was murdered one summer day on Oyster Key by a Florida plume hunter; that the killer was set free by an indulgent local jury was an indication that the millinery trade was not as yet defunct. The Millinery Merchants' Protective Association was protecting itself as best it could, having failed in an earlier attempt at compromise negotiations with the militant Audubons, and took full advantage of the contradictory and ineffective state laws. So foolish were some of these that the *New York Times* for March 20, 1910, was moved to an uncustomary sarcasm in regard to the Albany bird-feather hearings: "Birds-of-paradise and ostriches are not protected in New Jersey," it observed, "a fact which will cause consternation among the native ostriches and birds-of-paradise." The same hearings, nevertheless, led to the passage of the Bayne Law barring possession for sale, offering for sale, or actual sale of wild-bird plumage in the state; since the milliners' headquarters were in New York, their defeat was now a matter of course. Minor loopholes excepted, the defeat was consummated three years later with the enactment of the Federal Tariff Act, one provision of which read in part, "The importation of birds-of-paradise, aigrettes, egret plumes or so-called osprey plumes and the feathers, quills, heads, wings, tails, skins or parts of skins of wild birds, either raw or manufactured, and not for scientific or educational purposes, is hereby prohibited." The same triumphal year, 1913, witnessed the passage of the Weeks–McLean Act which, in awarding to government agencies responsibility for migratory game birds, laid the basis for ultimate protection of the beleaguered waterfowl and shore birds.

In twenty years great progress had been made, but in the three centuries previous a much greater amount of damage had been perpetrated, and Americans had not yet relinquished the philosophy of devil-take-the-hindmost. "Travels through Europe, as well as over a large part of the North American continent," had convinced Henry Fairfield Osborn, President of the New York Zoological Society, "that nowhere is Nature being destroyed so rapidly as in the United States. Except within our conservation areas, an earthly paradise is being turned into an earthly hades; and it is not savages nor primitive men who are doing this, but men and women who boast of their civilization. Air and water are polluted, rivers and streams serve as sewers and dumping grounds, forests are swept away and fishes are driven from the streams. Many birds are becoming extinct, and certain mammals are on the verge of extermination.

CAROLINA PARAKEET

Vulgar advertisements hide the beauty of the landscape, and in all that disfigures the wonderful heritage of the beauty of Nature to-day, we Americans are in the lead.

"Fortunately, the tide of destruction is ebbing and the tide of conservation is coming in. . . . Yet we are far from the point where the momentum of conservation is strong enough to arrest and roll back the tide of destruction; and this is especially true with regard to our vanishing animal life. . . ."

Dr. Osborn, one of that small, honorable band of zoologists who had ventured onto the firing line of the conservation cause, wrote this in a preface to *Our Vanishing Wildlife*, an excited work which appeared just prior to the key federal legislation just mentioned. Its author, Dr. William T. Hornaday, Director of the New York Zoological Park, was a bristling and articulate successor to G. O. Shields, and he prefaced his chapter on extinct North American birds with the statement that "fully ten per cent of the human race consists of people who will lie, steal, throw rubbish in parks, and destroy forests and wild life whenever and wherever they can do so without being stopped by a policeman and a club." Dr. Hornaday himself was an exponent of the club technique, and was not given to mincing his words. "Today," he continued, "the thing that stares me in the face every waking hour, like a grisly spectre with bloody fang and claw, is *the extermination of species*. To me, that is a horrible thing. It is whole-sale murder, no less. It is capital crime, and a black disgrace to the races of

civilized mankind. I say 'civilized mankind,' because savages don't do it!
. . . It has remained for the wolf, the sheep-killing dog and civilized man
to make records of wanton slaughter which puts them in a class together. . . ."

The most recent North American species listed on Hornaday's roster of
birds effectively extinct were the passenger pigeon, the Eskimo curlew, and
the Carolina parakeet. The latter species seems somehow out of place, for it
is not properly identified with any one of the various forms of mass slaughter which had characterized the previous half-century. Yet we have seen
that it was killed or captured commonly from earliest times, and Audubon remarked of it that "the husbandman commits great slaughter among
them." [14] Coues warned of its extinction, and Baird, Brewer, and Ridgway,
in their book, said, "There is little doubt but that their total extermination
is only a matter of years, perhaps to be consummated within the lifetimes
of persons now living," a prophetic statement in view of the fact that the
last captive specimen was in the possession of Dr. Ridgway when it died.

Actually, this lovely bird, as Frank M. Chapman suggested, was persecuted for a variety of reasons: "First, it was destructive to fruit orchards,
and for this reason was killed by agriculturists; second, it has been trapped
and bagged in enormous numbers by professional bird-catchers; third, it has
been killed in myriads for its plumage; and fourth, it has been wantonly
slaughtered by so-called sportsmen." [15] At the time of this account, the
parakeets were still seen occasionally in Florida, and, as it happened, it was
Dr. Chapman himself who was to see the last wild band, thirteen unlucky
birds, in April 1904, at Taylor Creek on the northeast side of Lake Okeechobee. (The parakeet was "rediscovered" in the swampy wilderness of
the Santee River, South Carolina, in the thirties. Unlike most sightings
of species long presumed extinct, this one was made by experienced observers, including Alexander Sprunt, but the light was poor and all the
evidence against it, and this record is considered very dubious at best,
even by Robert P. Allen, who accompanied Sprunt at the time.) Ten
captive birds remained alive at the time of Hornaday's writing, and the
last Carolina parakeet died in 1914.

John Muir died in that same year, only a few months after Martha, the
last passenger pigeon on earth, blinked a final time in the Cincinnati Zoo.
Muir was primarily a botanist, a lover of trees and mountains, and his
technical knowledge of wildlife was inconsiderable. Nevertheless, he understood the role of living creatures in the silences of the open, and the

awe inspired in him by the mighty flocks of migrating birds, which died in his own dying years, passes easily to those of us for whom the spectacle must remain forever in the accounts of others:

> It was a great memorable day when the first flock of passenger pigeons came to our farm. . . . I have seen flocks streaming south in the fall so large that they were flowing over from horizon to horizon in an almost continuous stream all day long, at the rate of forty or fifty miles an hour, like a mighty river in the sky, widening, contracting, descending like falls and cataracts, and rising suddenly here and there in huge ragged masses like high-splashing spray. How wonderful the distances they flew in a day— in a year—in a lifetime! [16]

The buffalo is gone, and of all his millions, nothing is left but bones. . . . Those discordant serenaders, the wolves that howled at evening about the traveller's camp-fire, have succumbed to arsenic and hushed their savage music. . . . The rattlesnakes have grown bashful and retiring. The mountain lion shrinks from the face of man, and even grim "Old Ephraim," the grizzly bear, seeks the seclusion of his dens and caverns.

—FRANCIS PARKMAN (1892)

9 : The End of the Wilderness Road

IN THE SECOND HALF of the nineteenth century, several of the western states established closed seasons on game animals. California defended the antelope and tule elk, Nevada the mountain goat and bighorn sheep, and Idaho, after 1864, attempted to protect all its hoofed mammals from February 1 to July 1, including the then abundant bison. Within fifty years the tule elk and the bison had become so rare that killing either, in California or Montana, respectively, was considered a felony punishable by two years in prison, and the antelope was no longer a legal game animal anywhere within its United States range. Farther east, the elk in Michigan were granted a ten-year respite as of 1879, and steps were taken to perpetuate the woodland caribou in Maine. Both animals were subsequently exterminated, and, as things turned out, the measures to protect them may well have contributed less to the national population of large mammals than did hunting laws passed in both states just after the turn of the century prohibiting "the careless shooting of human beings."

Clearly, the states were unable to enforce their laws, and it was only the intervention of federal agencies, cooperating with private organizations in the early days of the present century, that slowed the swift decline of native creatures.

Previously, federal wildlife aid had been primitive and uncoordinated, and the record of Congress toward its dumb constituents had been callous, to say the least. Its resistance to protection for the bison has already been noted, and in 1886 it jealously forbade the legislatures of the Territories to pass laws protecting fish and game. Twenty years later, when Theodore Roosevelt's committee on natural resources required fifty thousand dollars to complete its report, the lawmakers withheld the appropriations and, disdaining halfway measures, ordered the several government agencies involved to deny further material to the committee. The latter maneuver, it must be said, was atypical of the Congresses under Roosevelt, the fine record of which in regard to conservation should be required reading for its members today.

The first evidence of Congressional concern with wildlife was an act in 1871 establishing the Commission of Fish and Fisheries. Though the fisheries were of growing economic importance, scientific study of individual species had scarcely begun, and the first comprehensive texts on American fishes, by Dr. George Brown Goode (*American Fishes*, 1887), and by Drs. David S. Jordan and Barton W. Evermann (*The Fishes of North and Middle America*, 1896–1900) remain standard works to this day. A great many regional studies are in print, but there is still no modern natural history of American fishes, a situation which should be remedied. Similarly, the amphibians and reptiles had been treated regionally and rather casually, when they were treated at all: Audubon's notorious account of the pursuit, capture, and constriction by a rattlesnake of a gray squirrel in a tree suggests the primitive state of the natural history of these classes in the first half of the nineteenth century. But the National Museum of the Smithsonian, which first published Jordan and Evermann, also brought out E. D. Cope's *The Batrachia of North America* in 1889, and in 1900 his *The Crocodilians, Lizards, and Snakes of North America;*

TULE ELK

subsequently, Raymond L. Ditmars and Thomas Barbour did what they could to counteract public apathy about these creatures. Lack of interest in the cold-blooded vertebrates, which Ditmars, encouraged by Roosevelt, did much to offset, was reflected among the biologists themselves, for, by comparison with the treatisees on mammals and, more particularly, on birds, the systematic studies of fishes, amphibians, and reptiles came very late, and are still far short of completion.

For this reason it seems curious that the Fish Commission, as it was known, should have preceded parallel agencies having to do with the economically significant birds and mammals, but the work of the National Museum of the Smithsonian Institution was a partial compensation. The Museum, which had weathered a maneuver on the part of William Cullen Bryant, Horace Greeley, and other figures to make the showman Phineas T. Barnum its director, was reorganized in 1876 according to the educational concepts of Harvard's Louis Agassiz, and, under S. F. Baird and George Brown Goode, engaged in unofficial research on the latter orders. The Division of Economic Ornithology and Mammalogy of the Department of Agriculture was set up in 1886, and a decade later the name of this organization was changed to the Division of Biological Survey. The Division was given Bureau status in 1905. (A Bureau of Fisheries had also been created, and under the terms of the Reorganization Act of 1939 the two were merged the following year in a joint organization called the Fish and Wildlife Service.)

The first work of the new agency was general research, including a biological survey of the nation. The Survey concerned itself chiefly with the economic effect of birds and mammals on agriculture and other interests, and its early contribution to conservation, with one important exception, was negligible. The exception came about indirectly, through Merriam's interest in the relation of hawks, owls, and small mammal predators to the populations of rodents detrimental to the farmers.

Another concern was the problem of uncontrolled importations of exotic species. These are thought to have begun in 1790, when Benjamin Franklin's son-in-law, Richard Bache, made a vain attempt to establish the Hungarian partridge on his New Jersey estate. The European brown trout was an immigrant in the next century, and with it a remarkable array of other fish, birds, and mammals from the Old World. The Fish Commission was responsible for the introduction of the carp, and the Brooklyn Institute for the doughty English sparrow. Other New Yorkers, for reasons unclear, liberated forty pairs of starlings in Central Park in 1890, despite all the evidence presented by the A.O.U. against the sparrow, and by this time the rock dove, or common pigeon, was also a familiar figure in the streets. The pheasant, first released in Oregon and Massachusetts, was established by century's end, and subsequently the Hungarian partridge, with the chukar partridge of Asia, became locally abundant in various parts of the United States and Canada. Among the mammals, not including the Norway and black rats and the house mouse, which arrived long ago as stowaways, and the wild mustang and burro, which escaped the Spanish in the West, locally successful importations have included the European hare, European wild boar, Barbary sheep, fallow deer, and the aquatic nutria. Other exotics, both bird and mammal, have thrived on small islands and on similar very limited territories; the European goldfinch, for example, refuses to extend its North American range beyond the environs of Garden City, on western Long Island, nor will the crested mynah bird forsake the immediate vicinity of Vancouver.

As opposed to these successful species, however, there are literally hundreds which failed to establish themselves, including all manner of game birds and game animals, parrots, linnets, skylarks, monkeys, elephants, and camels. The money wasted in distribution of these creatures on a trial-and-error basis amounts to millions of dollars which would have been far better spent toward the restoration of creatures which belonged here. The exotics that do thrive in strange environments are apt to be dangerously "plastic," or adaptable, and too often increase to a degree detrimental to native fauna or fan out into regions where they are undesirable, bearing with them new parasites and diseases, and a whole galaxy of acquired habits which the conditions of their original environments had held in check. It is no coincidence that, among the imported creatures now widely established in this country—the brown trout, carp, pheasant, street pigeon, English sparrow, starling, house mouse, black rat, and Norway rat—only the trout and pheasant could remotely be considered welcome additions to our fauna, and even these, in certain areas, have provided excessive competition for desirable native creatures: the brown trout was a factor in the extermination of the grayling from Michigan, and the pheasant has reduced the quail in several states to remnants. The carp, imported as a food fish at a time of post-Civil War famine, is a coarse browser of submerged plants, and so muddies its waters as to render them uninhabitable for more desirable species; in addition, it destroys the sago pondweed, wild millet, and other plants crucial to wild waterfowl. The English sparrow, which was heralded as a foe of the cankerworm, turned out to be a confirmed consumer of agricultural seeds; its aggressive habits, harsh voice, and affinity for horse manure require no description, even for those who unwillingly set foot outside the cities. Followed closely by the starling, which is overtaking it rapidly these days, it may now be our most numerous bird, the squat, shrill bane of birdhouses, agriculture, and city sanitation departments. The pigeons, descendants of the wild Eurasian rock dove, also present a sanitation problem. The rats and the house mouse, of course, accompanied the first families, and for the present their destructive presence must be lived with, like the common cold.

North America, in turn, has sent poor ambassadors abroad. The muskrat, a harmless and valuable fur bearer on its native soil, has proved a serious pest in Europe, where it undermines dikes and roadbeds, and assails gardens. Our handsome gray squirrel is also a pest, both in South Africa, where it has taken to crippling orchards, and in England, where it is driving out the popular native red squirrel. The mink, in Iceland and Scandinavia, is extremely destructive to wildlife, and the white-tailed deer are among the exotic imports which have overrun New Zealand, where the government provides free shells to anyone who will shoot them.

Experience with exotic plants and insects has been even more unhappy than with animal importations. The South American water hyacinth, imported originally as an ornament, got entirely out of control and has overgrown waterways throughout the South; foreign insect pests, arrived by accident, include the European cornborer, elm-leaf beetle, gypsy moth, cabbage aphis, Japanese beetle, and a dismaying assortment of alien cut-

HAWAIIAN GOOSE, or NENE   LAYSAN TEAL

worms. Thus it might safely be said that redistribution of living things not
preceded by careful study of all conceivable eventualities should be avoided
wherever possible. This has been common knowledge ever since two dozen
European rabbits, left to their own devices in Australia in 1859, were
greeted by no predators worthy of their mettle and increased to thirty thousand in six years. The object of the introduction was to provide the Australian settlers with Old World hunting. Australians have been hunting
desperately ever since, while the rabbits proceeded to devastate vast areas
of sheep range, and provided fatal competition for primitive Australian
marsupials such as the wallaby and bandicoot.

Even so, the European rabbit, long after the Australian fiasco, was invited to this country. It made short work of San Juan Island, Washington,
undermining the entire Navy installation there, but fortunately could
make no headway in competition with the native rabbits of the mainland.
Similarly, the mongoose, brought to the West Indies by mankind to combat the rats brought long before, reduced the black-capped petrel and
many other bird, mammal, and reptile species to near-extinction and
encouraged a plague of the smaller pests which these creatures had formerly preyed upon; nevertheless, it was shipped to Hawaii on the same
errand, where it swiftly performed the identical disservice to the specialized
island fauna. (The mongoose had been preceded in Hawaii by the house
cat and Norway rat; these animals all attacked the remnant populations
of indigenous birds still surviving in the dwindling forests of the islands,
with the result that sixty per cent of the known forms of Hawaiian birds,
including at least twelve distinct species, are now utterly extinct; many
others, such as the *nene* or Hawaiian goose and the Laysan teal, are seriously endangered.) Attempts to let the mongoose try its luck on the wild-

life of this continent have so far been held in check, though single specimens have escaped here from time to time, and there is always the risk that some deranged admirer of this savage little beast will loose a pair upon the country. The Lacey Bill, one of the first measures to control the millinery traffic, also provided the federal government with authority to determine which exotic creatures would be welcomed to the United States, and the mongoose most emphatically is not one of them.

However well-intentioned, then, man's efforts to improve upon the natural scene have usually succeeded in upsetting the balance of nature, and, with few exceptions, the only projects in which his interference has been truly beneficial were those which tried to restore a balance already upset. The repeal of the Pennsylvania "scalp act" is a negative illustration of this sad lesson, just as the promotion of conservation programs and legislation is a positive one.

Movements and legislation related to conservation were under way, of course, throughout the late nineteenth century, but neither popular opinion nor the prestige of the presidential office were strongly operative on conservation's behalf until after 1901, when Theodore Roosevelt succeeded to the Presidency upon McKinley's assassination. McKinley, like Cleveland, had responded to a mounting national interest in the natural resources, and had set aside a number of large forest preserves, a program which Roosevelt expanded. Actually, the necessity for forest conservation, directly related to the conservation of wildlife, dated back to the warnings of William Penn. In the nineteenth century it was referred to increasingly, most farsightedly, perhaps, by George P. Marsh, whose *The Earth as Modified by Human Action*, in 1874, was a prototype of the numerous modern texts—by Fairfield Osborn, Harrison Brown, Paul B. Sears, and others, all of them lamentably unheeded—treating the conservation of renewable natural resources as a crucial factor in any intelligent confrontation of the world's increasing political and economic ills. The government had established a Bureau of Forestry in 1891, but no broad program of federal conservation was formulated until Roosevelt took office.

The President's steps in this direction were advised and implemented by Frederick H. Newell and Gifford Pinchot, respective chiefs of the Reclamation Service and the Forest Service. The Reclamation Service, set up originally to irrigate vast, arid regions of the West, later provided waterfowl refuges on certain of its impounded waters, but it was to have an uneven

WOOD DUCK

effect on wildlife, and especially on the western fishes, the habitats of which were often destroyed; its incidental victims, unlike many of their contemporaries, were nevertheless casualties of a worthy cause.

Gifford Pinchot, later head of Roosevelt's National Conservation Committee, was the chief architect of the President's reforms. Set up under his direction, the Forest Service encouraged a utilitarian approach to the use of public timberlands and watersheds. If it has not always acted in the best interests of wildlife, it has unquestionably preserved a great amount of wilderness habitat, particularly in the inviolate "roadless areas" of the national forests. To Pinchot, who invented it in this usage, the term "conservation" meant sound economic exploitation and renewal of a resource, and the wilderness was anything but inexpendable. Against the outraged opposition of John Muir and others, he was to encourage the flooding of Yosemite's Hetch Hetchy Valley as a reservoir for San Francisco. Furthermore, he resisted the formation of a separate National Park Service under the Department of the Interior, though this idea became law at last in 1916; Pinchot and his successors felt that the national parks and monuments could be most effectively administered in conjunction with the national forests, under the Department of Agriculture. Since the national forests are open to commercial leasing and exploitation—supervised hunting, lumbering, mining, and other operations are permissible—it is probably just as well that the unique monuments and parks were sequestered when they were.

Meanwhile, the Biological Survey, most notably in the person of Theodore S. Palmer, was encouraged by Roosevelt to apply its research to the conservation battle. Merriam's early statement on the economic value of predators was beginning to take root in the state laws, though the eagles, when the present century began, were protected in two states only. The Survey also issued a call in 1901 for a closed season on the disappearing wood duck, to which New York, New Jersey, West Virginia, and all of New England but Rhode Island immediately responded. More and more, the states were assuming responsibility for their wildlife, and state game commissions, originated in 1878 by California and New Hampshire, were making room for departments of conservation. The concepts of rest days for waterfowl, bag limits, resident and nonresident hunting licenses, and other modern controls were already in effect, though these measures were far from uniform in every state, and were subject to repeal wherever they were not ignored entirely. Nevertheless, enforcement was gaining ground, perhaps because it was now supported by national opinion, and the recommendations of the federal biologists were listened to in the states with a respect they have not always been shown since. In the early 1900s, Nevada, then Oklahoma, placed game protection on the curriculum of public education, and state wildlife refuges were created in Indiana, Pennsylvania, Alabama, Massachusetts (the heath-hen sanctuary on Martha's Vineyard), Idaho, and Louisiana. The western states, in 1909, cooperated to save the antelope, and by 1911 wildlife legislation in every state but Maryland was generally constructive. Maryland, in that year, still permitted spring shooting, the shooting of does and non-game birds, the sale and export of game, and unlicensed hunting by state residents; Sunday shooting, to the state's credit, was forbidden, if only to children and servants.

The years between 1900 and 1913, which culminated in the Seal Treaty, the Federal Tariff Act, and the Weeks-McLean Act, witnessed the first significant federal intervention in the cause of wildlife conservation, and the foundation of a federal refuge system which was to restore from near-extinction a number of our most rewarding creatures. The first federal refuge, sponsored jointly by the Biological Survey, the A.O.U., and the Audubon Society, was at Pelican Island, Florida. Authorized by President Roosevelt in 1903 for the protection from the plume hunters of a breeding colony of brown pelicans, this islet in the Indian River was four acres in

PRAIRIE FALCON

PEREGRINE FALCON, or DUCK HAWK

extent, a small beginning when one considers that the federal refuges in
the United States and Alaska now total in the millions of acres. In the
next few years, many other water-bird colonies received protection, and
in 1908 the first small Alaskan refuges were established. In the same year
a waterfowl breeding area was reserved, at Lower Klamath and Malheur
Lakes, on the Oregon–California border and the National Bison Range, in
Montana, was established in cooperation with the American Bison Society.
The first national monuments were set aside in this period, some of which,
like the Grand Canyon and Fort Jefferson (Dry Tortugas) National
Monuments, were of particular benefit to certain wildlife species. The
basis for the great national forest, park, monument, and wildlife refuge
systems of the present had been laid.

The beneficent attitude toward wildlife which flourished in this time did
not apply equally to all species; paradoxically, a certain element of the
fauna now fell victim, as never before, to widespread animosity. These
were the predatory animals and a few others of unlucky habits, which were
branded "criminals," "murderers," and "vermin" even by such professional
zoologists as Dr. Hornaday. The birds of prey, it is true, enjoyed an uneasy
sanctuary in some parts of their range, but the carnivorous mammals were

everywhere assaulted. The smaller carnivores—the weasels and skunks, the raccoon and the foxes—were persecuted on a local scale, as they are today, and were never seriously hampered in their operations; they have never been more than peripheral casualties of that uncertain tool of wildlife management known today as predator control.

Predator control is, in effect, a systematic reduction of species competing with mankind in the exploitation of other forms of life, wild or domestic, and, as such, is a scientific extension of the bounty system. The unhappy consequences of the Pennsylvania "scalp act" notwithstanding, the control of predators has often been a necessary evil—necessary, that is, because man's prior interference with the balance of nature has made it so. The shooting of hawks on the Martha's Vineyard heath-hen refuge and the occasional destruction of golden eagles on western bighorn ranges are among the very rare instances where predator control seems justifiably applied to birds of prey. In the case of the large carnivorous mammals, however, the frequent and continuing abuse of the practice does not mean that it is never valid; indeed, had war not been waged successfully against the gray wolves of the West, American cattle ranching would still be an uncertain, perhaps even unprofitable enterprise.

The plains gray wolf or buffalo wolf, essentially the same animal which had plagued the colonists in the East, stalked the pioneer encampments for strayed stock, and commonly invaded the settlement enclosures; its great numbers, its inferior pelt, and a chronic shortage of ammunition were factors which, in frontier days, encouraged defensive rather than aggressive action against the huge, wild dogs.

The situation changed with the advent of the cowmen. With the slaughter of the bison and other hoofed animals in the late nineteenth century, the wolves and coyotes, grown fat on man's leavings, turned their full attention to his livestock, which was already abundant on the grasslands. The wolves did not vanish in the wake of the bison, as had been predicted, and neither did the coyotes, though these more numerous, smaller animals were less destructive. On the contrary, the wolves thrived upon the cattle, and were said to have killed nearly half of one year's calf crop. The cowmen attacked the wolf with trap, bullet, and arsenic, but, as the manager of the Standard Cattle Company complained in 1896 to the Biological Survey, "the number of wolves has become so considerable that all means of extermination used for the last five years have only succeeded in keeping them at a standstill. . . . I consider that the extent of the loss to the community is much greater than is commonly supposed, and that it is greater than that from cattle thieves, which I estimate to be very heavy indeed. There is absolutely no way of estimating the extent of the loss to a state like Wyoming, but I should judge it to be not far from a million dollars a year, four times the entire revenue needed to run the state government." [1]

Another rancher, writing from New Mexico the following year, estimated that half a million head of livestock were annually destroyed by western wolves, and asked that the government provide free poison. Meanwhile, the sheep industry had developed rapidly, and these smaller animals were promptly set upon by both wolves and coyotes. Anyone familiar with the personality and habits of domestic sheep can sympathize with their plight only in principle; cropping all available forage to the roots, they destroyed wide areas of range, for cattle and for game animals as well. Nevertheless, the sheep ranchers had their rights, and brought added pressure on the Biological Survey for government intervention. The bounty system, traditionally shot through with fraud—dog, coyote, and even stretched fox and rabbit ears commonly passed as those of wolves, animals killed in one state were submitted for bounty in another, and female wolves enjoyed an early form of conservation in order that a future bounty crop might be insured—had never afforded much relief, and in the early 1900s the Survey concluded that only a concerted interstate campaign could materially reduce the menace. The annual loss was now in the millions of dollars, and an additional million was being squandered every year in bounties. The first recommendation of the Survey was that wolf dens be hunted out and the young destroyed, and, in addition, the

rangers on the national forests were authorized to begin widespread trapping operations. In 1907 the combined efforts of private and federal personnel accounted for eighteen hundred wolves and over ten times that number of coyotes, but remained inadequate. In 1914 federal funds were finally appropriated for the purpose of controlling injurious animals. These funds were assigned to the Survey which, though essentially a research agency, was considered responsible for all wildlife problems having to do with agriculture, forestry, and livestock. The western ranges were divided into supervised districts; state, federal, and private monies were coordinated; and within ten years the wolf problem had been eliminated.

The last wolves died very hard indeed. Unlike the unsophisticated packs of early days, which readily accepted crude baits of all kinds and blundered into the clumsiest of traps, these renegade animals learned to disdain manmade enticements. The last of them, in fact, were almost invariably taken in "blind-sets"—scented traps buried painstakingly along predetermined wolf runs, or hunting routes, some of them more than one hundred miles in circumference. Many wolves avoided even blind-sets over periods of years, and individuals with their own peculiarities earned names which became notorious. Rags the Digger, a shaggy old male given to unearthing traps unsprung, killed ten thousand dollars' worth of Colorado stock over a term of fourteen years. Old Whitey, pursued for fifteen years, would playfully snap the tails off other calves after feeding on one of their number. Whitey's mate, one of numerous three-toed outlaws which had benefited from past experience with traps, continued her work for two more years, and was the last of the renegades in Colorado.

The most famous of these animals was the Custer wolf (shown in the drawing by Bob Hines at the head of this chapter) which did away with over twenty-five thousand dollars' worth of stock in a ten-year reign on the Wyoming–South Dakota border, and had a five-hundred-dollar bounty on its head. It persistently outwitted the best hunters in the country, and was said to be accompanied by a parasitic pair of coyotes which, flanking it on both sides, allegedly served as sentinels. The ranchers appealed at last to the Biological Survey, and a hunter named H. P. Williams was assigned to the Custer wolf by Dr. Edward W. Nelson, the famous mammalogist. Williams discovered that the coyote legend was true. He shot both coyotes, and in October 1920, after six grueling months of tracking and trap-setting over an area of twenty-six hundred square miles, he caught up at last with the Custer wolf itself.

RED WOLF

Within several years the wolf had vanished from the American West, and today the last native gray wolves in the nation roam the northern forests of Michigan, Wisconsin, Minnesota, and possibly Oregon. These scattered bands cannot long survive. A few wolves also wander north from Mexico into New Mexico and Arizona, and they persist in some strength in wilderness areas of western Canada and Alaska. The red wolf, a species of southern woodlands, survives in diminishing numbers in east Texas and western Louisiana, with stray populations in Oklahoma, Arkansas, and southern Missouri, but it is much disliked by turkey ranchers, among others, and will doubtless trail its larger relative into oblivion.

The wild dogs of North America are all held in ill repute, and only the wily and widespread woodland foxes (and especially the red fox which, adapting better to civilization, has replaced the gray fox over much of their common range), the arctic fox, and the coyote have successfully withstood man's encroachments. The resilient coyote, though outlawed everywhere, has even contrived to extend its historic range as far east as upper New York State and as far north as Alaska. The kit and desert kit foxes are restricted in habitat as well as resourcefulness, however, and are endangered. These small, large-eared animals were once abundant in the deserts and on the Great Plains from Chihuahua and Baja California north to Alberta, Saskatchewan, and Manitoba. "Like the kit, the desert fox has little of the sophisticated mental ability of the red fox and falls an easy prey to the trapper. It is nowhere numerous . . . ," E. W. Nelson wrote in 1916,[2] and fifteen years later another authority added, "These little foxes . . . are so unable to cope with the advanced civilization that they are rapidly disappearing from the face of the earth." [3] The advanced civilization, in the case of the kit foxes, has appeared largely in the form of poisoned baits set out for more imposing predators, chiefly the coyote, which has learned to leave them for the edification of its small relative. The kit fox is said to have recovered somewhat in the last few years, but its future is uncertain.

The wild cats, as predators, are less important than the canine animals, though with the decline of the wolves their presence has been more noticeable. Of the seven species occurring in North America, four are essentially tropical (see Chapter 2), and the lynx of the northern border, Canada, and Alaska, is of chief economic consequence as a fur animal. The fierce bobcat, prolific and resourceful, has matched the success of the coyote in its efforts to circumvent man and remains widely distributed, though not plentiful. But the cougar, mountain lion, or puma, which once prowled every state in the nation and, ranging south to the Argentine, had the most extensive range of all North American mammals, is a species in full retreat.

In early times the cougar was confused extensively with the African lion (until the chronic absence of a lion with a mane encouraged a reappraisal), a fact which may have led to the observation, in 1800, that "it is fierce and ravenous in the extreme, and will swim rivers to attack cattle even in their enclosures." [4] Actually, it is the most timid of the world's large cats, and, as in the case of the North American gray wolf, and despite the wild-eyed tales in today's outdoor magazines, the documented instances of cougar attack on human beings, in all the history of North America, can be counted on the fingers of one hand. Nevertheless, it is a skilled killer of game and, more rarely, of domestic animals, and as such has been out-lawed. Solitary, and never numerous enough to warrant the campaigns which banished the wolf, it is nonetheless destroyed wherever found and is hunted commonly in the name of sport. A few still skulk, as we have seen, in hinterlands east of the Mississippi, and it persists here and there in Texas, in the wilder regions of the Western mountains, and in Vancouver and British Columbia.

Ill-advised control of predators had, by 1924, insured the almost total destruction of the Kaibab game preserve, established in 1906 on the north rim of the Grand Canyon, where some twenty thousand sheep and cattle had been introduced, where over six thousand large predators—wolves, cougars, coyotes, and bobcats—and uncounted golden eagles had been systematically eliminated, and where the deer, increasing in the two decades

KIT FOX

previous from four thousand to twenty-five times that number, overcropped and killed the available forage growth. The starving animals died by the thousands, and the attempts of the Forest Service to cut down the herds were impeded, tragically enough, by the enthusiastic but uneducated conservation groups, which for several years could not be made to understand that the victory won in the establishment of the preserve was fast becoming Pyrrhic. Control measures, in any case, were much too late. "The whole country looked as though a swarm of locusts had swept through it, leaving the range . . . torn, gray, stripped, and dying." [5] The stunted deer dwindled to ten thousand, and the ruined range has only recently recovered.

The lesson of the Kaibab had to be learned over and over again throughout the West, and it was not until the thirties that the National Park Service, at least, made it official policy that "every species shall be left to carry on its struggle for existence unaided, as being to its greatest ultimate good, unless there is real cause to believe that it will perish if unassisted," and that "no native predator shall be destroyed on account of its normal utilization of any other park animal, excepting if that animal is in immediate danger of extermination, and then only if the predator is not itself a vanishing form."

The wolf, by this time, had been exterminated almost everywhere in the United States. The cougar, however, still could be restored. Under normal conditions, its diet has been shown to consist chiefly of deer and, to a lesser extent, of porcupine, and since both of the latter animals, in excessive populations, are exceedingly destructive to timberlands, persecution of the cougar has done much more harm than good. In Yellowstone Park, where Buffalo Jones once wiped out forty cougar during a single campaign and where it is now absent, the excess elk have always constituted a serious problem, and some seven thousand—over half the so-called northern herd—had to be killed or otherwise removed in 1956 and 1957, to prevent further overgrazing of their territory. Like the wolf, the cougar served, and could still serve, a valuable purpose in weeding out sick, deformed, and excess animals from wild herds; if predator control in the case of the gray wolf has been excessive, in the case of the cougar it has been nothing short of stupid.

The role of the government agencies in predator control, after an incautious start, has been more or less responsible. Quite early the federal biologists in the West discouraged the indiscriminate use of poison, since it destroyed a great number of harmless animals such as the kit fox; furthermore, the complete extermination of a species had never been their intent. "Except on local areas where wolves have continued to present a pressing economic problem . . . little wolf control work is now justified. There still remain, even in the United States, some areas of considerable size in which we feel that both the red and gray species, in their respective habitats, may be allowed to continue their existence with little molestation." [6] The same attitude would surely apply to the cougar, but it is too rarely shared by the state game commissions and other appointive organizations, which keep a wet finger to the winds of political pressure.

Another victim of predator control, from the Rocky Mountains to Alaska, has been the grizzly bear. Like the cougar, the grizzly was never pursued in systematic fashion but was killed on sight by the ranchers, and died as well from poison baits intended originally for wolves. The fact that men die periodically beneath the great claws of grizzlies has also inspired

COUGAR, or MOUNTAIN LION

persecution, although the bears dislike the taste of human flesh, and almost invariably have killed men when cornered, provoked, or wounded. The individuals which attack man's livestock are also very rare; the grizzly's chief diet consists of small mammals, the sick and young of hoofed animals, fish, and considerable vegetable matter. A notable exception was Old Mose, which prior to its death in 1904, in the Black Mountains of Colorado, was credited with a kill including eight hundred head of cattle and no less than five human beings.

"Nature does not care whether the hunter slay the beast or the beast the hunter," John Burroughs once remarked. "She will make good compost of them both, and her ends are prospered whichever succeeds." [7]

The Act of Congress authorizing federal intervention against predators permitted expenditures for "experiments and demonstrations in destroying wolves, prairie dogs, and other animals injurious to agriculture and animal husbandry." The prairie dog, of course, is anything but a predator, and it is somewhat surprising that man has so exerted himself to destroy it. A relative of the marmots, it originally occupied "towns" often hundreds of miles in extent—the Chisholm Trail was said to have been surrounded by one huge dog town—throughout the short-grass plains from southern Saskatchewan and North Dakota south to southeast Arizona and Texas. Expanding with the introduction of cattle, which cropped the forage to a favorable height, and with the simultaneous destruction of predators, the prairie dog became a menace to cattlemen through its consumption of food grasses. Its extermination has since proceeded so rapidly that it is already extinct in Arizona and extremely uncommon elsewhere in its wide range, though a few small colonies are protected in the national parks and in such state reserves as the Mackenzie Park, in Lubbock, Texas. Its disappearance has brought about a parallel decline of the western burrrowing owl and the black-footed ferret, which frequent the dog towns for shelter and food, respectively; it has even been suggested that its disappearance in Arizona contributed to the decline of such game birds as the Merriam's turkey and the scaled, Gambel's, and harlequin quails by forcing the coyote into the mountains in search of food. The white-tailed prairie dog, a species of the Rocky Mountain foothills farther north, has also been reduced, though not as yet endangered.

The prairie dog is not the only small creature which from time to time has impeded man's economic progress. The passenger pigeon was a potential

BURROWING OWL

BLACK-TAILED PRAIRIE DOG

menace to farmers in colonial times and after, not only in the grain fields but in the hardwood forests, which were often stripped clean of the acorns, beechnuts, and other mast serving as hog feed. The Carolina parakeet and the redheaded woodpecker, as we have seen, were considered inimical to orchards, and the bobolink was an important pest in the days when extensive rice planting was conducted in the South. The gray squirrel was once as unpopular as the wolf for its forays into the settlers' corn, a problem upon which Pennant commented rather tartly just after the War of Independence: "Pennsylvania paid from January 1749 to January 1750, *eight thousand pounds* currency [in bounties]; but on complaint being made by the deputies that their treasuries were exhausted by these rewards, they were reduced to one half;—from three pence to a penny and a half. How improved must the state of Americans then be, in thirty-five years to wage an expensive and successful war against its parent country, which before could not bear the charges of clearing the provinces from the ravages of those insignificant animals!" [8] Today the mole, field mouse, California ground squirrel, and cottontail rabbit are among the small species which incur man's frequent wrath. Unlike the prairie dog, which in its communal towns is vulnerable to systematic poisoning, these species have managed to weather man's technology through the sheer exuberance of their breeding habits.

At least one creature, however, has been subjected to persecution unmotivated by financial considerations. *Heloderma suspectum*, the Gila monster of the American Southwest, and its near-relative, *H. horridum*, of Mexico, are the only venomous lizards in the world, and the former, at

GILA MONSTER

least, has paid dearly for its singularity. In its desert range in southwest Utah, south Nevada, New Mexico, and Arizona, it is usually killed on sight, and has become so scarce that the state of Arizona, in 1952, passed an unprecedented act protecting the Gila monster from molestation and even from commercial sale or exploitation in a live condition.

Not all Americans will immediately agree that the salvation of the Gila monster is desirable. *H. suspectum*, which Raymond Ditmars called "a highly dangerous brute to tamper with," [9] seems a doubtful addition to any community, and the loss to the world upon its extinction would be difficult to argue. Nevertheless, the loss would be there. Like the more pleasing creatures to which wildlife conservation is customarily applied, the Gila monster is a dumb animal, arrived in its desert world by a long process of evolution, or by the hand of God, if one prefers. Like the chickadee and the chipmunk, it has its place in its own environment, and attempts to remove it from the face of the earth place man in the uncomfortable position of deciding which animals besides himself are desirable inhabitants of the globe. "The world, we are told, was made especially for man—a presumption not supported by the facts. A numerous class of men are painfully astonished whenever they find anything, living or dead, in all God's universe, which they cannot eat or render in some way useful to themselves." [10] The Gila monster is just such a phenomenon as John Muir had in mind, and the conservation movement which was consolidating itself in the early 1900s would come of age when it advocated protection not only of a reasonable population of the predators but of a thick-bodied, pink-black, and poisonous reptile as well.

The soil, impoverished by the war and the tenant system which followed the war, was still drained of fertility for the sake of the poor crops it could yield. Spring after spring, the cultivated ground appeared to shrink into the "old fields," where scrub pine or oak succeeded broomsedge or sassafras as inevitably as autumn slipped into winter. —ELLEN GLASGOW (1925)

. . . the lightless and gutted and empty land . . .
—WILLIAM FAULKNER (1942)

All the day the dust sifted down from the sky, and the next day it sifted down. An even blanket covered the earth. It settled on the corn, piled up on the tops of fence posts, piled up on the wires; it settled on roofs, blanketed the weeds and trees.   —JOHN STEINBECK (1939)

10 : Old Fields

IN THE FIRST QUARTER of the century the science of conservation remained quite primitive, dependent more on restrictive legislation than on constructive action; except for the reservation of wilderness areas and the establishment of wildlife refuges, increasingly important as civilization consumed the land, conservation was characterized by such expensive and ineffective panaceas as indiscriminate predator control, introduction of exotic species, and the transplanting of native animals in conjunction with artificial propagation.

The first two programs were generally discredited by 1930, but the widespread attempts to infest one part of this continent with creatures which Nature, for her own excellent reasons, had developed in another, continued. The latter program achieved frantic proportions before biologists determined that the mortality rate of wild creatures transplanted without extensive prior study was almost as high as that of those raised in captivity and released.

In a California experiment, some years ago, three groups of valley quail were turned out on a private preserve. The first group was composed of wild birds native to the grounds which had been trapped, banded, and set free again. The second group represented wild birds transplanted from not far away. The third sample consisted of artificially propagated game-farm birds, in the same number. By the hunting season in the following year, not a single survivor of the last group could be found. Only 1.7 per cent of the transplants were retaken, as opposed to 7.7 per cent of the birds native to the area. These statistics have been paralleled in similar experiments elsewhere. Even in cases where transplants manage to take root, the results are not always beneficial. It is now thought, for example, that the few survivors among the hosts of Texas quail imported to the northeast for the purposes of introducing "new blood" accomplished, if anything, a weakening of the hardier northern strain which properly belonged there.

On the other hand, transplanting based on careful study is often desirable, especially where a suitable ecological niche exists but where the species in question is, for one reason or another, absent. The wild turkey, elk, and a few other forms have been successfully stocked not only in parts of their original range but in areas entirely new to them where conditions were determined in advance to be conducive. The strange environment, however, was invariably related closely to the original.

Unsuccessful transplantings, however disheartening to the hunters who have subsidized them, have contributed much to the understanding of the principle of range quality, or carrying capacity, which is now a basic premise of wildlife management. Wild creatures are explosive breeders, ordinarily producing many more young than the range can possibly support. "The life expectancy of new-born small game or fur animals," one ecologist points out, "is considerably *less than a year*, and, as a reasonable average, a full-grown individual in hunting season stands less than *one chance in*

three of being alive a year later." The animal numbers on a given range
are precisely controlled by its quality, which in turn is determined by the
available food, cover, water, and other variable factors controlling both
productivity and survival. "The turnover of wild individuals in an established population is a drastic weeding out of animals that are either unfit
or unlucky. This takes place on a large scale every year that is favorable for
breeding. If we toss more animals into this system, one of two things must
happen to a released individual. Either it is eliminated along with the
naturally produced surplus, or it can survive as one of those animals most
fit and favorably situated. If it does survive, it probably does so *in place of*
a wild individual that might have been there otherwise." [1] The population
of predators, in turn, is directly controlled by the numbers of their prey,
and on range of good quality their effects on game-animal populations are
negligible, since any surplus they fail to remove will be taken in any case
by the fine screen of nature. In the case of larger and longer-lived animals
such as deer, this elimination, in the absence of predators, takes the painful
form of disease and mass starvation.

It must be assumed, then, that, unless hunters are on hand to shoot
down the newcomers almost as fast as they leave their crates, the stocking
of a range already inhabited by the species will be most noteworthy for its
expense. Transplanting and artificial propagation, like the bounty system,
have provided their most significant rewards not to the hunter but to the
state officials, for whom they demonstrate a more spectacular evidence of
zeal than the creation, restoration, and protection of good habitat which
would actually benefit the game. In the Thomasville region of Georgia, for
example, superb quail and turkey shooting is maintained without benefit
of artificial stocking or even systematic predator control, but rather through
the encouragement, along field edges, wood lots, and roadsides, of valuable
food and cover plants such as the bicolor lespedeza. In some states, enlightened sportsmen's groups are coming to appreciate the importance of
wildlife habitat, but the fact remains that over three million dollars are
spent annually in this country for artificial propagation and transplanting,
a very minor part of which goes to the occasional program in which these
methods have been determined in advance to justify their cost.

Three million dollars, on the other hand, is only a quarter of the amount
devoted each year to the rearing and transplanting, for the public diversion, of fish. A few upland game birds excepted, the fishes include the only

SAN GORGONIO TROUT

game species which lend themselves readily to the indignities of mass culture, and incredible sums have been poured away in the form of ill-fated fingerlings and fry.

Originally these hatchery fish were distributed almost at random, and were commonly cast, with the best of intent, upon waters not "fished out" at all, but so polluted or silted that no sport fish worthy of the name could live there. The stocking later became more selective, but, as in the case of the game animals, only specialized situations—new waters, or those empty of the same or competing species, or those where conditions have been manipulated in advance—would seem to justify the practice, unless the fish have been raised to legal size and are introduced yearly, not to propagate their kind, but to be removed again as quickly and efficiently as possible by the taxpayers.

A pond, lake, or stream, like an area of land, can support a given population of a species, depending upon natural conditions. Again, it is the conditions or quality of the habitat rather than the number of breeding adults which determines population growth, a fact made more evident when one considers that a nest of the largemouth bass can contain six thousand eggs, and that a female walleyed pike, given a modest amount of milt and complete protection for her spawn, would overpopulate a large lake in one season. Overpopulation, with resultant stunting and disease, can be a consequence of ill-advised stocking in waters where conditions, natural or manipulated, permit the unchecked expansion of a species; in fact, biologists have learned that intense fishing pressure, rather than closed seasons, stocking, and other superficially constructive measures, is often the solution in bodies of water which, apparently fished out, are actually so full of fish that few individuals find enough to eat to attain a respectable size.

Nevertheless, fish culture has generally proved more profitable than propagation and transplanting of game animals and birds, and myriad bass, bluegill, trout, and other desirable forms now provide human diversion in waters in which they were formerly absent. Unhappily, their debuts have often been made at the expense of more delicate species or races already inhabiting the waters; the rainbow and cutthroat trouts in particular have brought about the decline and, in several cases, the complete extermination of other fish for which their competition proved too strong. This has been especially true in Western waters, where the variety of trouts found in the distinct river systems of the Rocky Mountains and elsewhere had suffered little or no predation or competition in their more isolated environments, and thus were poorly equipped to deal with aggressive newcomers.

Competition among fishes takes various forms, not the least of which is open assault by one competitor upon another, or upon its young. More often, there is competition for the available food, whether plant or animal. Sometimes the competition comes about in the insidious guise of hybridization, in the course of which the less dominant race is absorbed as completely as if it had been eaten, though if the races are not too closely related the victim may leave a mute record of its passing in the changed characters of the hybrid.

The emerald, San Gorgonio, and Gila trouts are among the western forms affected by the several manifestations of competition, though the Gila trout still survives. Its plight has been compounded, however, by siltation produced through deforestation of the watershed which feeds the New Mexican river of the same name.

Another game fish which has suffered the combined ravages of competition and siltation is the grayling, a northern species with a remarkable dorsal "sail." Quite common in Canada and Alaska, it was left behind by the retreat of the Pleistocene glaciers in certain cold streams of northern Michigan and Montana. (The rare Sunapee and blueback trouts, in the northeast, are also thought to be glacial relics, related to the Arctic char.) The Michigan grayling was exposed to competition from the rainbow and European brown trouts, as well as overfishing, but its disappearance in the

1930s was largely in consequence of logging operations, which opened its cool, clear woodland waters to silt and the warmth of the sun. The Montana population still survives, most notably in the Red Rock Lakes, a remote mountain sanctuary which it shares today with the last large flock of trumpeter swans in the United States.

Siltation, which coats stream bottoms with sterile slime and, shutting out the sun, kills aquatic plants supplying both food and oxygen to certain species, is probably the single most destructive enemy of American freshwater fishes. In many regions, particularly in the Midwest, desirable fish have been replaced in their native waters by such coarse forms as the catfish and European carp, which are better adapted to fouled conditions, and wholesale redistribution of fish populations has taken place in the great river systems as a consequence of watershed erosion. The harelip sucker of the central and southeastern states, the blue sucker of the Mississippi Valley, and the copper redhorse of the St. Lawrence drainage are edible fish which have suffered acutely from deterioration of their habitat; the first of these, a more desirable species than its name would indicate, is probably extinct. The redhorse, a specialized mollusc feeder, may have been declining of its own accord before man found it, and is now confined to clear waters in the vicinity of Montreal.

In Western environments irrigation and dam construction, which drastically alter water levels and, in times of drought, produce dry river beds, have contributed their effects to those of siltation, and the dams are particularly harmful when, as in the Pacific Northwest, they block the spawning runs of anadromous species such as the salmons and the steelhead trout. The large cui-ui (pronounced "kwee-wee") of Nevada's Pyramid Lake and the white salmon, or Colorado River squawfish (not a salmon at all, but a giant minnow attaining a weight of eighty pounds) are irrigation and dam victims, respectively, and are slipping toward extinction. The latter once was so abundant that Indians used it commonly as food, and farmers could pitchfork it out of the canals for use as fertilizer.

Overfishing, of course, has played a part wherever circumstances permitted, but most fish are virtually impossible to extinguish in this manner alone, since the waters will be forsaken by the fishermen long before the last breeding pair is taken. The larger fish of the Great Lakes were seriously reduced as commercial species in the past century, but the danger of their complete extermination is recent, and is not the work of man;

GILA TROUT

EMERALD TROUT

SUNAPEE TROUT

BLUEBACK TROUT

should it occur, it will have been accomplished by a far more efficient enemy, the sea lamprey, *Petromyzon marinus*.

The lamprey, a primitive eel-like parasite which attaches itself to its prey by means of its mouth sucker and sharp teeth and feeds on the blood and body juices with a voracity usually fatal to its host, was present in the St. Lawrence River and Lake Ontario for a number of years before entering Lake Erie. It invaded Lake Huron in the thirties, and Lake Michigan and Lake Superior in the forties, devoting particular attention to the lake trout, the Great Lakes whitefish, and several kinds of ciscoes, all of them large species of commercial significance. In 1943 the lake trout landings in Lake Michigan totaled seven million pounds. In 1954 twenty-two pounds were taken, and the trout fishery was dead.

The whitefish is cyclic in its numbers, but nevertheless its decline has been apparent. It will probably resist extermination, however, since, unlike its parasite, it frequents shallow water. The ciscoes are already virtually extinct in Lake Huron and Lake Michigan, and may, with the trout, disappear from Lake Superior if the lamprey is not soon controlled. Toxic compounds, electric weirs, and other methods have been tried by the Fish and Wildlife Service in over ten years of lamprey investigations, and it is now thought that the creature can be successfully combated. The restoration of affected species will be difficult, but no other fish has replaced the lake trout in the specialized ecological balance of the Great Lakes, and this species, at least, can presumably be reintroduced from elsewhere in its wide range. It will find an ample supply, if so, of one of its favorite foods, a nondescript cisco called the bloater which, disdained by the lamprey and freed from trout predation, is enjoying its finest hour in the Lakes.

The fresh-water fishes of North America are chronic victims of men's activity, and are subject also to climatic changes, as well as to damage to their environments through drought, flood, and other natural phenomena. Furthermore, they tend to be more primitive and vulnerable than their marine relatives; the lake sturgeon and the paddlefish, for example, grow very slowly, and are often exterminated before they can reach sexual maturity. Fresh-water habitats contain relatively few of the modern spiny-rayed fishes, a fact which supports the theory that fishes originated in fresh water and later invaded the sea.

In any case, man's alteration of the inland waters, through pollution, siltation, dredging, drainage, damming, irrigation, stream-straightening, and

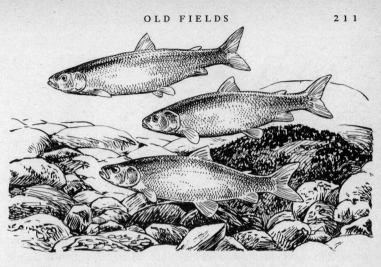

(*Top:*) DEEPWATER CHUB   (*Center:*) LONGJAW CHUB   (*Bottom:*) KIYI

These species, like the prairie chickens, differ only in minor characters

other practices, have been extremely harmful to our native species. It is only in the destruction of the Great Lakes fishes that he has not been the primary agent, an exception to the general rule which is qualified considerably by the existence of the Welland Ship Canal bypassing Niagara Falls. The lamprey almost certainly gained access to the inland seas by this unnatural route, so that, in the end, the responsibility for its ravages is ours.

The construction of the Welland Ship Canal, like the extensive irrigation and dam construction in the West and the widespread transplanting of game fish for public diversion, cannot be regretted simply because certain innocent fishes have been fatally injured. Members of the other vertebrate classes have also been necessary victims of man's progress across the continent. The entire range of the Las Vegas frog, for example, was entombed by the construction of that city. The bison and passenger pigeon hordes, had they survived the waste and greed of the commercial slaughters, would have had to give way in any case, in the present century, as obstacles to man's agricultural interests. Man, like the rat and the mosquito, can adapt himself to virtually all terrestrial climates, and less resourceful creatures have no choice but to make room for him during his stay on earth. He cannot be condemned for adjusting to his world as

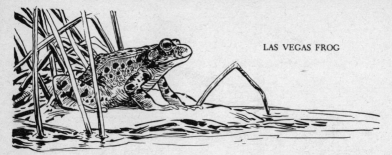

LAS VEGAS FROG

best he can, for all animals do that; he *can* be condemned for fouling his own nest, and he has been. In the words of the British ornithologist James Fisher, "Man is the filthiest animal that has ever trod the face of the earth. Man is ineradicably, utterly filthy. And every great nation in every part of the world has made a colossal mess as it has exploited its way through its own country."

Mr. Fisher made these irascible remarks at a panel discussion, *Pollution Control in Relation to Wildlife*, sponsored in 1956 by the National Audubon Society. He was speaking in reference to the menace to sea birds, ducks, and other creatures represented by the waste oil and sludge dumped off the coasts by ships at sea. Floating oil, killing thousands of wild birds every year, is a marine phase of the general problem of water pollution, which has changed the character and fauna of almost all the important streams and rivers in the United States.

At the turn of the century, in Chicago, there was opened a splendid "Sanitary Canal," designed to carry the industrial wastes and sewage of that city to the Des Plaines and Illinois Rivers. The lower Des Plaines and the upper Illinois almost immediately became

a vast open sewer with water grayish in color, offensive in odor, and containing in summer only septic organisms . . . characteristic of foul water. Sludge becoming 8 ft. or more deep collected along the bottom in slack waters and in late summer contained millions of tubificid worms. . . . Before the Sanitary Canal opened in 1900, the first green plants characteristic of clean water appeared in summer between 35 and 46 miles from Lake Michigan; in 1911 they were found only from 80 to 110 miles downstream, and optimum conditions for such plants were to be found 145 miles away; by 1918, this had receded about 25 miles farther. . . .

Unfortunately this is not atypical in America; in the upper Mississippi River, about 100 miles of flow is needed to allow the stream to recover from the sewage dumped into the river by Minneapolis and St. Paul, and for the first half of this distance, the river is grossly polluted.[2]

The Water Pollution Control Act of 1956, providing federal aid for communities willing to act on sewage and industrial pollution problems, is a belated and expensive remedy.

The senseless destruction of waters through the excessive construction of dams is another notable illustration of human progress gone awry. Dams may serve as emergency controls of flood, though the solution to flood lies farther upstream, and dams providing reservoirs and hydroelectric power are sometimes necessary. But too often expedience replaces responsibility in their purposes and location. Dams have been erected as monuments to political administrations, or out of gratitude to special interests, politically sophisticated, for which the inevitable alteration of the land above and/or below the dam site would afford an immediate gain. Others are sponsored by ambitious federal agencies, sometimes with total disregard for the recommendations of other arms of government. The Echo Park Dam, under the Bureau of Reclamation, which would have impounded the wild rivers of the Dinosaur National Monument on the Utah-Colorado border and demeaned great regions of scenic value, and the Bruces Eddy Dam of the Army Corps of Engineers, which would have submerged important tracts of Idaho elk range and other wilderness and sealed off the run of steelheads and Chinook salmon to their spawning grounds on the north fork of the Clearwater River, were two shortsighted projects blocked recently by the vigilance of conservationists, including a small, honorable band of senators and congressmen who took the trouble to ascertain the facts. These legislators might look carefully at the huge Central and Southern Florida Flood Control Project of the same agency, a thinly disguised development scheme affecting an area larger than Connecticut, New Jersey, and Delaware together. This latest assault on the Everglades, with the accompanying destruction of its flora and fauna, may cost the taxpayer an estimated $362,000,000, and will be of chief benefit to the few wealthy men who control almost all the land involved.

Again, dams and levees for the control of floods would be largely superfluous were the watersheds given proper attention. But many of the watersheds have been denuded; according to a Forest Service estimate made in 1931, the virgin forest in the United States, exclusive of Alaska, is one hundred million acres, or about one-eighth what it is thought

to have been before the white man came. The spring rains, unchecked
by forest roots, reach flood proportions as they accumulate downstream.
The Army Corps of Engineers spends millions every year to contain the
rampaging Mississippi; a fraction of this money applied toward land and
forest management north to the headwaters, including the elimination
of poor agricultural practices, would do much to alleviate not only the
disastrous inundations but the loss of those awesome amounts of topsoil
which pour away yearly in the form of sediment into the Gulf of Mexico.
One inch of topsoil requires from fifty to three hundred years to form, and
yet according to the Soil Conservation Service, established belatedly in
1935, the soil loss by erosion in the United States each year comes to
nearly five and a half billion tons, and the loss from farmlands alone
would fill a freight train which would circle the earth eighteen times. Anyone who has ever had to purchase topsoil from a contractor will appreciate
the value of such a cargo in billions of dollars; the effect on fish, animal,
and plant growth, which depends to a great extent on the mineral content
of this humble but intricate substance, is more difficult to define. We
might keep in mind, however, that rabbits frequenting regions of fertile
soil can weigh a third again as much as those on nearby impoverished
lands, and that trout attain their maximum size in waters which drain
the rich mineral land of fertile valleys.

Not satisfied with deforestation (as distinct from selective cutting and
reseeding), man furthers erosion by the drainage, usually for agricultural
ends, of marshes, potholes, ponds, and lakes. Millions of acres have been
drained in this country in the present century alone. The seasonal rains,
pouring away through dikes, ditches, and straightened streams instead of
collecting in natural basins to nourish the land through the long summers,
have compounded not only the flood problem but, succeeded by drought,
the scourge of erosion by wind as well. In terms of wildlife, the primary
victims of drainage have been fish, aquatic fur animals, and waterfowl: over
a third of all North American ducks once bred in the grassy sloughs and
potholes of the northern prairie states and the wheat provinces of Canada,
now ruthlessly bled away. "The constantly shrinking marsh area," one

BAND-TAILED PIGEON

conservationist concludes, "has crowded the remaining waterfowl population into smaller and smaller areas. This great concentration of birds on
the remaining water areas has had several harmful results: It has undoubtedly increased the toll taken by botulism; it has made it easier for hunters
to find and take the remaining birds; and worst of all, it has by the very
density of these concentrations led many to believe that no decrease of the
waterfowl population has occurred and that therefore no remedial measures are necessary." [3] Botulism, a mass poisoning of waterfowl brought
about by overcrowding and stagnation of shallow feeding grounds, is a
grim illustration of the lesson that ample habitat is a primary requisite of
wildlife abundance.

The decrease of the waterfowl population, which shrank rapidly after
the turn of the century, occasioned the last spectacular battle of the early
conservation movement, and split the conservationists themselves into two
camps. Unfortunately, the drainage of waterfowl breeding and wintering
areas was not recognized as the first cause of the decline—though drainage
of the Malheur refuge on the Oregon–California border occasioned the
celebrated Malheur Fight, waged from 1920 to 1934—and enormous quantities of money and emotion were expended on determining the bag limit
and other restrictive legislation which, like flood control by dam and
levee, was never a solution but a palliative. The struggle to enforce and
reinforce conservation legislation was severely handicapped, not only by
public apathy and political expedience but by ignorance and division
among the crusaders themselves.

The bag-limit fight, as it was known, commenced about seven years
after the Weeks-McLean Act of 1913, which awarded control of migratory
birds to the federal government. In 1916 a convention was ratified between
the United States and Britain, awarding the Canadian government similar

control, and establishing full protection for the swans, cranes, and the band-tailed pigeon, a species then in serious straits, as well as for all shore birds but the snipe, woodcock, the greater and lesser yellowlegs, and the blackbellied and golden plovers. (Among the shore birds, only the snipe and woodcock are still considered game birds.) Two years later the Federal Migratory Bird Treaty Act entrusted the Biological Survey with the execution of its provisions, which included the permanent prohibition of spring shooting as well as a prescribed limit of twenty-five ducks and eight geese per hunter per day over the course of the long state hunting seasons.

These limits were certainly too high, and by 1920 eleven states had been forced to reduce them below the allowed federal maximum. The states in which the birds were concentrated made no attempt to do this, much to the disgust of the terrible-tempered Dr. Hornaday, whose views on the rascality of his fellow man have been intimated earlier. In 1922 a "public shooting grounds bill" sponsored by Dr. Nelson of the Biological Survey and Ray P. Holland of the American Game Protective Association further incensed Dr. Hornaday; it provided for the purchase, with federal hunting-license fees, of waterfowl refuges upon which certain areas would be set aside for public hunting.

The concept of federal hunting licenses and federally maintained shooting preserves for what Hornaday was pleased to call "the Armies of Destruction" was to this aging warrior anathema. "Dr. Hornaday," as he himself recounted, "launched an intensive campaign to arouse all American sportsmen to the decrease and progressive extinction of game, and the necessity to make at once 'large reductions in bag limits and open seasons,' everywhere in the United States where no reductions had been made." [4] He also assaulted the sponsors of the shooting-grounds bill, averring that the Survey was interested chiefly in controlling the license monies and consolidating federal power, and that the American Game Protective Association was a nefarious front for "the manufacturers of guns, gunpowder, and loaded cartridges." He was supported most notably, though not without trepidation, by his own Permanent Wildlife Fund, *Outdoor Life* magazine, a newly created sportsmen's group called the Izaak Walton League, naturalist Edward Howe Forbush, Aldo Leopold of the Forest Service, and a scattering of legislators, including a young representative from New York named Fiorello H. La Guardia. The ensuing struggle wore on until 1929, during which time his opposition was led variously by Dr. Nelson, *Field and Stream*, the Camp-Fire Club, the Boone and Crockett

Club, and, rather surprisingly, the National Association of Audubon Societies. It was Dr. Nelson's contention that duck food was scarce on the wintering grounds, and that any increase in duck numbers would bring about mass starvation among them; the positions of the other groups were even more debatable, but the general feeling seemed to be that the number of birds taken was an ethical concern of the sportsmen or even, perhaps, of the states, and was on no account to be regulated by the government beyond the setting of the maximum figure. This, at least, was the view set forth by Charles Sheldon in the Audubon "Bulletin No. 6" dealing with the subject; Sheldon was also a power in the Boone and Crockett Club and a staunch admirer of the Biological Survey, which was later to name for him an antelope reservation in Nevada, and his opinion was evidently more popular among the sportsmen's conservation groups than was that of the ascetic Dr. Hornaday. Since Hornaday treated malingerers on his own side as intemperately as he did the opposition, one wonders that he kept the support he had.

As a matter of fact, the Izaak Walton League went over to the enemy, as had the Camp-Fire Club before it. Nevertheless, the shooting-grounds bill was defeated, and Dr. Hornaday had the eventual satisfaction, which he hastened to express, of witnessing a simultaneous attempt on the part of the Survey, the Audubon Societies, and the Izaak Walton League to claim credit for the reduced bag limit and other provisions he himself had advocated. Hornaday's recommended limit of fifteen ducks and four geese per hunter per day, adopted at last in 1930, has since been reduced to four and two, respectively; his revised open season, cut from fourteen to eight weeks, has remained more or less effective.

Despite his ingenuous attitude toward the predators, which he called "vermin" to the end, Dr. Hornaday's contribution to the fight for American wildlife was considerable, no less so for being carefully documented by himself. He decried the self-crippling disputes among conservation groups, federal, state, and private, including those skirmishes to which he himself had lent such flavor. Even today these organizations, insisting peevishly on their own prerogatives and accomplishments, occasionally do damage to the common cause. The divisions are not always petty, of course: the science of conservation is still young, and the differences of opinion are usually honest, and if these differences are at times emotional, one must remember that the conservation cause, so stark and final are the consequences of its failure, is a very emotional one indeed.

It would be pleasant to record that the efforts of Dr. Hornaday, his cohorts, and his converts, initiated a golden age for waterfowl and other wildlife, but such was not the case. The cumulative deterioration of the land and waters, slowed but by no means halted by federal legislation, became visible across the length and breadth of the continent; in the early thirties, the plight of American waterfowl, at least, became darker than at any time before or since.

The emergency of the Depression, commencing in 1929, absorbed the proposed appropriations of waterfowl refuge funds authorized by the Migratory Bird Conservation Act of that same year, a circumstance made still more serious by the subsequent drought which crept across the West. Drainage had already leached away much of the water resources of the Great Plains grain belt. Farther west, the short-grass plains, a land of low rainfall already severely damaged by overgrazing, were senselessly plowed under for the further production of wheat, a commodity which now plagues our economy in the form of huge annual surplus; the Soil Bank Act, which in 1958 authorized subsidies to farmers who would permit their land to revert to the natural state, is the ironic consequence of irresponsible production for quick profit.

The short-grass sod, laid bare, was no match for the wind of the dry years. "With the turf gone and the cycle of moisture past its peak, with the winds maintaining their normal behavior, the country literally started to blow out of the ground." The huge dust storms of lost soil which, in 1933, darkened the skies of a continent, from the Rocky Mountains to New York and Washington, left in their wake the mighty man-made desert called the Dust Bowl, and, because man is ever slow to learn his lesson, pain and poverty in a great area of the nation was exacted all over again by the cycle of drought which recurred in recent years. "Unless the dust is seen as a symptom and a symbol instead of a direct problem in itself, the misery which it has caused is of no avail. It is precisely the clever, efficient, and speedy solving of immediate problems, without regard to their general setting, which has brought us where we are." [5] The same, of course, could be said in reference to flood, which is erosion's other face. And wherever man suffers by unleashing upon himself the cumulative great forces of natural destruction, the wildlife falls inevitable victim.

Man, the land, and wildlife, in the dark days of the dust storms, profited much by the timely appearance on the scene of Franklin Roosevelt. Though not a crusader for conservation of the stature of his cousin, he was

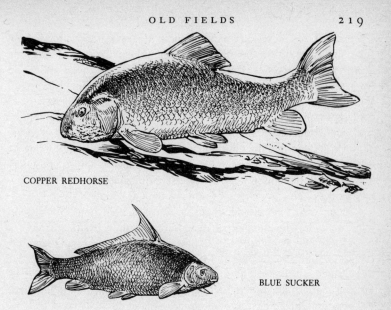

COPPER REDHORSE

BLUE SUCKER

exposed to information unavailable to the latter, and well understood the role of renewable resources in the dangerous future already taking shape. "Conservation," he was to say, just prior to his death, "is a basis for permanent peace." Roosevelt saw conservation in terms of the nation's economy and welfare, but the effects on wildlife of his anti-depression measures were nonetheless considerable. The Tennessee Valley Authority, a mighty experiment dedicated to the restoration and economic exploitation of the impoverished Tennessee River watershed, its forests, soil, water, and wildlife, was an early example of resource management and the "multiple use" concept, whereby conservation is practiced not according to dogmatic rules but according to the mutual, balanced interests of the local community and of the land. The TVA experiment, amended to include more recent data, has since been repeated on the Columbia, Colorado, and Missouri rivers. At the same time, Roosevelt's Civilian Conservation Corps and Works Progress Administration put to work a great body of unemployed in the construction of windbreaks on the plains and other measures, including reclamation work on many farmed-out and otherwise submarginal lands which were later to become part of the growing wildlife refuge system.

In 1934 Roosevelt set up a national committee on waterfowl restoration, two members of which were Aldo Leopold and Jay N. "Ding" Darling, the great political cartoonist. Darling's special interest was conservation, and his caricatures of lone waterfowl seeking places to light amid forests of bristling guns are memorable and biting. It was Darling who persuaded his large public that measures on behalf of waterfowl would help combat the fierce effects of drought as well, and who gained control of the Oregon land which permitted the reflooding of the Malheur Refuge. His influence was such that he was appointed Chief of the Biological Survey, and under his administration the waterfowl restoration program was neatly coordinated with emergency relief programs. In the CCC and WPA, the necessary labor was provided, and large sums were allotted from drought and relief funds for the purchase of ruined areas in drought-stricken regions. But the money to improve these lands, by halting erosion and restoring the water table, was lacking, and the Migratory Bird Hunting Stamp Act was enacted as a solution. The stamp is, in effect, a federal hunting license. Darling himself designed the first stamp, and an eminent wildlife artist has been conscripted for this purpose each year since.

Another step forward in 1934 was the so-called Coordination Act, by which lands and waters under the administration of other government agencies—the Forest Service, the Bureau of Reclamation, and so forth— might be developed as refuges, provided such a program did not interfere with the primary purpose of the area. Although the refuge system was considerably augmented before 1940 by direct purchase, its subsequent expansion has been accomplished almost entirely in the form of easement on other federal holdings. The economy in this arrangement outweighs the disadvantages, which might be likened to those created in any household sheltering two earnest housekeepers. The Fish and Wildlife Service, born of the Biological Survey and the Bureau of Fisheries in 1940, is apt to come off badly in any major dispute, not only because it is ordinarily the guest agency but because its needs are too often dismissed as inconsequential by comparison with those of more newsworthy agencies. Within the Department of the Interior, it differs at times with the Bureau of Land Management, with which it shares authority over the large game ranges in the West; also, the practices of the Bureau of Reclamation in regard to irrigation and damming, road-making and drainage, are at times injurious to the native animals. The Fish and Wildlife Service has difficulties with some of the other agencies with which it shares administration of public

The Happy Farmer and His Sportsman Friends
by Jay N. Darling ("Ding")

land, but these are minor by comparison with the threats to its refuges posed by the armed services.

The armed services, operating under cover of that shining panoply called national defense, have become the rich, arrogant landlords of vast areas of the United States, their legitimate and necessary use of which is chronically accompanied by wasteful and destructive abuses. The equivalent of a strip of land thirteen miles across and extending from coast to coast is now under their control, and present requests for further withdrawals from public territories would, if granted, widen this hypothetical domain by four more miles. In addition to the conservation agencies, lumbermen, cattle ranchers, miners, and other interests, a growing American public with huge recreational requirements has been entirely excluded from the petty kingdoms of the Defense Department, even in cases where multiple and simultaneous use was proven possible. In regard to wildlife, the attitude of the services is perhaps best demonstrated by the recent removal of deer from Fort Bragg, North Carolina, to Fort Benning, Georgia, for the diversion of Army nimrods, in direct contravention of the laws of both states. Especially in the West, the military reservations abut commonly on game ranges and federal wildlife refuges, which are often considered fair targets for artillery practice. The Army, which in its sheer bulk is undoubtedly the most insatiable of the services, recently attempted to gain control of over ten thousand acres of the Wichita Mountains National Wildlife Refuge, in Oklahoma, which unluckily adjoins the missile ranges of Fort Sill, and the Air Force, which has already swallowed up large sections of Nevada's Desert Game Range, now claims to require more for gunnery practice. Whatever the merits of such claims, it has been the finding of the House Committee on Interior and Insular Affairs that the armed services make small attempt to coordinate their activities in order to make best use of their already enormous holdings; in addition, the Committee's chairman has spoken sharply of "the military's disregard, even contempt, of the laws relating to the management and conservation of fish and wildlife." [6]

Serious as the encroachments by the military have become, they are only one factor in the over-all political problems confronting the Fish and Wildlife Service and other agencies administering public lands. These lands, supported by and for the taxpayers, are preyed upon incessantly by political and private interests, all of which support lobbies in the Capitol dedicated to the acquisition, by inexpensive lease, of commercial rights to

What a Few More Seasons Will Do to the Ducks
by Jay N. Darling ("Ding")

territory rightfully belonging to all Americans. Indeed, the fees paid by cattle, timber, oil, and mining companies, among others, are ordinarily nominal, so that the letter rather than the spirit of the applicable laws is in effect. Such leases are granted for the most part on the extensive national forests, but the game ranges and wildlife refuges are also invaded frequently, and the Fish and Wildlife Service, politically impotent, is often powerless to defend its own and the public interest. As an arm of the civil service, dependent on Congressional appropriations, it can enter the political arena only obliquely, and its recommendations must usually be carried to the public not by its own publicity department but by such private "watchdog" organizations as the Wildlife Management Institute and the National Wildlife Federation, which serve as informal lobbies for the protection of natural resources against the excesses of political patrimony, self-interest, and stupidity.

The taint of politics in conservation is not peculiar to the federal agencies. In many of the states the conservation, fish, and game commissions are shot through with the rot of the spoils system, and their personnel, because it is transitory, is of very uneven quality. The wildlife posts are favorite objects of party patronage, and loyal party workers, however ignorant of the basic information required for their work, are paid well to spend as spectacularly as possible the income derived from state hunting and fishing licenses. A favorite method, as has been indicated, is the well-publicized promotion of game farms and fish hatcheries.

Special privilege is another consequence of politics in conservation. In Kansas not long ago, two exclusive hunting clubs, owned and operated by wealthy Kansans and completely equipped with heated hunting blinds, were established in the very heart of a new state waterfowl refuge. The Kansas Forestry, Fish, and Game Commission brought condemnation proceedings against this singular arrangement, but its authority to condemn was contested by one of the clubs, and had finally to be validated by the United States Supreme Court. At this point, having won its case, the Commission was somehow made to see the error of its ways, and dropped condemnation proceedings with the sheepish assertion that the hundreds of acres comprising club properties were not necessary to the refuge after all.

For the wildlife of the nation at large, however, the infiltrations of politics have been most destructive in regard to the Fish and Wildlife Service. It must be remembered that the Service not only is responsible for the welfare of migratory fish, birds, and animals, but operates, in addition,

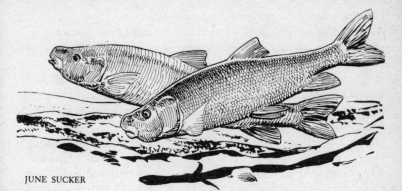

JUNE SUCKER

CUI-UI

COLORADO SQUAWFISH

a complex system of wildlife refuges and game ranges throughout the states and territories. It also administers research stations, including the Wildlife Research Refuge at Patuxent, Maryland, and subsidizes extensive programs of state and university studies and resource management, the latter supported with funds obtained through an excise tax on sporting arms, ammunition, and fishing tackle, under the Pittman-Robertson Federal Aid in Wildlife Restoration Act of 1937, and the Dingell-Johnson Fish Restoration Act of 1950. The Fish and Wildlife Service without question is the nerve center of the growing American conservation body.

Unhappily, the significance of the Service is still largely unrecognized, if Congressional appropriations can be taken as evidence. This remains true even though political recognition of the public's recreational and aesthetic needs contributed to a recent reorganization, rendering distinct a Bureau of Sport Fisheries and Wildlife from a Bureau of Commercial Fisheries and elevating the head of the former to the position of Assistant Secretary of the Interior. There seems every reason to expect, however, that the Fish and Wildlife Service, as the organization is still generally known, will remain a political starveling, and that much critical work will go unaccomplished for want of funds.

Congress has ever been niggardly when little or no evidence of electoral sentiment is presented to justify more generous appropriations. But the sentiment, as has been shown repeatedly when conservation groups have got the facts of a dispute before the public tribunal, is there. What is more, it is overwhelmingly in favor of any measure tending to preserve the natural heritage of the nation, wildlife included. That the Service does not always profit by this sentiment is due largely to the fact that its spokesmen in the Department of the Interior, in many cases political appointees, are too prone to place the policy of the incumbent administration above the recommendations of the trained personnel beneath them. The Eisenhower administration, in the Washington parlance, has been "cold" to conservation. "In a year and a half," Bernard De Voto concluded, in 1954, "the businessmen in office have reversed the conservation policy by which the United States has been working for more than seventy years to substitute wise use of natural resources in place of reckless destruction for the profit of special corporate interests." [7]

This point cannot be stressed too heavily. The federal civil service, like the state political machine, is subject to political patronage, and when this malodorous system is permitted to run riot in an intricate organization of dedicated specialists, the effects on efficiency and morale are ruinous. The Fish and Wildlife Service until recent years was relatively immune to the spoils system, since it is patently nonpolitical in character, and since its essential personnel was composed of experts not readily replaceable.

With the appearance on the scene of Secretary of the Interior Douglas McKay, however, the situation changed. A political vendetta of the most vicious sort was instituted, and the morale of the Service—and presumably of the other bureaus in the Department—suffered damage which, according to one private conservation official in Washington, it will take at least ten years to repair.

McKay's sole recommendation for his new job was his fortuitous support of President Eisenhower. Though innocent of experience, he brought to his task a lack of humility which proved disastrous, and it is his inglorious achievement that, prior to his expedient retirement, he found reason to lease away more public land than any Secretary of the Interior in the history of his country. In fact, the two hundred and seventy-four leases granted on refuge land between August 1953 and December 1955 alone very nearly equaled the total number of leases in the previous history of the refuge system. "There is a cynicism in the Interior," De Voto remarked, "which reminds observers of the aromatic days of the General Land Office. Yet some things that look like cynicism may be mere ineptness. Thus Secretary McKay at a moment when all the conservation organizations in the country—national, nonpartisan, and representing hundreds of thousands of votes—were denouncing his recommendation of Echo Park Dam. Seeking for *le mot juste* to characterize conservationists, he came up with 'punks.'" [8]

Meanwhile, the men beneath McKay were paying the penalty for political inexperience. Alfred M. Day, the Director of the Fish and Wildlife Service for seven years, was made assistant to his successor, who was, in turn, and through no fault of his own, the first political appointee ever to head the Service. Day, with Clarence Cottam, Durward Allen, and a number of other key men whom the Service could ill afford to lose, found compromise with the new regime impossible. As the *Washington Post and Times-Herald* wrote of Day's retirement in 1955, "His experience was an object lesson for young men who are considering a career in government. They should know what they're getting into. Political expediency, political vengeance still rule the roost, not only in waterfowl jobs but throughout the establishment. Day was no politician. In his time he'd worked for both parties, but most of all he'd worked for the birds. . . ."

McKay's successor and the present incumbent, Fred A. Seaton, is also a political appointee, but, unlike his predecessor, he values the presence and opinions of men better informed in his new field than himself. Among the factors which have restored the faith of conservationists in the Department of Interior have been Mr. Seaton's support of new restrictions on the leasing of public lands and his fine record in the face of political pressures.

There is no place in an effective civil service for politicians who carry into it their petty party practices. The all too frequent characteristics of the political appointee—ignorance, inexperience, and inability to listen to subordinates—are already damaging enough, and a time must come when these crucial positions in federal government, increasingly important as populations rise, resources decline, and the nation strains its uneasy economy, are given to informed and principled professionals in the service, not of the party in power, but of the people.

"The worst enemies of wildlife," as "Ding" Darling once remarked, "are the Republicans and Democrats." [9]

The interest in wildlife abroad in the land is evidenced by the growing number and membership of conservation groups, bird clubs, and related organizations, as well as by the increased influence these groups now bring to bear on legislation affecting natural resources. The older groups referred to in this text are almost all still active, and the newer groups, of local, state, or national significance, are numerous. Many organizations are more or less specialized in their interests: Ducks Unlimited, for example, is concerned almost entirely with restoring water to Canadian breeding grounds damaged by drainage. The Welder Wildlife Foundation is dedicated to the maintenance and study of a natural tract of Texas plains and river woodland north of Corpus Christi, in order to determine the effects of overgrazing as well as the degree of grazing best suited to the mutual interests of the land, livestock, and wildlife. The American Museum of Natural History, in New York, is a seat of biological field research whose contributions to conservation knowledge, if indirect, are still important; the Museum staff, which has always included naturalists of the highest caliber, has been active in this field for many years, as have the personnel of the National Museum in Washington and other vital institutions throughout the country, including the numerous and well-equipped biology, zoology, and conservation departments in American universities. Among other projects, the Wildlife Management Institute sponsors the North American Wildlife Conference, the annual transactions of which, since 1936, have become standard reference material. With the National Wildlife Federation, which coordinates the policies of local conservation groups all over the country, it also serves as an unofficial influence on federal legislation affecting the national resources. The Conservation Foundation, allied to the New York Zoological Society, approaches its subject from an international viewpoint, and sponsors research studies of foreign as well as domestic problems. The Wilderness Society promotes the concepts of Aldo Leopold, Robert Marshall, and others who, after 1920, advocated the sequestration of inviolate primeval wilderness for posterity; it is presently sponsoring the crucial Wilderness Bill, which would establish on the public lands a wilderness preservation system invulnerable to special interests or political expedience. The National Parks Association is an articulate defender of the institution which gives it its name, and lends its voice as well to other conservation programs. These groups are important, but they are only a few of the many like them in a nation maturing to its responsibilities toward future generations.

The task of the conservation groups is endless, and the sum of their efforts has unquestionably spared, and continues to protect, wild creatures of this continent which would otherwise have long ago disappeared. The basic principles of conservation are now quite clearly understood, and it is only the details of their application which, here and there, are still disputed. Many of these disputes are purely academic, since funds are wanting in almost every area of applied conservation practice; the movement remains needy, and, as a result, a great deal of its effort must be confined to the protection of past gains. The major concern of conservationists at present is the massive dissemination of pesticides across the land, which one zoologist has called "the greatest threat North American wildlife has ever faced, perhaps greater than all the rest put together." [10]

The broadcasting by airplane of chlorinated hydrocarbons, a family of chemicals related to the terrible nerve gases developed in World War II, has achieved dangerous proportions since 1945, when the relatively innocuous DDT came into general use. Since that time the use of more and more potent pesticides has expanded wildly, and in 1957 alone, sixty-five thousand tons of dieldrin, heptachlor, and other chemical poisons were strewn across the fields and forests of the nation.

The chief agent of pesticide distribution is the United States Department of Agriculture, which has been granted large sums by Congress for the control of injurious insects, and which to date has supported the claims of the prospering pesticide manufacturers that the effects of their products upon creatures other than the "target" animal are of small consequence. The Fish and Wildlife Service, the National Audubon Society, the Izaak Walton League, and other groups in a better position to judge the question fairly disagree. Investigations by the Service, hampered seriously for want of Congressional appropriations, have nonetheless indicated startling wildlife mortalities in sprayed areas: the thirteen quail coveys known to exist on one tract studied were wiped out entirely, with a serious loss of all other vertebrate animals. The poisons may remain in the soil or water for years, so that their effects are cumulative; they have also been shown to affect fertility in creatures exposed to less than lethal doses, and may seriously upset the balance of nature by killing harmless insects and other food animals crucial in the chain of life.

In 1954, in a park area in Michigan, 185 pairs of robins were known to nest. In 1957, after several applications of pesticide toward control of the Dutch elm blight, the area supported but six nests, at least five of which produced no young. The earthworms on which the robins fed had absorbed the poison residues in the leaf litter; crayfish fed experimentally on earthworms from this area perished instantly.

The salmons of certain New Brunswick rivers and the trouts of Yellowstone Park have been seriously reduced by the presence in their waters of pesticides used in the control of the spruce budworm. A veterinarian in Climax, Georgia, reported that massive spraying in the region toward control of the imported fire ant took the lives of one hundred cattle, and that an equivalent number of brood sows suffered total reproductive failure; in Texas, four bulls and eleven calves were killed on a treated area. The Montgomery *Alabama Journal* interviewed thirty-six families in the village of Monroeville in October 1958: their losses as a result of fire-ant control included "697 dead chickens, 10 roosters, 20 turkeys, 11 cats, 7 puppies, and 2 ducks." The destruction of wildlife and domestic animals brought about by pesticides in Alabama has led its Department of Conservation to demand that spraying be stopped "until methods can be devised to safeguard wildlife, song birds, fish and human populations."

At a meeting on November 10, 1958, sponsored by the National Audubon Society, a zoologist, Dr. George Wallace, predicted that, should the immediate ambitions of the Department of Agriculture and the pesticide manufacturers be realized, "we shall have been witnesses, within a single decade, to a greater extermination of animal life than in all the previous years of man's history on earth." When one considers that, according to the Fish and Wildlife Service, a pound of poison per acre may suffice to eliminate a quail covey, and that the Department of Agriculture has considered the use of twenty pounds per acre for effective insect control, Dr. Wallace's dark view seems very reasonable.

The Department of Agriculture is apparently unconcerned about the growing apprehension. It is its ambition to "eradicate" the imported fire ant from the twenty-seven million acres of the South which it now infests, even though no insect, imported or indigenous, has ever been entirely exterminated in the United States. "Experience to date," the Department avers blandly, "indicates that a successful program can be carried out without serious consequences to wildlife resources." [11]

But it now seems clear that research into every aspect of the fire-ant problem has been totally inadequate; in the opinion of many authorities, in fact, no problem exists at all. The sting of the fire ant has been grossly exaggerated, as has the damage it has done to crops; the fire ant is essentially a feeder on other insects and their larvae, and is considered a beneficial creature in its native South America. In any case, an irresponsible control program has been set in motion without sufficient information as to its future effects. Congress, goaded into action by public outcry, has recently called for an investigation of the use of pesticides, but serious damage may have been done to the wildlife, livestock, and even the human beings of the nation before this frantic broadcasting of poison into our environment can be brought under control.

The success of any conservation measure is directly dependent on the degree of public opinion mustered to its support. A fair presentation of questions affecting the national resources will invariably evoke a constructive public response; setbacks of recent years, such as the flood of commercial leases on the wildlife refuges and other lands, have transpired largely behind the scenes in federal or state government, without benefit of open hearing. One reason for the general enlightenment has been the spread of conservation education; the knowledge gained by the professionals in the field is reaching a wide audience through films, newspapers, magazines, and other outlets, in a capsule form no less salutary for being lightly sugared.

In addition, a healthy minority of Americans has proved itself willing to purchase books on one phase or another of the world of nature. Many of these books are purely decorative, but others—the excellent field guides by Roger Tory Peterson, Richard H. Pough, and others are good examples—implement a growing trend toward animal study by amateurs, of which the best-known manifestation is bird watching. The diagrammatic illustrations in such books permit that accurate identification in the field which formerly was impossible without a shotgun, and wildlife art of a high caliber may be found in any number of volumes for use in the amateur's library. Artists such as Louis Agassiz Fuertes and the Canadian Major Allan Brooks, who stood virtually alone in their abilities a few decades past, have been succeeded by a phalanx of expert illustrators, among whom Roger Peterson, Francis Lee Jaques, Bob Hines, and T. M. Shortt are only a very few. That there are so many able and successful people in this field can indicate only the growing demand for their talents.

Among the writers, such adept interpreters of nature as Edwin Way Teale and Loren Eiseley, Sally Carrighar and Joseph Wood Krutch, continue to satisfy the tastes of people whose parents liked William Beebe and Aldo Leopold, and whose grandparents were partial to John Burroughs and John Muir. A most meaningful omen is the success of general treatises like Rachel Carson's *The Sea Around Us*; that Miss Carson has reached so many minds is evidence not only of her unusual lyric gift but of the human need in these headlong days to understand and identify with the continuity of earth and time.

The wildlife of America, pinned in or chivied out of its last redoubts by the convulsions of blind progress, is finding its most potent defenders among individuals, or rather in those groups of individuals banded together in defense of the natural environment—wild flowers and trees, wild shorelines, swamps, savannas, deserts, wild rivers, mountains, forests—as a nonmaterial need. That the need seems to be felt so commonly is only partly the achievement of those who, ever since the first warnings of Alexander Wilson, have worked painfully toward the illumination of their countrymen. It is also the reaction of a people entrapped by the apparatus of its own progress, and seeking a passage back to more permanent values, to the clean light of open air. The wild creatures of the open spaces, of clear water and green northern wilds, of gold prairie and huge sky, embody a human longing no less civilized for being primitive, no less real for being felt rather than thought.

At the same time that we are earnest to explore and learn all things, we require that all things be mysterious and unexplorable, that land and sea be infinitely wild, unsurveyed and unfathomed by us because unfathomable. . . . We must be refreshed by the sight of inexhaustible vigor, vast and titanic features, the sea-coast with its wrecks, the wilderness with its living and its decaying trees, the thunder-cloud, and the rain which lasts three weeks and produces freshets. We need to witness our own limits transgressed, and some life pasturing freely where we never wander.

—HENRY DAVID THOREAU (1854)

Wild Alaskan peaks, deep under snow and glacial ice, slid beneath our big airliner. . . . Except for parts of Arctic Canada, Alaska is certainly the wildest remaining part of wild North America.

—ROGER TORY PETERSON (1955)

11 : Land of the North Wind

IN THE NEW STATE of Alaska, America has a splendid chance to demonstrate that the hard lessons of conservation have been learned, for the great part of it is still under federal jurisdiction and, protected from the excesses of private exploitation, remains unspoiled. The effects of statehood on this unique wilderness should not be the responsibility of its inhabitants alone, for the future of Alaska is crucial to the nation.

The "Great Land," as the Russians called it, is truly monumental. Transposed onto a map of the United States, its rude expanses would extend east and west from Georgia to California, north and south from Canada to Mexico. One-fifth the total area of the first forty-eight states, it encompasses an astonishing range of climate and terrain, from the evergreen coasts of Southeast Alaska to the brown barren of the Arctic Slope; the valleys, tablelands, and alpine tundra of the Interior, walled by the Brooks Range to the north and the Alaska Range to the south, roughly separate these regions, and it is characteristic of Alaska's unruly nature that temperatures on the Yukon have ranged from seventy degrees Fahrenheit below zero to one hundred degrees above.

For the most part, with exceptions to be noted, the wildlife of Alaska represents northern populations of species found also in Canada and the United States. As such, its creatures are hardy and adaptable; a number of mammals, including the wolf, wolverine, and grizzly, hunt simultaneously in such separate environments as forest and barren tundra. Travelers acquainted with the fauna of the United States will find few species new to them; on the other hand, they will find many which are elsewhere rare or seldom seen, including large numbers of breeding sea birds such as jaegers and phalaropes.

To all but a few amphibians and reptiles the Alaskan climate is hostile, and only one species is peculiar to it: the Alaska worm salamander, of the southeast coastal strip, is known from a single specimen collected in 1889 near Hassler Harbor. There are no snakes at all.

Alaskan fishes, on the other hand, are plentiful, and most of the state's species abound in the waters of more southerly latitudes as well. Exceptions include endemic forms of the Arctic char and the Dolly Varden trout in the streams of the northwestern tundra, and the great white shee-fish, or inconnu, an anadromous salmon-like giant which wandered eastward long ago from the rivers of Siberia. The shee-fish has established itself quite commonly in deltas and rivers emptying into the Arctic Ocean and the Bering Sea, but remains the least known of all North American game fishes.

Eurasian birds stray also to Alaska. The rare, rose-tinted Ross's gull, a native of the Asian steppes, occurs periodically at Point Barrow, often in numbers, in the course of a mysterious annual journey eastward along the Arctic ice pack, but there are no breeding records for North America. On the other hand, the very scarce Aleutian tern (unknown in the Aleutians) is among several species simultaneously resident on the Siberian and

ALASKA WORM SALAMANDER

Alaskan coasts, and a number of Asian birds, including songbirds, cross the Bering Sea annually in small numbers to breed on the Alaskan mainland. These include the wheatear, a Eurasian thrush which also comes yearly from the opposite direction to breed in Labrador, arriving by way of Greenland and returning across the Atlantic to winter in Spain and Africa. Such birds are listed among North American species, "rare" only in the technical sense that few trouble to make the trip.

The northern marine mammals are common to both Asia and North America, but on the latter continent the Pacific walrus and the rare ribbon seal are peculiar to Alaska. Among land animals, only a few shrews and small rodents are confined to Alaska, the rest occurring also in Canada and in many cases in the United States as well. It is the sheer numbers of the larger forms—the furbearers, great carnivores, hoofed animals, seals, walruses, and whales—that distinguish the Alaskan fauna, representing as they do one of the mightiest congregations of wild beasts to be found anywhere on earth. This is true despite the fact that their exploitation dates from the eighteenth century, shortly after Bering's expedition of 1741 had rediscovered North America from the west.

As indicated in Chapter 5, the first Alaskan animal exploited by the white man was the sea otter, skins of which were brought back to Kamchatka by the survivors of the Bering Expedition. The sea otters on the Siberian coasts were already in decline, and the local fur traders, brutal, ignorant men called *promishleniks*, set off immediately in their rude craft for the new hunting grounds. They first attacked the populations of otters at Bering Island and the Commander Islands, then struck eastward across the Bering Sea to North America. Attu, in the Aleutian Islands, was discovered in 1745, and in 1761 a trader named Pushkareff and his men became the first whites to winter on the Alaska mainland. Pushkareff enslaved some twenty-odd aborigines, a number of whom soon jumped into the sea to escape his cruelty and the rest of whom, with two exceptions, he threw after the first in irritation. The atrocities perpetrated by the *promishleniks*

ALEUTIAN TERN

were usually at the expense of the gentle Aleut peoples, conscripted in numbers to hunt down the otters in their kayaks; the mainland Indians, less resigned to their fate, killed *promishleniks* at every opportunity, and the century of Russian occupation of Alaska was notable for its bloodshed. In 1862 the imperial charter of the Russian American Fur Company, a trading concern which represented the *de facto* government of Alaska, was refused renewal in direct consequence of the company's stubborn history of abuses.

The Russian American Company had succeeded to the power of the original Shelikoff Trading Company which after 1790, under Alexander Baranoff, had established trading posts up and down the Alaska coast, and in 1812 had purchased land from local Indians at Bodega Bay, north of San Francisco. The "Ross," or Russian, Settlement there was established as an agricultural community, the chief purpose of which was to grow grain and other foods for the Alaska posts and trading ships. Its presence in California was resented, by the Spanish at first and afterward by the Americans, who, with the British and even the French, had attempted for a number of years to insinuate themselves into the rich Alaska fur trade. The Convention of 1824 establishing the 50° 40′ boundary as the southern limit of Russian influence also revoked a Russian ban against the presence of ships of other nations in its Alaskan waters; the position of the Ross Settlement became uncomfortable in 1834 when Russia, outraged that certain American traders had sold liquor and firearms to the restless natives, temporarily renewed the maritime restrictions against American ships. In 1841 the Ross Settlement was abandoned.

Meanwhile, the American whalemen had invaded the North Pacific. In

1848 a Captain Royce, of the ship *Superior* out of Sag Harbor, Long Island, ventured through the Bering Straits into the Arctic Sea. The baleen whales were plentiful along the ice floes, and the following year the *Superior* was joined by no less than one hundred and fifty-four American ships, which turned home, it is said, with an average cargo of twelve hundred barrels of oil and ten tons of baleen.

The sea otter was now shy and scarce and the fur seals had been markedly diminished, while farther south the elephant seals and Guadalupe fur seals were disappearing all along the temperate coasts. These factors, in combination with the administrative problems of the remote settlements, persuaded the Russians to accept the idea of selling their claims in North America. In March 1867, after relatively brief negotiations, Secretary of State Seward received the following communication from the Russian diplomat Edouard de Stoeckl:

> Mr. Secretary of State:— I have the honor to inform you that by a telegram dated 16–28 of this month from St. Petersburg, Prince Gortchakoff informs me that his Majesty the Emperor of all the Russias gives his consent to the cession of the Russian possessions in the American continent to the United States for the stipulated sum of seven million two hundred thousand dollars in gold, and that his Majesty the Emperor invests me with full powers to negotiate and sign the treaty.
>
> Please accept, Mr. Secretary of State, the assurance of my very high consideration.   STOECKL

One wonders still why Russia relinquished so readily a land which had already produced for her in furs alone many times the amount received

WHISKERED AUKLET

NORTHERN RIGHT WHALE

in payment. "The fur trade of Alaska," as William Dall was to point out three years later, "has been widely known for a century. Its history is almost a history of the country. The furs were the principal, if not the only objects which led to its exploration and settlement." In the splendid days in which Dall wrote, wolf, muskrat, and ermine skins had "a certain value, though hardly to be classed as furs." [1]

Dall was a member of a surveying expedition inspecting possibilities for telegraph routes to Alaska, and he wrote upon his return an exhaustive account of the new territory's resources, its past history, the nature and customs of its Indians and Eskimos, and its prospects for the future. At this time there were fewer than five hundred Americans in Alaska, not counting a detachment of Army troops, and, despite the extensive fur trapping and gold mining which had already been conducted by the Russians, the extent of Alaska and its resources must still have seemed unlimited. In addition to the fur and whaling trades, Dall saw great potential in the cod, herring, and salmon fisheries—at least two million salmon, and probably twice that number, he said, were taken annually by the natives at the mouth of the Yukon alone. He also spoke warmly of a time "when eggs, salted birds, eider and swan's down, may occupy some space in the commerce of Alaska. . . . Milliners may obtain thousands of wings and breasts of the most delicate colors and rarest beauty, from the northern marshes. . . ." Elsewhere he notes that "The quantity of walrus-tusks annually obtained will average one hundred thousand pounds." [2]

Charles M. Scammon, who was captain of Dall's research vessel, wrote his own book four years later on the marine mammals of the Pacific coast and on American whaling. Already he was far less optimistic than Dall had been about the future of the walrus and other species, pointing out that

RIBBON SEAL

the whalemen had turned upon the walrus about 1868, with the rapid decline of the Arctic whales. "Already the animals have suffered so great a slaughter at their hands that their numbers have been materially diminished . . . making it difficult for the Eskimaux to successfully hunt them. . . ." [3] This view was borne out by E. W. Nelson of the Biological Survey, who estimated that half the walrus population of Alaska had been exterminated in a single decade after 1871. John Muir, who accompanied Nelson on an Alaska research trip in 1881, has left us a vivid account of walrus slaughter:

> A little schooner has a boat out in the edge of the pack killing walruses, while she is lying a little to east of the sun. A puff of smoke now and then, a dull report, and a huge animal rears and falls—another, and another, as they lie on the ice without showing any alarm, waiting to be killed, like cattle lying in a barnyard! Nearer, we hear the roar, lion-like, mixed with hoarse grunts, from hundreds like black bundles on the white ice. A small red flag is planted near the pile of slain. Then the three men puff off to their schooner, as it is now midnight, and time for the other watch to go to work.
>
> These magnificent animals are killed oftentimes for their tusks alone, like buffaloes for their tongues, ostriches for their feathers, or for mere sport and exercise. . . . [4]

In this same period an American counterpart of the Russian trading concerns, the Alaska Company, was carrying on a systematic exploitation of the remaining sea otters and fur seals, which were to require full protection within a half-century of the Alaska Purchase. Even before 1867, explorers and whalemen had helped the Eskimos of the northern coasts wipe out the Alaska race of the musk ox, but the animals of the Interior still absorbed without difficulty the incidental food and fur harvests of the aborigines and scattered whites.

In 1900, with the discovery of gold at Nome, this situation changed. The white men descended upon the Territory in packs, turning to trapping in the winter time when the mines and streams were frozen. Both food and fur animals declined rapidly. The Alaska Civil Code, which until now had only prohibited the export of bird eggs, was amended, in 1902, to include restrictions on the slaughter of brown bears and other animals, after Theodore S. Palmer of the Biological Survey and Madison Grant of the New York Zoological Society had announced that Alaska game animals were in a fair way to disappearing entirely.

In the United States, where native creatures, the commercial fishes excepted, are no longer of economic importance, we are somewhat startled to learn that the dressed wild meats consumed annually in Alaska still amount to several million pounds, exclusive of the tonnage of beluga, whale, walrus, seal, and other marine creatures eaten yearly in the coastal villages. In addition to meat and blubber, an average family of Eskimos on the Bering deltas will dry and cache a ton of salmon annually, and in regions where fish are their chief source of food will eke out their winter store in the lean days of early spring with emperor, white-fronted, and other species of geese as these arrive on the great coastal breeding grounds. The threat of famine in the remote villages is very real, and the Fish and Wildlife Service, which officially outlaws spring shooting, unofficially condones such native practices. Though conservationists are never pleased to learn that much of the harvest of wild flesh is used to feed the half-wild huskies, these sled dogs are crucial to survival, too. Alaskan wildlife, everywhere but in the few large towns, still plays today the part in the economy that the passenger pigeon and the heath hen in the East and the bison and bighorn in the West played on those earlier frontiers. In the wilderness, or "bush," moose, caribou, and Dall sheep are shot commonly in the name of survival, and a bear slaughtered in "self-defense" tastes just as good as one killed on a hunter's permit.

Prior to this century wildlife protection was unheard of in Alaska, and it is understandable why the rough sourdough society took unkindly to the first Alaskan Game Act of 1902, representing, as it did, interference on the part of a remote government agency called the Biological Survey. This was true even though the Game Act permitted an annual kill of two moose, three sheep, three caribou, and six deer, or a total of fourteen large hoofed animals per hunter; no limit at all was placed on killing by Indians, Eskimos, miners, prospectors, trappers, and others claiming dependence on wildlife for survival. The Act, to be sure, was generally disregarded: in 1911 an Indian was observed with eighty-two caribou tongues he was offering for sale, and a report on Alaskan game conditions a decade later described a

KODIAK BEAR

recent slaughter of one hundred moose near Kantishna for use as dog food. Nevertheless, the insulting implications of the Act rankled in the breasts of most Alaskans, who felt that the native fauna would thrive best under their own ministrations.

This view was contested, inevitably, by Dr. Hornaday. The latter, after years of dire warnings and imprecations, entered the Alaskan skirmishes in 1918, in spirited opposition to the Sulzer Bill, a measure advanced beneath the banner of patriotism "to help win the WAR!" According to Sulzer, an Alaskan delegate who had acquired the support of Dr. Nelson of the Survey, the war effort would be forwarded materially were the storage and sale of game to be permitted in the Territory throughout the year, thus relieving the citizens of Fairbanks and other towns of the necessity of importing beef. The Sulzer Bill died in committee, but four years later a would-be delegate named Dan Sutherland who had sympathized with Hornaday was defamed in the Juneau *Empire* by such epithets as "A vote for Sutherland is a vote for Hornaday and the Alaskan Brown Bears!" The great brown bear, and particularly the Kodiak form, was at this time nominated commonly as a candidate for extinction; it was an alleged slayer not only of salmon and livestock but also of a few unlucky hunters who had perished in attempts upon its life. Sutherland was nonetheless elected, and it is to his credit that he subsequently prepared, in collaboration with the politic Dr. Nelson, the new Alaska Game Law of 1925.

BARREN-GROUND CARIBOU

The Alaska Game Law instituted wildlife legislation more or less equivalent to that obtaining in the United States; it also established the Alaska Game Commission, composed today of one representative from each of four Alaskan districts, plus the director in Alaska of the Fish and Wildlife Service. This body, taking into account the opinions of Service personnel, recommends to the Secretary of the Interior any changes in Alaskan wildlife laws which seem to it desirable; although these changes, over the years, have reflected the interests of the salmon fisheries and other groups more faithfully than those of the Service, they have nonetheless been regularly approved by the Department of the Interior. The Service can, and has, offset certain undesirable Commission-inspired legislation with new rulings of its own. When a bounty was placed on the dwindling wolverine, for example, the Service countered by establishing a trapping season on it, making the killing of wolverines at other times illegal. At the moment, game protection in Alaska seems adequate enough, though one wonders about the provision permitting an unlimited kill of caribou found within the Arctic circle. A third of the state lies north of this imaginary line, and the region will not long remain remote.

The barren-ground caribou, once incredibly abundant, was already decreasing when the Game Law was first enacted. On the Kenai Peninsula it declined, then disappeared, after the great fire of 1883, which destroyed the edible lichens it requires, and the importations of reindeer in the next decades provided damaging competition in northwest Alaska. Tundra fires, including a prolonged burn which in 1957 smoked the skies of the western Interior throughout much of the summer, have destroyed much lichen ground. Farther east, the great Tanana herd has been driven constantly northward by the surge of civilization toward the Yukon. The crossings by caribou millions, blocking passage on the great, gray rivers for days at a time, are long since spectacles of the past.

Though still the most abundant of Alaskan game animals, the caribou is the only one which continues a serious decline. The moose, which occupied the Kenai Peninsula after the caribou had deserted it and has flourished most notably there, is still extending its Alaskan range north and west. The mountain goat and the Dall sheep have maintained fair numbers on their stark, high terrains: a spectacular habitat shared by both beautiful white animals are the peaks and cliffsides surrounding the huge Skilak glacier on the Kenai, where the bands can be approached quite closely in a small airplane. The region is bordered by the Russian River, and the scars of old Russian gold diggings are still visible along the gorge. In southeast Alaska, the small Sitka mule deer has survived the early years of commercial slaughter and is now doing quite well.

All other hoofed mammals in Alaska are imported. The reindeer was introduced in the 1890s, after three whole villages of Eskimos had starved to death on St. Lawrence Island. The St. Lawrence famine actually occurred in the winter of 1878–1879, and once again we are indebted to John Muir for a forceful description:

> The scene was indescribably ghastly and desolate, though laid in a country purified by frost as by fire. Gulls, plovers, and ducks were swimming and flying about in happy life, the pure salt sea was dashing white against the shore, the blooming tundra swept back to the snow-clad volcanoes, and the wide azure sky bent kindly over all—nature intensely fresh and sweet, the village lying in the foulest and most glaring death. The shrunken bodies, with rotting furs on them, or white, bleaching skeletons, picked bare by crows, were lying mixed with kitchen-midden rubbish where they had been cast out by surviving relatives while they yet had strength to carry them. . . .
>
> Mr. Nelson went into this Golgotha with hearty enthusiasm, gathering the fine white harvest of skulls spread before him, and throwing them in heaps like a boy gathering pumpkins. . . .[5]

It was thought that semi-domestic reindeer herds might strengthen the desperate Eskimo economy, but the natives turned out to be indifferent herdsmen, unable to cope with the problem of wolves and a tendency on the part of the closely related caribou to lure the domestic stock into their own wild herds. Both animals were damaged by resultant hybridization, the reindeer becoming wilder and the caribou weaker. Meanwhile, the combined herds laid waste the available lichens, and an immediate increase in the reindeer to a high point of over a million was followed by a long decline which still continues.

Importation of exotics had its heyday, however, with the establishment of the Game Commission, at a time when the redistribution of wildlife was still popular in the United States. In 1928 small bands of Olympic elk and bison were introduced to Afognak Island and the Big Delta Valley, respectively, and in 1930 a band of Greenland musk ox was moved to Fairbanks, then Nunivak Island, via New York City. All these animals have done well, though the bison increase has tapered off; the musk ox may eventually be transferred to the mainland tundra, but the elk, which would certainly provide disastrous forage competition for the caribou should probably be left where it is.

Alaska, in its accelerated fashion, has experimented with all the usual conservation panaceas except artificial propagation; the latter, aside from being superfluous, has yet to strike the fancy of the Game Commission. On a large scale, if commercial fur farming is discounted, the practice can be applied successfully only to the upland game birds and the fishes, and in Alaska the various grouses and ptarmigans which comprise the game-bird group are plentiful and relatively unpersecuted. The innumerable waterways, many of them still virgin, abound with five species of salmon, a variety of trouts, the grayling, the shee-fish, and the northern pike; in these rich waters the pike is considered so inferior that it is not rated as a game fish even in the eyes of the law. Attempts made to improve matters by importing the eastern brook trout have been in vain, not at all surprisingly, except in a few streams and lakes where the native forms were absent. Native rainbows have been successfully transplanted in the state.

The control of predators, and particularly the bounty system, has been pursued enthusiastically. The bald eagle was bountied until recent years as a fellow scapegoat of the brown bear in the destruction of salmon, the decline of which has actually come about through commercial overfishing. The hair seals have also been bounty victims, as alleged consumers of salmon in the sea, and the coyote, which invaded Alaska only quite re-

GRAYLING

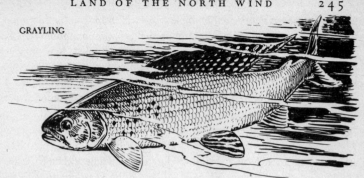

cently, has met its usual reception. Undaunted, it has spread in a few decades to the Arctic and to the Bering Sea.

But the great Alaskan predator is the gray wolf. The serious war against the wolves commenced in defense not of the native animals but of the reindeer. In early days the packs had concentrated on the caribou, but the semi-domestic, smaller animals were easier prey. The ensuing reduction of the wolves contributed inevitably to severe overgrazing by both reindeer and caribou of the slow-growing lichens, but nevertheless the wolf bounty was increased from fifteen dollars in 1921 to the present fee of fifty. The Alaska Native Service approves the bounty, just as it approves the exploitation of walrus by the Eskimo, as an asset to the native economy, and political pressure supports it also. In the winter of 1953–1954 over two hundred wolves were killed in the Kotzebue area alone. The great majority of the wolves are shot down on the winter snow from airplanes, often in areas where many wolves but no real wolf problems exist. Neither reindeer nor caribou have benefited significantly, since lack of forage has been the secret of their distress. Formerly, the predator-control agents of the Fish and Wildlife Service scattered poisoned baits around by plane, killing bears and valuable fur animals as well as the intended victims. In recent years they have been more discriminate in both attitude and method; in the Nelchina River area, where the caribou has outgrown its range, the wolves are now protected, in order to spare the hungry caribou from themselves. Meanwhile, control of the Kenai Peninsula wolf, largest of all North America races, has brought about its complete extinction, and the Kenai moose, predictably, have begun to overbrowse their range.

Alaska has been tardy in conservation progress, not only because her politics have been dominated by the commercial fishing and other interests but also because until after World War II there was no authoritative body of biologists to document unbiased conservation opinion. For many years previously, only two Fish and Wildlife Service biologists had been assigned to the more than half a million square miles of the Great Land. This situation has been bettered, and profitable studies of the salmon fisheries, caribou herds, and other resources are now under way, but the Service, especially in the law-enforcement branch, remains woefully undermanned. The game agent for the western Interior, for example, must patrol alone an area larger than New England, including the whole Yukon-Kuskokwim delta, and a sketch here of a typical mission in his ceaseless surveillance of the region will give some idea of the task confronting wildlife agents in Alaska. One must keep in mind that, in addition to their ordinary duties, these men perform the functions of the game wardens in the older states.

The delta formed between the mouths of the Yukon and Kuskokwim is a remote, foggy world of dark tundra pools, bleak, faceless shore, and isolated volcanic peaks rising mysteriously above the waste; its wilderness of water rivals the sloughs and potholes of the Canadian prairie provinces as the great North American nesting grounds for waterfowl, though only a relatively narrow strip behind the beach is heavily populated by the birds. While the Canadian grounds favor ducks over geese, the reverse is true on the Yukon-Kuskokwim, and emperor, white-fronted, and cackling geese, in company with large numbers of whistling swans, are the dominant birds. There are black brant, too, and a variety of ducks, including such sea ducks as eider and old-squaw, as well as innumerable lesser sandhill cranes, shore birds, jaegers, and gulls.

The land, relentlessly monotone in all but a few summer weeks of feverish flowering, is almost uninhabited. The distances are so great that the game agent must fly endless rounds in suitable weather if he is to touch at each scattered Eskimo settlement and fishing camp even once a year. Much of the work can be done only in season, when the waters are free of ice. On the rare clear days, the fishing camps on the outer deltas may be detected from a distance by the red racks of drying salmon and the flapping of white canvas tents, but at other times there are no landmarks, only the black faces of the ponds shifting evilly in the Bering mists. Poor flying weather may ground the agent for many days at a time.

Nor are the natives always glad to see him. They line up silently on the river bank as he sets his pontoons on the roiled waters, the ceaseless wind stirring the fur trim on the parkas. The agent singles out the village leader and tells the purpose of his visit. Gently, insistently, almost apologetically, he confiscates a wolverine pelt submitted for bounty out of season, then lectures the round-faced, resigned group on the waterfowl laws which preserve sport shooting for the white man in faraway America. Since the waterfowl, for them, may mean survival, they cannot be expected to understand the laws, and the agent does not really expect them to obey. Apologizing in their turn, they tell him again as they had told him the year before that they must take the geese in early spring if they are not to starve before the great silver king salmon makes its run in from the sea. One says he is proud to be an American and to obey the American law, but that his children must be allowed to eat; he offers to tell the agent how often the law is broken here, if that will be of service to the government, but he repeats that it will be broken. The agent counsels them obliquely against waste, repeats the letter of the law, and smiles. Immediately the fishermen smile, too, and remember the pidgin English they had forgotten so long as his presence posed a threat. One asks him in a sing-song voice, "Why is it the birds go away so many in the fall of the year, and come back to us so few?" And the agent patiently explains, using his hands. Like all the Service personnel one meets in remote places, he is dedicated, and does not begrudge his time.

The problems of the Service in Alaska closely parallel those it must deal with in the United States. Among the most recent is the matter of private leases on the fourteen Alaskan wildlife refuges. Some of these refuges are bird rocks and seal rookeries, like the Pribilof Islands and the remote islets attached to the Aleutian chain, but the Kenai moose range, Kodiak Island, Nunivak Island, and the Hazen Bay refuge of the Yukon-Kuskokwim include great areas of land. Prospectors for gold have largely been replaced by timber agents and geologists in search of oil and other minerals; in 1957 oil was discovered in quantity on the Kenai, in the very heart of the great moose range. Disturbing as this is to conservationists, the fact remains that the Alaskan economy needs the oil industry and income, and a lease had to be granted; already a raw road stretches like a scar across the spruce forest and muskeg, laying open the inner wilderness. The moose, an unpredictable creature not in the least averse to whiling away an hour or even a week among the buildings of a settlement, will probably take the oil development in its great stride, as will the adaptable black bear. The scarce Kenai brown bears, however, may well disappear, and the few trumpeter

WOLVERINE

swans which now raise long copper-stained necks to the whine of occasional airplanes may vanish also. Probably this chance must be taken. The moose range, it is pointed out, is three times the size of Rhode Island, and not more than five per cent of it would be likely to undergo development. The development, in turn, is to be supervised by the Fish and Wildlife Service, and for the moment one can only hope that the overworked Alaska branch of this key agency can resist the political pressures which have hampered Alaskan conservation until this time.

The resources of the new state, spared to date by the virtual absence of roads north and west of Fairbanks, are still largely intact, and are still there to be saved by proper management. The salmon runs, though much reduced by overfishing in the spawning rivers, continue to support the leading fishery. The fisheries, which include a large harvest of halibut, crabs, and shrimp, are in turn the leading commerce, though oil may soon compete. Meanwhile, the fur trade is still flourishing. In a twenty-year period after 1925, over six million fur animals—muskrat, beaver, mink, marten, and blue fox are the most important species, in that order—valued at more than forty-two million dollars were shipped out of Alaska; these figures are exclusive of the numerous furs used locally, and of the 1,258,021 fur seals taken in the Pribilofs in the same period, with an additional value of forty-eight million dollars. Timber for wood pulp is also a growing source of income, and the game animals and fishes have helped to make the tourist trade Alaska's second industry.

Man's habitations in Alaska, the few large towns excepted, are garish and unkempt, modern versions of the settlements which sprang up one by one on the westward course of the American frontier; cluttered with tin

cans, oil drums, even garbage, the muddy streets of such diverse settlements as Bethel on the Kuskokwim and Point Barrow on the Arctic Ocean
seem somehow symptomatic of a ruthless invasion of a land by a transient
population. The situation is changing rapidly, however. More and more
Americans are remaining in Alaska and taking pride in it, and great unspoiled areas have already been set aside, in national parks and monuments,
refuges and forests. It is in the interest of all Americans, Alaskan and
otherwise, to see that these are protected and even augmented.

The most recent reserve is one of the most important, including as it
does a large part of primeval Alaska lying north of the Arctic Circle. The
Arctic Game Range, established in 1958, will do much to protect the bare
wilderness of the huge Brooks Range, and the caribou and other animals
exposed on the brown barrens of the Arctic Slope which stretches away
northward toward the blue ice packs of the Beaufort Sea. Glimpsed from
the air between banks of cold rolling fogs, the region is beautiful and
forbidding. Its tundra is desert of a kind, but the great beauty of Alaska
lies in its bleakest areas—tundra, ice pack, glacier, and bare mountain, with
their unique and precious complement of life.

In Canada, the history of wildlife exploitation and conservation has run
more or less parallel to events in the United States, ever since the first
fishery stations and fur-trading posts were established along the St. Lawrence. That Canada has been spared the terrible animal losses of her neigh-
bor, in extinct species as well as in general numerical reduction, is probably
due less to superior foresight than to the resistance of her wilderness to her
sparse population. Though the wildlife of Canada has been seriously diminished, the Dominion, like Alaska, is still in a position to reserve for the

GLACIER BEAR

future representative populations of virtually all her fauna. The great auk and the Labrador duck are perhaps the sole North American species to the final demise of which Canada's contribution has been significant, but a few others within her domain are presently imperiled.

Actually, Canada harbors very few creatures not found elsewhere on the continent. This is because the prairies and wooded provinces of her temperate regions are extensions of very similar terrains found south of her border, and her huge expanses of thinly inhabited spruce muskeg and Arctic tundra are duplicated in Alaska. In consequence, her few amphibians and reptiles are almost entirely species more or less common within the United States, and her fishes, though abundant, are similarly endemic to the United States or Alaska, or both. Even those birds such as the whooping crane and Ross's goose which breed only within her boundaries are birds of the United States for more than half the year; her Arctic birds, without exception, occur also in Alaska.

A few mammals, on the other hand, are purely Canadian in distribution. These include localized forms such as the Gaspé shrew, British Columbia red-backed vole, and Vancouver marmot, as well as the scattered Mackenzie and Ungave phenacomys, small mouselike creatures of central and eastern Canada, respectively. The woodland caribou have been exterminated in their limited range within the United States, and are now, for all practical purposes, creatures of Canada alone. Since they continue to decline, their prospects for the future must depend on the determination of Canadian conservationists.

Conservation in Canada commenced, as in the United States, with the establishment of large national parks, and since both countries worked together almost from the beginning, Canadian progress in this field need only be sketched briefly.

The Canadian Pacific Railway, completed in 1885, encouraged the authorization in that year of the Banff National Park, first of its kind in the country. The magnificent Jasper National Park, in the same region, was among five parks set up by 1908, and a number of others, both national and provincial, now preserve wild areas of the land. The Waterton Park and the Quetico Forest Reserve adjoin and complement Glacier National Park, in Montana, and the Minnesota National Forest, their respective counterparts in the United States, and there are, as well, a number of enormous game preserves in the Yukon and Northwest Territories on which hunting and trapping is restricted to Eskimos and Indians. The total

WOODLAND CARIBOU

area of these preserves is more than half a million square miles, or nearly twice the extensive national forest holdings in the United States. The Thelon River Game Sanctuary, also in the Northwest Territories, is inviolate; it shelters such precarious forms as the musk ox and the barren-ground race of the grizzly bear. Waterfowl sanctuaries are numerous, with an especially important group protecting the breeding grounds at Hudson Bay; others in Saskatchewan and Alberta preserve the great prairie wetlands. Many special sanctuaries, including the home of the gannets on Bonaventure Island, Quebec, are scattered throughout the provinces, which maintain a number of refuges of their own, and it can fairly be said that the refuge system in Canada, including the incidental protection afforded by its parks, compares favorably with that in the United States.

Cooperation between Canadian and American conservation groups has been extensive and effective. The treaties protecting the fur seal and the migratory birds were fine early examples, and the Canadian breeding grounds of the latter are the joint concern of both nations, working together through such agencies as Ducks Unlimited. Canada entered early in the campaign to save the bison, and supplemented her own wild bands with the purchase of Montana bison in 1909. Wood Buffalo Park, established in 1922, in the Northwest Territories and Alberta, contains the last descendants of the dark "wood bison" race long since extirpated from the eastern United States; it also contains the last known breeding grounds of the whooping cranes. Over ten thousand square miles in area, it is several times the size of Yellowstone, our own largest national park.

Conservation legislation has run the same uneven course in Canada as it has elsewhere. The Northwest Game Act of 1906, which, as amended in 1917, controlled the take of fur animals among its protective measures, was a large step forward. On the other hand, when American states had cooperated in 1911 to spare the antelope, the provinces harboring this species still permitted hunting. As a result, the antelope is all but gone from Canada, where it was once common on the prairies. A few species— the grizzly and polar bears in particular—may still receive insufficient protection, and certain other resources require strict management in the Dominion. The Atlantic salmon fishery of the maritime provinces, the hair-seal commerce based in Newfoundland, and the take of edible, unwary birds such as the spruce grouse, ptarmigans, and prairie chicken are among the latter.

The Canadian naturalist R. M. Anderson remarked in 1924, "Of all the wildernesses, the man-made wilderness is the most desolate." [6] It does not seem unreasonable to hope, however, that this lovely northern land of clear waters, evergreen forest, and boreal wilderness will absorb, without fatal disfigurement, the invasions of development and commerce.

Bob Hines

The beauty and genius of a work of art may be reconceived, though its first material expression be destroyed; a vanished harmony may yet again inspire the composer; but when the last individual of a race of living things breathes no more, another heaven and another earth must pass before such a one can be again. —WILLIAM BEEBE (1906)

12 : *Another Heaven and Another Earth*

IN 1831, according to contemporary report, the whooping crane was common in the fur countries of Canada, and was even then so tenacious of life that there were known instances "of the wounded bird putting the fowler to flight, and fairly driving him off the field." [1] This information will be of small surprise to people familiar with this spirited species, which resembles superficially a huge heron but is actually allied closely to the much smaller rails found also in its marshes. The most statuesque of North American birds, standing over five feet tall, the whooping crane moves nearly a yard with each long, graceful stride; its fierce, fiery eye and javelin beak, backed by a mask of angry carmine skin, might well give pause to any creature wishing harm to it. Black wing tips excepted, it is otherwise satin white, and the plumes formed by the tertial feathers of its wings, accumulated at rest on its rump, make it one of the few creatures in the world as imposing from behind as from the front. John James Audubon, with a single shot, once killed seven of these birds, a number which would represent today nearly a quarter of all the whooping cranes remaining on the earth.

The whooper, understandably, was one of the first birds remarked upon by the explorers of this continent, and the wild horn note of its voice, of a volume suited to the bird's stature, contributed to its early legend. Its dislike of civilization, as evidenced by its swift disappearance from the East Coast, gave rise to such misconceptions as the following, authored in the early nineteenth century by Thomas Nuttall: "Ever wary, and stealing from the view of all observers, it is surprising, that furtive and inharmonious as owls, they have not excited the prejudice of the superstitious." Nuttall claimed to have observed these cranes in the Mississippi Valley, where "the passage of their nightly armies fills the mind with wonder." [2]

The great white bird, frequenting open water edge, could not, of course, be furtive if it tried, and it is doubtful, considering its wild and solitary nature and its habit of migrating in family groups rather than flocks, whether the word "armies" described it properly even then. In historic times it has always been much rarer than the sandhill crane, the bird with which Nuttall very likely confused it; probably there were no more than a few thousand of these birds in all America at the time of the first records, and it must be assumed that the species, declining slowly over thousands of years, was then only a few centuries from extinction.

This remnant population was set upon by the usual destructive forces of the white man, but was affected most by shooting for food and sport, by amateur oölogists, and by agricultural development and drainage over much of its breeding terrain. The early limits of its range are quite indefinite, but it is now thought to have nested from Illinois north and west across the prairie states and provinces to the Northwest Territories, wintering from Mexico and the Gulf Coast north along the eastern seaboard to New Jersey. During the nineteenth century it retreated west of the Mississippi, and by 1880 was a rare bird everywhere. It was last seen in Illinois in 1891, and a nesting in Hancock County, Iowa, four years later, was the last recorded in the United States. Forbush and Hornaday warned of its extinction just after the turn of the century, and John C. Phillips, by 1926, estimated that less than a dozen pairs remained in all North America. This figure has varied little in the thirty-odd years since. The Aransas

WHOOPING CRANE, with pintail ducks

National Wildlife Refuge, established on the Texas coast in 1937, sheltered in winter one of two remaining populations in this country. The existence of a separate, non-migratory flock in a Louisiana swamp was reported to the National Audubon Society some years earlier by Richard Pough, who had heard of it through local people; the presence of cranes in his region was vehemently denied, however, by Mr. E. A. McIlhenny, whose Avery Island sanctuary had been so important at the turn of the century in the salvation of the egrets. No action was taken, and a flock of cranes which might have been far easier to protect than the migratory individuals wintering at Aransas disappeared in the wake of a flood in 1939.

In 1945 a crane was recorded in Wyoming, and until the fall of 1958, when five transient cranes were reported at the Medicine Lake Wildlife Refuge in Montana, no specimen had been observed more than fifty miles from a migration route extending north from Texas through Oklahoma, Kansas, Nebraska, and South and North Dakota into Saskatchewan, where the last Canadian nesting had been observed in 1922. Apparently the birds continued northward, but for many years their final breeding grounds were to remain a secret of the wilderness.

This element of mystery, combined with the noble aspect of the crane, was of great assistance to the Cooperative Whooping Crane Project, set up in 1945 by the Fish and Wildlife Service and the National Audubon Society. The dramatic circumstances of the bird's struggle for survival, brought to light, inspired immediate national news coverage, and a great many Americans and Canadians still follow avidly the varying fortunes of the last flock. *Life* magazine ran a crane article, an oil company restricted its drilling operations in the vicinity of the wintering grounds, and not long ago the Air Force was persuaded by public outcry to forgo bombing practice at nearby Matagorda Island. The bombing, according to Robert P. Allen, "would undoubtedly have been fatal to *Grus americana*." [3]

Allen, who directed the crane project for several years, made a comprehensive study of crane habits, including the spectacular mating dance which, photographed, contributed not a little to the bird's publicity. This publicity achieved a sentimental peak in 1950, when two injured birds, placed together in an Aransas enclosure, produced Rusty, the first crane ever bred in captivity. Rusty perished on his third day, apparently the victim of a foraging raccoon, and further attempts to propagate the cranes were unsuccessful until 1957, when two young were raised successfully by crippled birds at the New Orleans Zoo. As of this writing, it seems quite likely that a captive flock can be built up and maintained, but as a wild species, exposed to the cumulative hazards of its existence, the crane still stalks precariously along the abyss.

An early achievement of the crane project, in addition to habitat research at Aransas, was the marking out of the exact migration route, township by township, from the Gulf Coast to Saskatchewan. This step was crucial in the attempt to locate the northern breeding grounds and as a means of encouraging and enforcing protection for the migrant family groups en route. Although the crane population by April 1950 was a hopeful thirty-three, twenty-four birds perished in migration in the next three years, a tragedy due apparently to shooting. A body of Saskatchewan farmers, in particular, was of the opinion that too much money was being wasted by the Canadian Wildlife Service and other groups on a bird which was doomed anyway, and vowed publicly to execute the cranes on sight. But the Audubon Society, in 1953, saturated the entire migration route with conservation propaganda, from educational leaflets to television films, and thereby aroused such a wave of protective sentiment that the flock returned unscathed that year to the salt flats of Aransas. The death of cranes by shooting has been negligible ever since.

In 1954 the secret of the summer grounds, unsolved despite many trips in search of it, was broken. A pilot for the Canadian Wildlife Service, investigating with forestry personnel a fire in the wild Wood Buffalo Park, sighted three cranes—a pair with young—in a region of spruce bog and tamarack. The next year more families were discovered, and it is now presumed that all remaining cranes nest in the same wilderness, which lies not far south of Great Slave Lake. That a national park should have surrounded these last nesting marshes was a circumstance as fortunate as it was blind, but nevertheless the seasonal poles of whooping crane existence are now both legal sanctuaries.

Grus americana, unlike *Homo sapiens,* lives out its life from day to day, quite unconcerned about its prospects for extinction. Each spring, as whooping cranes have done since long before man evolved, it rises, bugling, from the edge of the Gulf and flies to the northern horizon, pausing to rest on the sand bars of the River Platte, perhaps, before continuing on across the big skies of the prairies. Each November it sails down across the continent to settle once again on the Texas coast. This journey it must continue to perform, spring after spring, fall after fall, until, on some far, nameless day, the last solitary giant sinks down and fails to rise. Inert in the silence of the marsh, its broken plumes stirring in the silent air, it cedes the chemical remains of its long history to the swift obsequies of insects, to the ultimate cycle of life energy on earth. And this will occur with or without man's intervention, and whether or not the species survives its present crisis, for the crane is old, and its time, in geological terms, is short.

There is, to be sure, a certain logic in the view which advocates the relinquishment of doomed creatures to eternity. Despite the attentions of a nation, the crane shows little tendency to increase its numbers, and one may question whether, having been reduced to its low ebb, the species would do so even were its original habitats restored. Accident, inbreeding, storm, or any combination of these and other factors could bring the final band to a swift end and it is very likely that the crane has passed a point of no return. Thus, the efforts on the bird's behalf must be met with failure, and the large amounts of time and energy expended upon them would, in the view of some, be put to better use in another area of conservation.

But a great majority of naturalists, including many of those who have lost hope for the species and all those who have ever stopped short at the sight of so magnificent a creature, believe that the continent will be a finer place for every year the bird flies north and south. Leaving aside the merits of the question, it should nonetheless be pointed out that the whooping crane, as a symbol of lost wilderness, has unquestionably drawn more interest, even income, to the conservation cause than has been

HARELIP SUCKER

expended upon it; indeed, the unprecedented popular concern with wildlife owes much to the national sympathy with the crane.

In the whooping crane's mindless efforts at immortality, the fact that it is a bird, and a big, white, conspicuous bird at that, has probably been as helpful to it in recent years as it was harmful in the days when people sought it out with intent to kill. A number of species in the other vertebrate classes, as we have seen, find themselves in positions as precarious as that of the crane, without the consolation of a single line of newsprint, or the formation of Cooperative Harelip Sucker Projects, National Blind Salamander Societies, much less Gila Monsters Unlimited. Only large mammals of noblest mien, or those whose virtues have been sanctified in children's books and animated cartoons, elicit anything like the public's response to the plight of its feathered friends, and this is because the great majority of birds, unlike most other vertebrates, are lively and color-ful, and are readily observed throughout the country.

Even among birds, however, the whooping crane is blessed with unusually spectacular habits and appearance. The covert, erratic Bachman's warbler, which may be closer to extinction than the crane, can boast only a small, esoteric public, few members of which ever have seen it; it will not even cooperate with its admirers by congregating, like the crane, Colima warbler, and Cape Sable sparrow, in a national park or other accessible sanctuary, or even in one state. The Everglade kite, America's rarest bird at the pres-ent writing, enjoys a limited notoriety. Even the ivory-billed woodpecker has vanished quietly, though the history of its decline in numbers closely parallels that of the crane.

The ivory-bill, on a smaller scale, is actually as striking as the whooper.

GEORGIA BLIND SALAMANDER

Its beautiful white bill, valued as an ornament by the Indians, was a tool well suited to the chopping of its characteristic oval holes in heavy tree bark, and its strident voice was a memorable sound in the forests of the southeast. A "majestic and formidable species," as Alexander Wilson called it, "his eye is brilliant and daring; and his whole frame so admirably adapted for his mode of life and method of procuring subsistence, as to impress on the mind of the examiner the most reverential ideas of the Creator." [4]

Be that as it may, the bird was not adapted to the radical change in its habitat which came about through lumbering. It was so specialized that it fed almost exclusively on insects and grubs found only beneath the bark of trees a few years dead, which were often the very first ones to be felled. As such trees were inevitably scattered, it required a very wide territory, but its wilderness was slowly cut away. By the twentieth century the species was decidedly rare, and in 1941 but twenty-four individuals were thought to remain. The last accepted sighting was made five years later, in the Singer tract of northern Louisiana, where efforts by conservationists to prevent exploitation by timber interests were finally in vain. More recent reports from the Apalachicola Swamp of northern Florida are problematical, at best, though Herbert Stoddard, the quail authority, is said to know of a last pair or two somewhere not far from his home in Thomasville, Georgia. For obvious reasons, not excluding an invasion by well-intentioned naturalists, Stoddard will not disclose its whereabouts; quite possibly he is the only man who will ever hear again the ivory-bill's loud, wild cry in the dark cypress silences of southern swamplands.

It is no coincidence that the North American creatures in extreme peril of extinction, including the great majority of rare fishes, amphibians, reptiles, and mammals, and the rare birds without exception, share two consistent characteristics: they were localized or uncommon before the white man affected them, and they were unadaptable to change. The only

BACHMAN'S WARBLER

doomed form of recent years which does not seem to fall into either category is the Eskimo curlew, and this species was, for all practical purposes, a victim of the great commercial slaughters which ended the nineteenth century. For the curlew, protection came too late. Should extinction come for the rarest birds left—the ivory-billed woodpecker, Everglade kite, whooping crane, California condor, Cape Sable sparrow, and Colima and Bachman's warblers—it will come only indirectly by the hand of man. In the case of the last three, as a matter of fact, it would be difficult to establish any human guilt at all.

This realization may be taken as a measure of conservation progress; the general claim might even be made that, as a direct consequence of legislation and effort of the past half-century, no widely distributed species capable of restoring itself under favorable conditions has not been given the chance to do so. Though a few species perished in the early years of this century before the conservation movement found momentum, the plume birds, certain shore birds and waterfowl, the bison, elk, and antelope, the beaver, sea otter, fur seal, gray whale, and many others then in danger have all been returned to a safe level, and even those among them still sadly reduced are in no immediate peril. In other words, though we are left today with a broken wilderness and token populations of our wildlife, the only members of the latter we seem likely to lose entirely in the near future are those which, in the distant past, ceased their long process of evolution, became rigid in their habits, and, standing still in the face of change, began to die.

"Nature is dynamic and the evolution of an organism, in very general terms, may be described as a constant adaptation to change. When, for example, a certain environmental condition alters so that an organism is unable to secure its habitual food in the usual way, it must broaden the

IVORY-BILLED WOODPECKER

scope of its food preferences or find a new way of securing the food it is used to eating. Otherwise it will perish." [5]

The whooping crane may have insured its eventual doom by failing to move inland and upland from the water edge many thousands of years ago, as did its relatively adaptable cousin, the sandhill crane. The ivory-billed woodpecker and the Everglade kite, addicted, respectively, to a certain grub and a certain species of snail, could not survive a scarcity of these creatures; by contrast, the numerous and widespread mourning dove is known to use one hundred and forty-nine species of plant food, and the white-tailed deer five hundred and sixteen. The red-cockaded woodpecker of Southern States nests only in certain pines; these trees, cut heavily for pulpwood, are also afflicted by the red-heart fungus, and since it is most unlikely that the bird can change its habits, it seems doomed to perish with its pinelands. The special requirements of the rare songbirds are not as yet clearly understood, but it can be assumed with reasonable certainty that at some point in their past they were unable to effect that extension of their habits which would have permitted the further evolution of a more dynamic species. The same might be said of the California condor, which, unlike the other vanishing birds, is known to have disappeared from the larger part of its wide range long before the first white man ever landed.

Fossil remains of the California condor have been found as far east as Florida, and it circled the desert mountains from Nevada to Texas no more than two thousand years ago. It is now confined, however, to the coastal mountains of the Pacific. Lewis and Clark reported it from Oregon, where one was observed perched on a stranded whale, and in this period it may still have strayed north to the Canadian border and east as far as Utah. The appearance of the white man doubtless hastened its withdrawal, for it was last seen in the state of Washington about 1830, and in Oregon in 1913. Recently it has retired northward from Baja California, and is now present only in the Los Padres National Forest, in south-central California.

At the time of its disappearance from Washington, Richardson termed it common in California, and Coues, nearly half a century later, attested also to its abundance. In the first part of the nineteenth century, the condor's decline had probably been slow, although Indian tribes are said to have killed it as a burial fetish, a messenger from the living to the dead, and the Forty-niners apparently used its gigantic quills as containers for their gold dust. But the next half-century witnessed the general settlement of California, and by 1900 the condor was fading fast.

Like most members of its family, this huge vulture is not particular about its food, provided that the food is carrion. When the great game animals roamed freely in the West, it must have fed abundantly, and the sheep ranches operated by the Spanish also provided ample nourishment. As the sheep were replaced by the less numerous cattle, however, the domestic source of food decreased, and the game animals had already declined. The condor's plight was compounded further by the reduction of livestock mortality effected by modern treatment of diseases, and by the sanitary practice of burning or burying dead animals. The carcasses of marine animals became less frequent along the coast, and the coast itself, more and more populated, was gradually forsaken by the shy birds. In the present century the condors have come to depend for food on small mammal remains and other meager fare; a few ranchers have cooperated with conservationists by leaving dead stock unburied, and trappers have been asked to skin fur animals in the field, but the condors have dwindled to an estimated sixty in number, at which level they are presently maintaining themselves.

Food, however, is but one of the serious problems. The other great birds of the continent—the trumpeter swan and the whooping crane, the white pelican and the eagles—have all been seriously reduced, and, though the

causes vary, one common to them all is conspicuousness, which draws man's malevolent attention. The truly enormous condor, with its wing-spread of ten feet, is a tempting target for the idle rifle.

Furthermore, its optimum reproductive rate of one young every second year, per pair, is the lowest of all North American birds, barely offsetting the annual mortality. Conceivably, the condors could be helped by arti-ficial rearing, since experiments with the very similar Andean condor of South America, in which the removal of the first egg for artificial incuba-tion inspired the parents to produce another, and the removal of the second fledgling encouraged a nesting the following year, have shown that four young might be produced in the time required in the wild for one. In practice, eleven Andean condors were raised from a single pair over a period of six years. But efforts to assist the California condor in this manner have to date been resisted by the National Audubon Society and other groups, which apparently feel that the removal of eggs or a pair of adult condors from the remnant population might prove disastrous. The last nests are located almost entirely in the Sespe Wildlife Preserve of the Los Padres, to which even naturalists are forbidden access without special permit.

At least one authority believes that over two hundred condors still exist, many of them in the mountains outside the Preserve which stretch away northward toward San Francisco. The figure of sixty, presented originally in the Audubon Society's exhaustive monograph on the species, is more generally accepted. These forlorn survivors, scattered across the ridges of the coast range, seem badly suited to a world which has gone on without them. The birds have declined through long epochs of animal abundance dating back to the days of the giant bears and bisons, mammoths and mastodons, ground sloths, dire wolves, and saber-toothed tigers, and one may suppose that their last days began with the passing of this prehistoric fauna. The condor's ancient relative, *Teratornis*, with its wingspread of twelve feet, is long since gone, though it flew once in company with the

CALIFORNIA CONDOR

condor; the condor, in turn, shares its mountains today with the much smaller turkey vulture, a bird better adapted to the lean pickings of civilized landscapes. Silent, swaying patiently on intent wings, the turkey vulture remorselessly usurps the condor's range.

The ivory-bill, whooping crane, and condor may all be senile species, better suited to other ages, other climates, and too old to change. The last two, at least, were eking out the million and more years of their existence long before the first red nomads spread south from Bering Strait, and their history with the white man has occupied no more than one fleeting autumn of a great old age. In consequence, their passing, when it comes, will bear a quite different import from that of the passenger pigeon, a species cut down in the prime of its existence. But it is also true that, had mankind not altered the shape and nature of the land, their withdrawal from the earth would have been a slow one, lived out gracefully over centuries to come. And so we must assume responsibility, even for these.

The ancient condor, bare-headed and ragged, is not a pretty bird at rest, but in flight, soaring stiff-winged on the air currents of the Los Padres, it achieves all the dignity of its years. To see it—and one should—one must usually climb into the mountains which surround its last preserve. The most simple route, perhaps, is via Piru Canyon, which lies not far north of the city of Los Angeles. In the canyon one follows a road which traces the contours of the western face, reaching its highest point high above and beyond the lake at San Felicitas Dam. Forsaking the car, one climbs a fire break up the spine of the mountain, gaining a brushy summit in an hour's journey. Though the summit commands a view of many miles in all directions, no sign of man is any longer visible. Great rolling brown ridges mount, one upon another, to the westward horizon, and to the north the shadowed canyon narrows, disappears. Jutting cliffs form the eastern face of Piru Canyon, falling steeply from the distant high plateaus, and to the south the mountains open out into the bright open lands of the Santa Clara Valley. The world is as it was long, long ago, its life breathing quietly beneath the sun.

A light wind stirs the chaparral, muting an insistent rock wren, and raptors of several sorts—buteos, eagles, small falcons, turkey vultures—are almost constantly in sight, casting neat shadows as they slide across a canyon face, curl upward, and sweep slowly back, yet seeming to drift always in a fixed direction. A raven flaps aimlessly across the scene, and white-throated swifts swoop past in violent arcs. As the sun rises, so, often, do the birds, forsaking the early morning hunt with the drying of the dew and circling upward into oblivions of blue too bright to contemplate. But the great condor, sulking on some remote ledge in the fastnesses of its preserve, fails to appear. One by one its small relatives vanish, black specks which trick the eye, then are no more. Midday comes, and the songbirds sit stone still in the brush. There is sun, heavy silence, a pervasive scent of parched vegetation, a lizard materialized on a rock.

The condor, appearing, does not break the silence. There are two. They crest the horizon to the westward, several miles away, but even at that distance, seen through binoculars, they can be only condors or eagles, for their posture is too bold, their flight too firm, for hawks or vultures.

They sail down across the dry ravines, across this high country where few men have stalked and none have stayed, coming on swiftly, unswerving. A mile away, they no longer can be eagles, and the heart stops. Sweeping forward, a scant hundred feet above the brush, they descend the grade of ridges, one bird four wing spreads behind the other, and the definitive broad band of white of the wing's shoulder glints powerfully now in the hard light. They pass the ridge summit at eye level, implacably, and in that moment the naked orange of the head is bright. Then, as swiftly as they had come, they glide away, broad-backed as they sink across the canyon, alone in a world of gray-green brush, brown mountain, ocher cliffs, blue sky. The birds do not circle at the canyon but forge straight on, dark silhouettes against the pale plateaus in the far distance, as if, striking eastward on some ancient errand, they meant to return across the continent.

RED-COCKADED WOODPECKER

Appendices
Reference Notes
Bibliography
Index

Appendix I:

The Rare, Declining, and Extinct Vertebrate Animal Species of North America North of the Mexican Boundary

Main references to these species in the text may be found in the Index. Brief histories of obscure fish, amphibian, and reptile species not mentioned in the text, as well as pertinent supplementary information on other species, are provided here.

Of the numerous rare and extinct subspecies only a few are of sufficient interest to be included here.

FISHES

MARINE FISHES   (General discussion, Chapter 5)

Marine fishes, those confined entirely in range and habitat to salt water, are rarely or never threatened with total extermination by other than natural causes, since man has as yet been unable to damage the chemistry of the sea, and since the commercial fisheries cease being profitable long before a breeding stock adequate for the repropagation of a particular species has been destroyed.

ANADROMOUS FISHES   (General discussion, Chapter 5)

The anadromous fishes, those that ascend from salt into brackish or fresh water to spawn, have been reduced in number, in part from overfishing but mostly as a result of the ceaseless deterioration of their native streams through damming, siltation, and pollution; such valuable species as the shad, the sea sturgeons, the Atlantic salmon, the Pacific salmons, and the smelt have to date been endangered from a commercial rather than a natural-history point of view, with the exception below:

white sturgeon, *Acipenser transmontanus* Richardson

FRESH-WATER FISHES   (General discussion, Chapters 6 and 10)
The fresh-water fishes are chronic victims of civilization, and are also more subject than marine forms to climatic changes, as well as damage to their habitats by drought, flood, and other natural causes. Field research in regard to the very numerous forms is incomplete, and this list must be considered less comprehensive than representative. Fishes of local distribution are not included unless their numbers have seriously declined or unless, as in the case of the Devil's Hole pupfish, they are so very small as to be subject to sudden extermination.

The species are grouped roughly according to distribution—Eastern, Western, and Great Lakes. Fresh-water fish populations of Canada and Alaska remain largely intact. Nomenclature and classification are generally as recognized in Blair, et al. (*Vertebrates of the United States*, New York: McGraw-Hill, 1957).

FISHES OF THE EAST, INCLUDING THE MISSISSIPPI VALLEY

A number of species of the cave blindfishes, swamp fishes, and spring fishes (*Amblyopsidae*) of the central and eastern United States are potentially endangered by swamp drainage and other factors contributing to the lowering of the water table. Three other small fish of the eastern states have been affected by isolation and/or destruction of habitat. Two of these, a "pigmy sunfish" confined to one spring in the Tennessee River drainage (and possibly extinct) and a "darter" of swift southern mountain rivers, are not as yet scientifically described.

Maryland darter, *Etheostoma sellare* (Radcliffe and Welsh) [extinct]

Three eastern suckers have been affected by siltation of their waters:

harelip sucker, *Lagochila lacera* Jordan and Brayton [extinct]

blue sucker, *Cycleptus elongatus* (LeSueur)

copper redhorse, *Moxostoma hubbsi* Legendre

Two trouts, relict forms derived from the Arctic char, may be endangered through isolation:

Sunapee trout, *Salvelinus aureolus* Bean
A beautiful deep-water trout found originally in Sunapee Lake, New Hampshire, and in Floods Pond, near Ellsworth, Maine. Now confined, in its pure strain, to the latter pond, this fish has been known to hybridize with the lake trout, and mixed strains have been successfully propagated in New Hampshire.

blueback trout, *Salvelinus oquassa* (Girard)
A striking blue-and-salmon trout thought to have become extinct in the early 1900s in its known habitat, the Rangeley Lakes of western Maine, this species was rediscovered in 1948 in lakes farther north. Originally a victim of over-fishing as well as of the predations of land-locked salmon, the blueback is probably not now in danger, though further study is needed.

WESTERN FISHES

A number of small species found in isolated springs or holes throughout the Great Basin and other regions of the West must be considered endangered, due largely to their restricted and vulnerable habitats. The following are representative:

Devil's Hole pupfish, *Cyprinodon diabolis* Wales

OWENS PUPFISH

Owens pupfish, *Cyprinodon radiosus* Miller
  This species was formerly very abundant in the northern Owens Valley of
  California, in ditches, sloughs, and bog pastures, but suffered through introduction of large-mouth bass and through drainage. Unrecorded since 1939, it
  is probably extinct.

Leon Springs pupfish, *Cyprinodon bovinus* Baird and Girard
  Described from sixteen specimens taken near Fort Stockton, Texas, in 1851.
  Though searched for carefully in 1938 and 1950, it appears to have gone
  extinct, due probably to the introduction of exotic species.

Big Bend gambusia, *Gambusia gaigei* Hubbs [extinct]

Mohave chub, *Siphateles mohavensis* Snyder

thicktail chub, *Gila crassicauda* (Baird and Girard)
  Formerly in lowland waters of Central Valley, California, but much reduced
  by drier climate, irrigation, and introduction of predatory fishes. Only two
  have been collected in the last two decades, and possibly it is now extinct.

western topminnow, *Poeciliopsis occidentalis* (Baird and Girard)
  This species was once widespread in the Gila River basin of Arizona, but is
  now seriously reduced in range due to destruction of habitat and competition
  with an introduced eastern relative, *Gambusia affinis*.

MOHAVE CHUB

A number of larger forms are also endangered or extinct due to irrigation and
drainage:

  cui-ui, *Chasmistes cujus* Cope

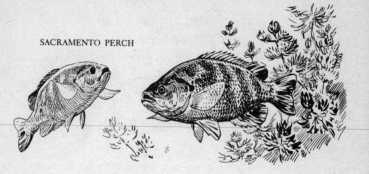

SACRAMENTO PERCH

June sucker, *Chasmistes liorus* Jordan
A small relative of the cui-ui once abundant in Utah Lake, but now extinct, or nearly so.

Colorado River squawfish, *Ptychocheilus lucius* Girard

Sacramento perch, *Archoplites interruptus* (Girard)
The only native sunfish west of the Rockies has decreased greatly in its original range in northern California due to competition of introduced species.

grayling, *Thymallus arcticus signifer* (Richardson)
Subspecies.

A number of western trouts are extinct or endangered, chiefly due to the introduction into isolated waters of competing forms, particularly the rainbow and the European brown trouts:

San Gorgonio trout, *Salmo evermanni* Jordan and Grinnell
This fish disappeared from the south fork of the Santa Ana River, California, about 1935, and is now presumed extinct; it could not compete or withstand a tendency to hybridize with the rainbow.

emerald trout, *Salmo smaragdus* Snyder
The status of this fish is uncertain; it may be a distinct species, or it may be a form of rainbow. Confined to Pyramid Lake, Nevada, where the last specimen was taken in 1915, it is now presumed extinct.

royal silver trout, *Salmo regalis* Snyder
Status as above. "A trout of immense size" (Jordan and Evermann) found in the deep waters of Lake Tahoe, California-Nevada. Unreported for many years, it is now presumed extinct.

Gila trout, *Salmo gilae* Miller
Status as above. Perhaps better regarded as a subspecies.

GREAT LAKES FISHES

lake sturgeon, *Acipenser fulvescens* Rafinesque
Extinct in United States river systems and very scarce throughout most of range. Still common in Lake Winnebago, Wisconsin, and in the St. Lawrence

River, but very rare in Great Lakes as a result of overfishing. Siltation and pollution of its spawning streams make its restoration there unlikely.

The large fishes of the Great Lakes, not including the sturgeon, have been most seriously reduced by the predations of the sea lamprey, but the lake trout, lake white-fish, and blackfin cisco are widespread elsewhere and are not endangered as species. The following ciscoes are confined to the Great Lakes and may be nearing extinction:

deepwater chub, *Coregonus johannae* (Wagner)

longjaw chub, *Coregonus alpenae* (Koelz)

kiyi, *Coregonus kiyi* (Koelz)

AMPHIBIANS AND REPTILES

Amphibians and reptiles, for the most part nocturnal and secretive, are not nearly so menaced by man's activity as are, for example, the birds and larger mammals. Only the common bullfrog among the amphibians and the green turtle among the reptiles are still economically significant, though the alligator, diamond-back terrapin, and hawksbill turtle were formerly commercial species, and a few small species of both groups are still taken commonly as pets.

A great many amphibian and reptile subspecies are of very local distribution, but only those generally recognized as distinct species are listed below; the Deep Springs toad and Las Vegas frog, the status of which is still disputed, are included. Nomenclature and classification follow the usages recognized by Conant (*A Field Guide to Reptiles and Amphibians of Eastern North America*, Boston: Houghton Mifflin, 1958) and Stebbins (*Amphibians and Reptiles of Western North America*, New York: McGraw-Hill, 1954).

The amphibians and reptiles of Canada and Alaska are relatively few in number and are, for the most part, northern populations of species common within the United States. A single exception, the Alaska worm salamander, is considered here, though others may appear with the advance of field research in these areas.

OCOEE SALAMANDER

AMPHIBIANS   (General discussion, Chapters 2 and 6)
A number of distinct species of salamanders are limited to single springs, pools, mountain sides or cave systems. The following are perhaps the rarest known at present, but others doubtless exist which have yet to be found.

Georgia blind salamander, *Haideotriton wallacei* [extinct?]

Ocoee salamander, *Desmognathus ocoee*
    Known only from Ships Prow Rock, Ocoee Gorge, in southeast Tennessee.

San Marcos salamander, *Eurycea nana*

Valdina Farms salamander, *Eurycea troglodytes*
    Known only from a cave, the Valdina Farms Sinkhole, in Medina County,

VALDINA FARMS SALAMANDER

Texas. Possibly a race of the Texas salamander, *E. neotenes*, a species which includes a number of very localized forms.

Mariposa salamander, *Hydromantes brunus*
A new species known only from one small area of hillside near the confluence of the Bear Creek and Merced Rivers, Mariposa County, California.

Alaska worm salamander, *Batrachoseps caudatus*

MARIPOSA SALAMANDER

One toad and one frog of doubtful status should probably be included:

Deep Springs toad, *Bufo exsul*
A small black toad confined to Deep Springs, in the dry desert valley between the White and Inyo Mountains of California, this form could easily be exterminated by climatic change, or by collectors. Probably a subspecies of the western toad, *B. boreas*.

Las Vegas frog, *Rana fisheri*
Endemic to springs since drained in the settlement of Las Vegas, Nevada, and last recorded in 1942. Presumed extinct. Probably a subspecies of the common leopard frog, *R. pipiens*.

DEEP SPRINGS TOAD

REPTILES   (General discussion, Chapters 2 and 6)

Two crocodilians occur in North America. One, the American alligator, *Alligator mississippiensis*, occurs sparingly in the Gulf States and north to North Carolina. The other, while still relatively common in the Greater Antilles, Central America, Ecuador, and Colombia, is in serious danger of extirpation from this continent.

American crocodile, *Crocodylus acutus* Cuvier

green turtle, *Chelonia mydas.*

Two American fresh-water turtles are of very narrow distribution:

bog turtle, *Clemmys muhlenbergii*
Formerly called Muhlenberg's turtle, this small, pretty species once occurred throughout the East, but the destruction of its swamps and sphagnum bogs through drainage has limited it to a few widely separated localities, from New York south to western North Carolina.

BOG TURTLE

flattened musk turtle, *Sternothaerus depressus*
"An extraordinary little turtle that looks almost as though a man with a heavy foot had trod upon it" (Conant). Extensive drainage in its small range in northwest Alabama could endanger it.

Like the salamanders, the lizards of North America, the Gila monster excepted, are endangered only when their distribution is very local:

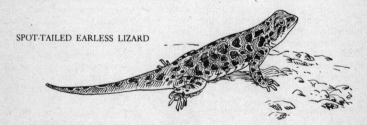

SPOT-TAILED EARLESS LIZARD

spot-tailed earless lizard, *Holbrookia lacerata*
Known from two scarce races in central and southern Texas (the southern race occurs also in Coahuila), this lizard may be a decadent form, declining slowly in numbers. Its status is uncertain: possibly it is a geographical race of one of the more common earless lizards.

alligator lizard, *Gerrhonotus* ——?
> A new species, not as yet scientifically described, "known only from Surprise Canyon on the west slope of the Panamint Mountains west of Death Valley" (Stebbins). Five specimens and three cast skins have been located.

Gila monster, *Heloderma suspectum*

Arizona worm lizard, *Bipes* ——?
> Possibly a form of the two-footed worm lizard, *B. caniculatus*, of Mexico.

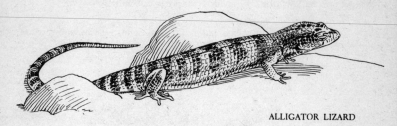

ALLIGATOR LIZARD

North American snakes, and especially the poisonous species, are persecuted regularly, and although a number of forms are localized or uncommon, only one is genuinely rare:

> Brazos water snake, *Natrix harteri*

BIRDS

With the possible exception of the large mammals, the birds of North America have been most seriously affected by the coming of the white man, largely as a consequence of wasteful exploitation for food and feathers but also because, in many cases, of the alteration or destruction of habitat. At least seven species are already extinct, and, although conservation measures in the past half-century have restored many forms to relative abundance, the myriad birds which awed the first explorers are gone forever.

The endangered birds to be treated here are not necessarily chosen on the basis of actual numbers, since what might be a healthy population for an inherently solitary or localized species could be extremely unhealthy for a widespread, gregarious, and economically significant form; except in cases where the scarcity of a particular species makes its peril implicit, emphasis will be placed on those birds still declining in the face of civilization. Subspecies and geographic races, except in a few specified cases of unusual historic or scientific interest (e.g. the heath hen), will not be considered; nor will the Eurasian or tropical species which appear more or less regularly in North America, particularly in Alaska, eastern Canada, south Florida and the Keys, and along the Mexican border—unless, of course, they are, or have been, well established. The great majority of these birds are common enough within their normal range, and on this continent are "rare birds" only in a technical sense; they might more properly be called "common accidentals."

Species are listed here by scientific orders, beginning with the most primitive groups and concluding with the perching birds. Nomenclature and classification follow usages adopted in the A.O.U. *Checklist of North American Birds* (see Bibliography).

GAVIIFORMES (loons):
  None (i.e., no recent species endangered).

COLYMBIFORMES (grebes):
  None.

PROCELLARIIFORMES (albatrosses and allies):
  short-tailed albatross, *Diomedea albatrus*
  Guadalupe petrel, *Oceanodroma macrodactyla* [extinct]
  Bermuda petrel (cahow), *Pterodroma cahow*
  black-capped petrel, *Pterodroma hasitata* [extinct?]

PELICANIFORMES (pelicans and allies):
  Pallas cormorant, *Phalacrocorax perspicillatus* [extinct]
    Hypothetical in North America.

CICONIIFORMES (herons and allies):
  great white heron, *Ardea occidentalis*
  roseate spoonbill, *Ajaia ajaja*

ANSERIFORMES (swans, geese, and ducks):
  trumpeter swan, *Olor buccinator*
  Ross's goose, *Chen rossii*
  Labrador duck, *Camptorhynchus labradorium* [extinct]

FALCONIFORMES (vultures, hawks, and allies):
  California condor, *Gymnogyps californianus*
  swallow-tailed kite, *Elanoides forficatus*
  white-tailed kite, *Elanus leucurus*
  Mississippi kite, *Ictinia mississippiensis*
  Everglade kite, *Rostrhamus sociabilis*
  short-tailed hawk, *Buteo brachyurus*
  white-tailed hawk, *Buteo albicaudatus*
  golden eagle, *Aquila chrysaetos*
  bald eagle, *Haliaeetus leucocephalus*
  Aplomado falcon, *Falco femoralis*

GALLIFORMES (grouse, quail, and allies):
  prairie chicken, *Tympanuchus cupido*
    subspecies: Attwater's prairie chicken, *T.c. attwateri*
                heath hen, *T.c. cupido* [extinct]
                northern prairie chicken, *T.c. pinnatus*
  lesser prairie chicken, *Tympanuchus pallicidinctus*
  masked bobwhite (subspecies), *Colinus virginianus ridgwayi*
  harlequin quail, *Cyrtonyx montezumae*

GRUIFORMES (cranes, rails, and allies):
  whooping crane, *Grus americana*

CHARADRIIFORMES.
  Suborder CHARADRII (shore birds):
    Hudsonian godwit, *Limosa haemastica*
    Eskimo curlew, *Numenius borealis* [extinct]
  Suborder LARI (gulls, terns, and allies):
    Aleutian tern, *Sterna aleutica*

Suborder ALCAE (auks and allies):
   great auk, *Pinguinus impennis* [extinct]

COLUMBIFORMES (pigeons and doves)
   passenger pigeon, *Ectopistes migratorius* [extinct]

PSITTACIFORMES (parrots):
   Carolina parakeet, *Conuropsis carolinensis* [extinct]

STRIGIFORMES (owls):
   None.

CAPRIMULGIFORMES (whip-poor-wills and allies):
   None.

APODIFORMES (swifts and hummingbirds):
   black swift, *Cypseloides niger*

CORACIIFORMES (kingfishers):
   None.

PICIFORMES (woodpeckers):
   ivory-billed woodpecker, *Campephilus principalis* [extinct?]
   red-cockaded woodpecker. *Deudrocopos borealis*

PASSERIFORMES (perching birds):
   Kirtland's warbler, *Dendroica kirtlandii*
   Sutton's warbler, *Dendroica potomac*
      Disputed species, not recognized by A.O.U
   Colima warbler, *Vermivora crissalis*
   Bachman's warbler, *Vermivora bachmanii*
   Townsend bunting, *Spiza townsendi* [extinct]
      Disputed species, not recognized by A.O.U.
   Cape Sable sparrow, *Ammospiza mirabilis*
      Disputed species, though recognized by A.O.U
   Ipswich sparrow, *Passerculus princeps*
      Disputed species, though recognized by A.O.U.

The following species, while not presently endangered, could become so with any significant decline:

American egret	limpkin
reddish egret	golden plover
glossy ibis	long-billed curlew
wood stork	upland plover
caracara	whiskered auklet
peregrine falcon	band-tailed pigeon
prairie falcon	burrowing owl
Franklin's grouse	raven
sage hen	

MAMMALS

The history of North American mammals closely parallels that of the birds, and a comparable reduction has taken place among those forms pursued for food and clothing, as predators, and in the name of sport, often in combination with the destruction of habitat. Though fewer species have become extinct, a number of sub-species have disappeared, all of them representing significant populations of their species. This is true of virtually all the large terrestrial mammals of the continent. The carnivores, which include the more valuable furbearers as well as the predators, have been seriously diminished as a group, as have the hoofed mammals, most of which are prized game species and all of which have the misfortune of being highly edible. The other orders have been less affected, though numerous marine mammals are threatened. The small mammals, like the small species of all the vertebrate classes, are not often endangered except when their distributions are so localized as to be subject to change. Three examples of particular interest, and two other small mammals now precarious for reasons not based on local distribution, are included here.

As in the case of the birds, the mammals are listed by order. Nomenclature and classification follow the usages adopted in Miller and Kellogg's *List of North American Recent Mammals* (see Bibliography).

MARSUPIALIA (opossums and allies):
    None.

INSECTIVORA (moles and shrews):
    Certain shrews are very limited in distribution, but none seem rare enough to justify inclusion here.

CHIROPTERA (bats):
    spotted bat, *Euderma maculata*

CARNIVORA.
  Family URSIDAE (bears):
    glacier bear (subspecies), *Euarctos americanus emmonsii*
    grizzly bear, *Ursus horribilis*
    Kodiak bear, *Ursus middendorffi*
      Disputed species, though recognized by Miller and Kellogg.
    Alaska Peninsula bear, *Ursus gyas*
      Status as above.
  Family MUSTELIDAE (weasels and allies):
    fisher, *Martes pennanti*
    sea mink, *Mustela macrodon* [extinct]
    black-footed ferret, *Mustela nigripes*
    sea otter, *Enhydra lutris*
  Family CANIDAE (wolves and allies):
    kit fox, *Vulpes velox*
    desert kit fox, *Vulpes macrotis*
      Disputed species, though recognized by Miller and Kellogg.
    red wolf, *Canis niger*
    gray wolf, *Canis lupus*
  Family FELIDAE (cats):
    ocelot, *Felis pardalis*
    jaguar, *Felis onca*
    cougar, *Felis concolor*

PINNIPEDIA (seals, sea lions, walruses):
  Guadalupe fur seal, *Arctocephalus townsendi*
  elephant seal, *Mirounga angustirostris*
  ribbon seal, *Phoca fasciata*
  gray seal, *Halichoerus grypus*
  West Indian monk seal, *Monachus tropicalis*
  walrus, *Odobenus rosmarus*
  Pacific walrus, *Odobenus divergens*
    Disputed species, not recognized by Miller and Kellogg.

RODENTIA (rodents):
  Kaibab squirrel, *Sciurus kaibabensis*
  blacktail prairie dog, *Cynomys ludovicianus*
  whitetail prairie dog, *Cynomys gunnisoni*
  Muskeget Island beach mouse, *Microtus breweri*
    Disputed species, though recognized by Miller and Kellogg.
  Gull Island vole, *Microtus nesophilus* [extinct]
    Status as above.

LAGOMORPHA (pikas, hares, rabbits):
  None.

ARTIODACTYLA (hoofed mammals):
  key deer (subspecies), *Odocoileus virginianus clavium*
  Merriam elk, *Cervus merriami* [extinct]
    Disputed species, though recognized by Miller and Kellogg.
  tule elk, *Cervus nannodes*
    Status as above.
  woodland caribou, *Rangifer caribou*
  Dawson caribou (subspecies), *Rangifer articus dawsoni* [extinct]
  bison, *Bison bison*
  musk ox, *Ovibos moschatus*
  bighorn sheep, *Ovis canadensis*

XENARTHRA (armadillos and allies):
  None.

SIRENIA (manatees and allies):
  manatee, *Trichechus manatus*
  rhytina, *Rhytina gigas*
    Not recognized as North American species by Miller and Kellogg.

CETACEA (porpoises and whales):
  Northern right whale, *Eubalaena glacialis*
  bowhead whale, *Eubalaena mysticetus*
  gray whale, *Rhachianectes glaucus*
  blue whale, *Sibbaldus musculus*
  Sowerby whale, *Mesoplodon bidens*
  Gervais whale, *Mesoplodon europaeus*
  Stejneger's whale, *Mesoplodon stejnegeri*

Appendix II:

A Chronology of Representative Legislation Affecting North American Wildlife

1616–1622 First New World wildlife protection: The government of Bermuda issues proclamations protecting the cahow and the green turtle.

1629 The West India Company grants hunting rights to persons planting colonies in the New Netherlands.

1630 First New World bounty system: Massachusetts Bay Colony authorizes payment of one penny per wolf.

1694 First closed season (on deer), in Massachusetts.

1708 First closed season on birds: in certain New York counties, on heath hen, grouse, quail, turkey.

1710 Massachusetts prohibits use of camouflaged canoes, or boats equipped with sails, in pursuit of waterfowl.

1718 Massachusetts establishes first closed term (three years) on deer.

1739 First warden system (Massachusetts). (New York, 1741.)

1776 First federal game law: closed seasons on deer established in all colonies except Georgia.

1782 Bald eagle recognized as national emblem.

1818 First law protecting non-game birds, establishing a closed season on larks and robins in Massachusetts.

1830 First closed season on moose, in Maine.

1831 Massachusetts establishes closed season on heath hen. A closed term of four years established in 1837.

1838 First law against use of batteries, or multiple guns, on waterfowl; later repealed (New York).

1846 First law against spring shooting (wood duck, black duck, woodcock, snipe); later repealed (Rhode Island).

1848 Massachusetts passes law protecting pigeon netters from molestation.

1851 Non-game bird protection established in Vermont; subsequently in Massachusetts (1855) and ten other states (by 1864).

1852 First closed season on antelope and elk, in California

1861 First closed season on mountain goats, mountain sheep, in Nevada. Closed term of ten years on heath hen, in New York.

1864 First protection of bison, in Idaho; closed season (February 1–July 1) on bison, deer, elk, antelope, goat, sheep.

1869   First pigeon protection, in Michigan and later Pennsylvania (1878): no fire-arms to be discharged within one mile of roosts.
New York establishes closed term of five years on moose (Long Island).

1870   First closed season on caribou, in Maine.

1871   Establishment of Federal Commission of Fish and Fisheries (later Bureau of Fisheries).
New York establishes thirty-dollar bounty on Adirondack wolves.

1872   First law providing rest days for waterfowl, in Maryland.
Establishment of Yellowstone Park, first national park.

1874   A Bill "to prevent the useless slaughter of buffaloes within the Territories of the United States" is passed by Congress but is pigeon-holed by President Grant.

1875   First law prohibiting market hunting of waterfowl, in Arkansas.

1877   Florida passes a plume-bird law prohibiting wanton destruction of eggs and young.

1878   First state game departments and commissions set up, in California and New Hampshire.
First law establishing bag limits on gamebirds, in Iowa.

1879   Ten-year closed term on elk established in Michigan.

1885   Establishment of Banff National Park, first national park in Canada.

1886   Territorial legislatures forbidden by Congress to pass laws protecting fish and game.
A.O.U. "Model Law" for bird protection first promoted.
Establishment of federal Division of Economic Ornithology and Mammalogy (later Division of Biological Survey).

1890   Ten-year closed term on buffalo, in Wyoming.

1894   Park Protection Act provides protection for wildlife in national parks of the United States.

1895   Modern system of resident and nonresident hunting licenses established in a number of states.

1896   The Supreme Court (Geer vs. Connecticut) decrees that game is the property of the state rather than the landowner.

1897   Law providing a two-year prison term for the "felony" of killing buffalo, in Montana.

1900   Lacey Bill forbids importation of foreign creatures without permit; also, interstate traffic in creatures killed in violation of state laws.

1901   New England states (except Rhode Island), New York, New Jersey, and West Virginia respond to alarm issued by Biological Survey, establish closed terms on wood duck.
Nevada places game protection in curriculum of public school education; also, Oklahoma (1905).

1902   First law protecting brown bears, in Alaska.

1903   First federal wildlife refuge established, at Pelican Island, Florida.

1905   Law providing a two-year prison term for the "felony" of killing elk, in California.

1906   Congress refuses appropriations for further investigations by President Roosevelt's Natural Resources Committee.
Canada passes Northwest Game Act, requiring the licensing of fur traders.

1908   President Roosevelt sets up National Conservation Commission under Gifford Pinchot.

1909   Antelope removed from list of game animals everywhere in its range except Arizona (which followed suit in 1911) and Canada.

1910   Federal act prohibiting the taking of sea otters in Alaskan waters.
New York establishes law prohibiting sale of wild game (Bayne Bill), also the possession for sale, offering for sale, or sale of wild bird plumage.

1911   "Seal Treaty" controlling the take of fur seals and sea otters (the latter still receive complete protection) signed by United States, Great Britain, Russia, Japan.
Elephant seal protected by Mexican government.

1913   Federal Tariff Act bars importation into United States of wild bird plumage.
Weeks-McLean Act awards responsibility for migratory game birds to the Biological Survey.

1914   Act of Congress authorizes funds for the control of wolves, prairie dogs, and other injurious animals.

1916   Ratification of Convention between United States and Great Britain for Protection of the Migratory Game Birds in United States and Canada, including full protection for band-tailed pigeon, cranes, swans, most shore birds (administered after 1918 by the Biological Survey).

1918   Federal Migratory Bird Treaty Act prohibits spring shooting, awards to government the right to prescribe bag limits of migratory birds.
United States and Canada give full protection to wood duck (until 1941).

1925   Passage of Alaska Game Law, setting up Alaska Game Commission under Biological Survey and establishing bird and mammal protection equivalent to state laws in the United States.

1929   Law for the protection of the diamond-back terrapin, in Maryland.
Norbeck-Andresen Migratory Bird Conservation Act provides for further acquisition of waterfowl refuge land.

1934   Migratory Bird Hunting Stamp Act establishes federal hunting license in form of "duck stamp."
Fish and game sanctuaries authorized in suitable National Forest areas.

1936   First North American Wildlife Conference called by President F. D. Roosevelt.

1937   International Whaling Convention establishes seasons, whaling grounds, etc., gives full protection to gray whale, right whales.
Pittman-Robertson Federal Aid in Wildlife Restoration Act establishes excise taxes on guns, ammunition, for use in wildlife projects in United States.
Treaty with Mexico for protection of migratory birds and mammals.

1939–   Reorganization Act transfers Bureau of Biological Survey and Bureau of
1940   Fisheries from Department of Agriculture and Department of Commerce, respectively, merges them under Department of Interior as Fish and Wildlife Service.

1940   Bald eagle receives full protection throughout United States. Also, Alaska (1952).

1950   Dingell-Johnson Fish Restoration Act (equivalent of Pittman-Robertson wildlife act).

1952   Law for protection of the Gila monster, in Arizona.

1956   Water Pollution Control Act, including grants-in-aid for communities willing to act on sewage and industrial pollution problems.

1957   Coordination Act separates Fish and Wildlife Service into Bureau of Commercial Fisheries and Bureau of Sports Fisheries and Wildlife.

1959?   Wilderness Bill, first introduced in 1956 but as yet unpassed, would protect for posterity wilderness areas now under government control but subject to change in administration, leasing, etc., and eventual deterioration.

Reference Notes

(For full information about incomplete references, see Bibliography. The abbreviated listing "America" refers to America: A Library of Original Sources [Chicago: Veterans of Foreign Wars, 1925].)

The lines from "Sunday Morning" on page 17 are from The Collected Poems of Wallace Stevens (New York: Knopf, 1954).

CHAPTER 1: THE OUTLYING ROCKS

Epigraph. Quoted in Joel A. Allen.
1. Aldo Leopold, A Sand County Almanac.
2. "Saga of Eric the Red," in America, Vol. I.
3. In America, Vol. I.
4. Labrador Journal, quoted in Fisher and Lockley.
5. Manual of the Ornithology of the United States and Canada.
6. Journals of Columbus, quoted in Welker.
7. Quoted in Bent, Life Histories of . . . Petrels. . . .
8. J. B. Labat, Nouveau Voyage aux Isles de l'Amérique, 1722 (ibid.).

CHAPTER 2: THE TROPICAL BORDER

Epigraph. The Whole and True Discouerye of Terra Florida, 1563, quoted in Lorant.
1. Quoted in Bakeless.
2. Lawson.
3. Brandt, Arizona and Its Bird Life.
4. "The World Encompassed by Sir Francis Drake," in America, Vol. I.
5. Captains Arthur Barlowe and Philip Amadas, report to Sir Walter Raleigh on the first voyage to Roanoke, 1685, in America, Vol. II.

CHAPTER 3: THE EASTERN SLOPE

Epigraph. History of Plimouth Plantation, quoted in America, Vol. II.
1. Ibid.
2. George Percy, Observations . . . , quoted in Nevins and Commager.
3. History of Plimouth Plantation, loc. cit.
4. Quoted in Bakeless.
5. Letter to England, 1621, in America, Vol. II.
6. New English Canaan.
7. Letters of George and Leonard Calvert, 1634, quoted in America, Vol. II.
8. "God's Controversy with New England."
9. Philosophical Transactions, quoted in Barton.
10. New England's Rarities, quoted in Forbush, Game Birds. . . .
11. Elsa G. Allen.
12. Quoted in Joel A. Allen.
13. Governor John Winthrop, quoted in Nuttall.
14. Wilson, The American Ornithology.

CHAPTER 4: FUR COUNTRIES AND FOREST LAKES

Epigraph. *Arctic Zoology.*
1. Quoted in Bakeless.
2. *Travels and Discoveries in North America,* quoted in *America,* Vol. II.
3. *A Journey from Hudson Bay to the Arctic,* 1795, quoted in Swainson and Richardson.
4. Nuttall.
5. *The Ornithological Biography.*
6. Coues.
7. ? Beltrami, *La Découverte des Sources du Mississippi,* 1825, quoted in Godman.
8. Quoted in *America,* Vol. III.
9. *A Natural History of Uncommon Birds. . . .*
10. Manly Hardy, in Beard et al.
11. *Journals of Captain Meriwether Lewis,* quoted in *America,* Vol. V.
12. Quoted in Godman.
13. Witmer Stone, with W. E. Cram, *American Animals* (New York: Doubleday, Page, 1902).

CHAPTER 5: OCEAN COASTS AND THE HIGH SEAS

Epigraphs. Secretary Edward Randolph, King's Commissioner, quoted in Stackpole. Melville, *Moby Dick.*
1. Quoted in Godman.
2. Quoted in Stackpole.
3. *History of Nantucket,* quoted in Stackpole.
4. Log of the *Phebe* (ibid.).
5. Quoted in Bakeless.
6. Journals of Steller, quoted in Golder.
7. *Contributions to the Natural History of Alaska.*
8. *Key to North American Birds.*
9. Quoted in Golder.
10. *Arctic Zoology.*
11. *Voyages and Discoveries in the South Seas.*
12. Ibid.
13. Blaine, 1890, quoted in *America,* Vol. IX.
14. Thompson.
15. *The Marine Mammals of the North-Western Coast of North America.*

CHAPTER 6: HIDDEN WORLDS

Epigraph. Quoted in Audubon, *The Ornithological Biography.*
1. Welker.
2. *Travels through North and South Carolina. . . .*
3. All Wilson quotations on pages 114–116 are from *The American Ornithology.*
4. From Wilson's diaries, appended to Vol. IX of *The American Ornithology* by Ord. Quoted in Welker.
5. *Key to North American Birds.*
6. Letter to Audubon, 1830, quoted in Herrick.
7. Schorger.
8. *The Ornithological Biography.*
9. Quoted in Ford.
10. *The Ornithological Biography.*
11. *Key to North American Birds.*
12. Hamilton.
13. *The Auk,* Vol. XV, 1898.
14. Cahalane, "Status of the Black-Footed Ferret."
15. *The Mammals of North America.*

CHAPTER 7: PLAINS, PRAIRIES, AND THE SHINING MOUNTAINS

Epigraphs. Cooper, *The Prairie.* Audubon, *Missouri River Journals,* quoted in Ford.
1. Quoted in Ford.
2. *Missouri River Journals,* quoted in Ford.

3. Alonzo Delano, *Life on the Plains and among the Diggings,* 1854, quoted in *America,* Vol. VII.
4. *Prairie and Forest.*
5. Lewis, quoted in Godman.
6. *A Journey from Hudson Bay to the Arctic,* 1795, quoted in Swainson and Richardson.
7. *Missouri River Journals,* quoted in Ford.
8. Cody, *True Tales of the Plains,* quoted in *America,* Vol. IX.
9. Durward L. Allen.
10. *Our Wild Indians. . . .*
11. Theodore Roosevelt, quoted in Cutright.
12. *Key to North American Birds.*
13. Quoted in Huth.
14. *Our National Parks,* quoted in Teale, ed., *The Wilderness World of John Muir.*

CHAPTER 8: THE HIGH AIR OF A CONTINENT

Epigraph. *Prairie and Forest.*
1. Hornaday, *Our Vanishing Wildlife.*
2. Aldo Leopold, *A Sand County Almanac.*
3. Forbush, *Game Birds. . . .*
4. A. C. Dent, quoted in Bodsworth.
5. *Key to North American Birds.*
6. Ibid.
7. Letter to Sarah Bache, Jan. 26, 1784.
8. Quoted in Welker.
9. *Key to North American Birds.*
10. "On the Decrease of Birds. . . ."
11. *Adventures in Bird Protection.*
12. Quoted in Cutright.
13. Ibid.
14. *The Ornithological Biography.*
15. *Handbook of Birds of Eastern North America.*
16. *Story of My Boyhood and Youth,* quoted in Teale, ed., *The Wilderness World of John Muir.*

CHAPTER 9: THE END OF THE WILDERNESS ROAD

Epigraph. Preface to *The Oregon Trail.*
1. Letter cited in Young.
2. "The Larger North American Mammals."
3. Vernon Bailey.
4. Thomas Bewick.
5. R. P. Boone, "Deer Management on the Kaibab," *Transactions of the North American Wildlife Conference,* 1938, quoted in Durward L. Allen.
6. Young.
7. *Birds and Poets,* quoted in Welker.
8. Pennant.
9. *Reptiles of the World.*
10. Muir, quote in Teale, ed., *The Wilderness World of John Muir.*

CHAPTER 10: OLD FIELDS

Epigraphs. Glasgow, *Barren Ground* (New York: Doubleday, 1925). Faulkner, "Delta Autumn," in *Go Down, Moses* (New York: Random House, 1942). Steinbeck, *The Grapes of Wrath* (New York: Viking, 1939).
1. Durward L. Allen.
2. Hesse et al.
3. Gabrielson, *Wildlife Conservation.*
4. *Thirty Years War for Wildlife.*
5. *Deserts on the March.*
6. Engle, Clair.
7. "Conservation: Down and Out."
8. Ibid.
9. Quoted by Clarence Cottam in conversation with the author.
10. George Wallace, address to the annual meeting of the Audubon Society, Nov. 10, 1958, New York City.
11. U. S. Dept. of Agriculture, in response to inquiries by the National Audubon Society.

CHAPTER 11: LAND OF THE NORTH WIND

Epigraphs. Thoreau, *Walden*. Peterson, *Wild America*.
1. *Alaska and Its Resources*.
2. Ibid.
3. Scammon.
4. *Cruise of the Corwin*, quoted in Teale, ed., *The Wilderness World of John Muir*.
5. Ibid.
6. "The Present Status . . . of the Larger Mammals of Canada."

CHAPTER 12: ANOTHER HEAVEN AND ANOTHER EARTH

Epigraph. *The Bird: Its Form and Function*.
1. Swainson and Richardson.
2. *Manual of the Ornithology of the United States and Canada*.
3. *On the Trail of Vanishing Birds*.
4. *The American Ornithology*.
5. Robert P. Allen, *On the Trail of Vanishing Birds*.

Bibliography

Bibliography is a necessary nuisance and a horrible drudgery that no mere drudge could perform. It takes a sort of inspired idiot to be a good bibliographer and his inspiration is as dangerous a gift as the appetite of the gambler or dipsomaniac—it grows with what it feeds upon and finally possesses its victim like any other invincible vice.

—ELLIOTT COUES (1892)

(USNMB: *United States National Museum Bulletin.* TNAWC: *Transactions of the North American Wildlife Conference.*)

Alexander, W. B. *Birds of the Ocean.* New York: Putnam, 1927.

Allen, Durward L. *Our Wildlife Legacy.* New York: Funk and Wagnalls, 1954.

Allen, Elsa G. *History of American Ornithology before Audubon.* Transactions of American Philosophical Society (Philadelphia), Vol. XLI, October 1951.

———. "New Light on Mark Catesby." *The Auk,* Vol. 54, 1937.

Allen, Glover M. *Extinct and Vanishing Mammals of the Western Hemisphere.* New York: American Committee for International Wildlife Protection, 1942.

Allen, Joel A. "On the Decrease of Birds in the United States." *Penn Monthly,* December 1876, pp. 931–944.

Allen, Robert P. *On the Trail of Vanishing Birds.* New York: McGraw-Hill, 1957.

———. "The Reddish Egret." *Audubon Magazine,* Vol. 56, No. 6–Vol. 57, No. 1.

America: A Library of Original Sources. Chicago: Veterans of Foreign Wars, 1925, 12 Vols.

American Ornithologists' Union. *The A.O.U. Checklist of North American Birds.* New York: American Ornithologists' Union, 1957.

———. "Destruction of Our Native Birds." A.O.U. Bulletin No. 1 of The Committee on Protection of Birds, 1886.

———. *Fifty Years' Progress of American Ornithology.* New York: American Ornithologists' Union, 1933.

Anderson, R. M. *Catalogue of Canadian Recent Mammals.* National Museum of Canada Bulletin No. 102, 1947.

———. "The Present Status and Distribution of the Big Game Mammals of Canada." *Transactions of the North American Wildlife Conference,* 1938, pp. 390–406.

———. "The Present Status and Future Prospects of the Larger Mammals of Canada." *Scottish Geographical Magazine,* Vol. XL, 1924.

Anthony, H. E. *Field Guide of North American Mammals.* New York: Putnam, 1928.

——— et al. *Animals of America.* New York: Garden City, 1937.

Audubon, John James. *The Ornithological Biography.* Edinburgh, 1831–1839, 5 Vols.

——— and Bachman, John. *The Viviparous Quadrupeds of North America.* 1849–1854, 3 Vols.

Bailey, Alfred M. *Birds of Arctic Alaska.*

Denver: Colorado Museum of Natural History, 1948.

———. "Notes on Game Conditions in Alaska." Reprint, 1921.

Bailey, Vernon. Mammals of New Mexico, North American Fauna No. 53, U. S. Department of Agriculture, 1931.

Baird, Spencer F. The Birds of North America. Philadelphia, 1860.

———. The Mammals of North America. Philadelphia, 1859.

———; Brewer, T. M.; and Ridgway, R. North American Land Birds. Boston, 1874, 3 Vols.

Baker, John H. "Fifty Years of Progress in Furtherance of Audubon Objectives." Audubon Magazine, Vol. 57, No. 1.

———. "The Greatest Threat to Life on Earth." Outdoor American, June 1958.

Bakeless, John. The Eyes of Discovery. Philadelphia: Lippincott, 1950.

Barbour, Thomas. The Crocodile in Florida. Ann Arbor, Mich.: University of Michigan Press, 1923.

Barton, Benjamin S. Fragments of Natural History of Pennsylvania. Reprint, Philadelphia, 1883.

Bartram, William. Travels through North and South Carolina, Georgia, East and West Florida. Second ed., London, 1792.

Beard, Daniel B., et al. Fading Trails. New York: Macmillan, 1947.

Bent, A. C. Life Histories of North American Birds of Prey. USNMB No. 167, No. 170, 1937.

———. Life Histories of North American Gulls and Terns. USNMB No. 113, 1921.

———. Life Histories of North American Petrels, Pelicans, and Their Allies. USNMB No. 121, 1922.

———. Life Histories of North American Wood Warblers. USNMB No. 203, 1953.

Bewick, Thomas. A General History of Quadrupeds. Fourth ed., 1800.

Bishop, Sherman C. Handbook of Salamanders. Ithaca, N.Y.: Comstock Publishing Company, 1943.

Blair, W. F., et al. Vertebrates of the United States. New York: McGraw-Hill, 1957.

Blake, Ernest R. Birds of Mexico. Chicago: University of Chicago Press, 1953.

Bodsworth, Fred. Last of the Curlews. New York: Dodd, Mead, 1955.

Bonaparte, C. L. American Ornithology. Philadelphia, 1825.

Brandt, Herbert. Alaska Bird Trails. Cleveland: Bird Research Foundation, 1943.

———. Arizona and Its Bird Life. Cleveland: Bird Research Foundation, 1951.

Brooks, James W. "The Pacific Walrus and Its Importance." TNAWC, 1953.

Brooks, Maurice. "George Sutton and His Warbler." Audubon Magazine, Vol. 47, 1945.

Burt, William Henry, and Grossenheider, Richard Philip. A Field Guide to the Mammals. Boston: Houghton Mifflin, 1952.

Caesar, Gene. The Wild Hunters. New York: Putnam, 1957.

Cahalane, Victor H. Mammals of North America. New York: Macmillan, 1954.

———. "Status of the Black-Footed Ferret." Journal of Mammalogy, Vol. 35, No. 3, 1954.

Carr, Archie. Handbook of Turtles. Ithaca, N.Y.: Cornell University Press, 1952.

——— and Goin, Coleman J. Reptiles, Amphibians, and Fresh-Water Fishes of Florida. Gainesville, Fla.: University of Florida Press, 1955.

Catesby, Mark. The Natural History of Carolina . . . Second ed., London, 1754.

Chapman, Frank M. Handbook of Birds of Eastern North America. New York: Appleton, 1909.

Clemens, W. A., and Wilby, G. V. Fishes of the Pacific Coast of Canada. Ottawa: National Museum of Canada, 1949.

Conant, Roger. A Field Guide to Reptiles and Amphibians. Boston: Houghton Mifflin, 1958.

Coues, Elliott. *Key to North American Birds*. Fourth ed., Boston, 1892.

Cutright, Paul R. *Theodore Roosevelt the Naturalist*. New York: Harper, 1956.

Dall, William H. *Alaska and Its Resources*. Boston, 1870.

Davidson, M. E. McLellan. "On the Present Status of the Guadalupe Petrel." *The Condor*, Vol. 30, 1928.

de Schauensee, R. M. *Rare and Extinct Birds in the Academy of Natural Sciences of Philadelphia*. Bulletin of, Vol. XCIII, 1941.

De Voto, Bernard. "Conservation: Down and Out." *Harper's*, August 1954.

Ditmars, Raymond L. *Reptiles of the World*. New York: Macmillan, 1937.

Dixon, James B., et al. "Natural History of the White-Tailed Kite in San Diego County, California." *The Condor*, Vol. 59, 1957.

Dodge, R. I. *Our Wild Indians*. . . . Hartford, 1882.

Dufresne, Frank. *Alaska's Animals and Fishes*. New York: A. S. Barnes, 1946.

Dutcher, William. "History of the Audubon Movement." *Bird-Lore*, Vol. VII, 1905.

Edwards, George. *A Natural History of Uncommon Birds* . . . London, 1743.

Everhart, W. Harry. *Fishes of Maine*. Department of Inland Fisheries and Game, 1950.

Engle, Honorable Clair. "Stopping the Military Land Grab," *National Parks Magazine*, October-December, 1956.

Fanning, Captain Edmund. *Voyages and Discoveries in the South Seas, 1792-1832*. Salem, Mass.: Marine Research Society, 1924.

Finch, L. Boyd. "The Florida Swamp That Swallows Your Money," *Harper's Magazine*, February 1959.

Fisher, James, and Lockley, R. M. *Sea-Birds*. Boston: Houghton Mifflin, 1954.

Forbush, Edward Howe. *Birds of Massachusetts and Other New England States*. Boston: Massachusetts Department of Agriculture, 1925-1929, 3 Vols.

————. *Game Birds, Wild-Fowl, and Shorebirds*. Boston: Massachusetts Board of Agriculture, 1912.

Ford, Alice, *Audubon's Animals*. New York: Studio-Crowell, 1951.

Friedmann, Herbert. *The Birds of North and Middle America. Part XI: Birds of Prey*. USNMB No. 50, 1950.

Gabrielson, Ira. *Wildlife Conservation*. New York: Macmillan, 1947.

————. *Wildlife Refuges*. New York: Macmillan, 1943.

Gibson, W. Hamilton. *Camp Life and the Tricks of Trapping*. New York: Harper, 1891.

Gillmore, Parker. *Prairie and Forest*. New York: Harper, 1874.

Gilmore, Raymond M. "The Whaling Industry," in *Marine Products of Commerce*, ed. by Donald K. Tressler and James McW. Lemon. New York: Reinhold, 1951.

———— and Ewing, Gifford. "Calving of the California Grays," *Pacific Discovery*, Vol. II, No. 3, 1954.

Godman, John. *American Natural History*. Philadelphia, 1831, 3 Vols.

Golder, F. A. *Bering's Voyages*, Vol. II. New York: American Geographical Society, 1925.

Greenway, James C., Jr. *Extinct and Vanishing Birds of the World*. New York: American Committee for International Wildlife Protection, 1958.

Grieve, Symington. *The Great Auk*. London, 1885.

Griffith, Richard E. "What Is the Future of the Sea Otter?" TNAWC, 1953.

Griscom, Ludlow, et al. *The Warblers of North America*. New York: Devin-Adair, 1957.

Gross, Alfred O. *The Heath Hen*. Memoirs of the Boston Society of Natural History, 1928.

Hamilton, Andrew. "Lost Lakes of the Desert." *Westways*, February 1955.

Hays, W. J. "Notes on the Range of Some of the Animals in America at the Time of the Arrival of the White

Man." *American Naturalist*, Vol. 5, No. 7, 1871.

Herrick, Francis H. *Audubon the Naturalist*. New York: Appleton-Century, 1938.

Hesse, Richard; Allee, W. C.; and Schmidt, Karl P. *Ecological Animal Geography*. New York: Wiley, 1951.

Hewitt, C. Gordon. *The Conservation of the Wildlife of Canada*. New York: Scribner, 1921.

Hoffman, C. H. "The Truth About Chemical Controls." *American Forests*, November 1958.

Hornaday, William T. *Our Vanishing Wildlife*. New York Zoological Society, 1914.

———. *Thirty Years War for Wildlife*. New York: Scribner, 1931.

———. *Wildlife Conservation*. New Haven: Yale University Press, 1914.

Hubbs, Carl L. "Back from Oblivion." *Pacific Discovery*, Vol. IX, No. 6, 1956.

——— and Lagler, Karl F. *Fishes of the Great Lakes Region*. Bloomfield Hills, Mich.: Cranbrook Institute of Science, 1947.

Huth, Hans. *Nature and the American*. Berkeley: University of California Press, 1957.

Jefferson, Thomas. *Notes on the State of Virginia*. Reprint, Philadelphia, 1825.

Jordan, David Starr, and Evermann, Barton Warren. *American Food and Game Fishes*. New York: Doubleday, Page, 1903.

Kortright, Francis H. *The Ducks, Geese, and Swans of North America*. Washington, D.C.: American Wildlife Institute, 1942.

LaMonte, Francesca. *North American Game Fishes*. New York: Doubleday, 1946.

Laut, Agnes. *The Fur-Trade of America*. New York: Macmillan, 1921.

Lawson, John. *History of North Carolina*. . . . Reprint, London, 1709.

Lehmann, Valgene. *Attwater's Prairie Chicken, Its Life History and Management*. North American Fauna No. 57, Department of Agriculture, 1941.

Leopold, A. Starker, and Darling, F. Fraser. *Wildlife in Alaska*. New York: Ronald, 1953.

Leopold, Aldo. *A Sand County Almanac*. New York: Oxford, 1949.

———. *Game Management*. New York: Scribner, 1933.

———. "On a Monument to the Pigeon," in *Silent Wings*. Madison, Wis.: Wisconsin Society for Ornithology, 1947.

———. *Report on a Game Survey of the North Central States*. Washington, D.C.: American Game Association, 1931.

Logier, E. B. S. *The Frogs, Toads, and Salamanders of Eastern Canada*. Toronto: Clarke, Irwin, 1952.

Lorant, Stefan, ed. *The New World*. New York: Duell, Sloan, and Pearce, 1946.

Matthiessen, G. C. "The Land and Nature as Reflected in American Literature." Unpublished.

Mershon, W. B. *The Passenger Pigeon*. New York: Outing Publishing Company, 1907.

Miller, Gerrit S., and Kellogg, Remington. *North American Recent Mammals*. USNMB No. 205, 1957.

Moffett, James W. "The Lake Trout." Washington, D.C.: National Wildlife Federation, 1956.

——— and Applegate, Vernon C. "The Sea Lamprey." *Scientific American*, April 1955.

Morton, Thomas. *New English Canaan*. Boston reprint, 1883.

Murie, Olaus J. *The Elk of North America*. Washington, D.C.: Wildlife Management Institute, 1951.

Murphy, Robert C. "John James Audubon." *New York Historical Society Quarterly*, October 1956.

——— and Mowbray, Louis J. "New Light on the Cahow." *The Auk*, Vol. 68, 1951.

National Audubon Society. "The Haz-

ards of Broadcasting Toxic Pesticides."
New York: November 1958.

Nelson, Edward W. "The Larger North American Mammals." *National Geographic Magazine*, Vol. XXX, No. 5, 1916.

———. *Natural History Collections Made in Alaska, 1877–1881*. Washington, D.C.: Dept. of Agriculture, 1887.

Nelson, Perry H. "The Grayling." National Wildlife Federation, 1956.

Nevins, Allan, and Commager, Henry Steele. *A Short History of the United States*. New York: Random House, 1945.

Nuttall, Thomas. *Manual of the Ornithology of the United States and Canada*, Vol. I. Boston, 1834.

Ord, George. In *Proceedings of the American Philosophical Society*, Vol. I, No. 13, 1840.

Osborn, Fairfield. *Our Plundered Planet*. Boston: Little, Brown, 1948.

Palmer, Theodore S. *Legislation for American Game Protection, 1776–1911*. Biological Survey Bulletin No. 41, 1912.

———. *Legislation for the Protection of Birds Other than Game Birds*. Biological Survey Bulletin No. 12, 1902.

Parkman, Francis. *The Oregon Trail*. New York: Modern Library, 1949.

Pearson, T. Gilbert. *Adventures in Bird Protection*. New York, Appleton-Century, 1937.

Peattie, Donald Culross, ed. *Audubon's America*. Boston: Houghton Mifflin, 1940.

Pennant, Thomas. *Arctic Zoology*. London, 1785, 2 Vols.

Peterson, Roger Tory. *A Field Guide to the Birds*. Boston: Houghton Mifflin, 1947.

———. *A Field Guide to Western Birds*. Boston: Houghton Mifflin, 1941.

——— and Fisher, James. *Wild America*. Boston: Houghton Mifflin, 1955.

Pough, Richard H. *Audubon Western Bird Guide*. New York: Doubleday, 1957.

———. "An Inventory of Threatened and Vanishing Species." TNAWC, 1937.

Rausch, Robert. "On the Status of Some Arctic Mammals." *Arctic*, Vol. 6, No. 2.

Reid, N. J. *The Black-Tailed Prairie Dog.* (Unpublished.)

Rhode, Clarence J., and Barker, Will. *Alaska's Fish and Wildlife*. Washington, D.C.: Fish and Wildlife Service Circular No. 17.

Scammon, Charles M. *The Marine Mammals of the North-Western Coast of North America*. New York: Putnam, 1874.

Schmidt, Karl P. *A Check-List of North American Amphibians and Reptiles*. Chicago: University of Chicago Press, 1953.

———. "Crocodiles." *Fauna*, Vol. 6, No. 3.

Schorger, A. W. *The Passenger Pigeon*. Madison: University of Wisconsin Press, 1955.

Scott, W. E. D. "The Present Condition of Some of the Bird Rookeries of the Gulf Coast of Florida." *The Auk*, Vol. 4, Nos. 3 and 4, 1887.

Sears, Paul B. *Deserts on the March*. Norman: University of Oklahoma Press, 1947.

Smith, Hobart M. *Handbook of Lizards of the United States and Canada*. Ithaca, N.Y.: Comstock Publishing Company, 1946.

Snyder, Dorothy E. "A Recent Colima Warbler's Nest." *The Auk*, Vol. 74, No. 1, 1957.

Sprunt, Alexander, Jr., and Chamberlain, E. B. *South Carolina Bird Life*. Columbia: University of South Carolina Press, 1949.

Stackpole, Edouard A. *The Sea Hunters*. Philadelphia: Lippincott, 1953.

Stebbins, Robert C. *Amphibians and Reptiles of Western North America*. New York: McGraw-Hill, 1954.

Stimson, Louis A. "The Cape Sable Seaside Sparrow: Its Form and Present Distribution." *The Auk*, Vol. 73, No. 1, 1956.

Storer, Tracy I. *General Zoology*. New York: McGraw-Hill, 1951.

———— and Tevis, Lloyd P., Jr. *The California Grizzly*. Berkeley: University of California Press, 1955.

Sutton, Ann and Myron. "The Adventures of Steller." *Natural History*, Vol. LXV, No. 9, November 1956.

Swainson, William, and Richardson, John. *Fauna-Boreali Americana*, Vol. II. London, 1831.

Tanner, James T. *The Ivory-Billed Woodpecker*. New York: Audubon Research Report No. 1, 1942.

Taverner, P. A. *Birds of Canada*. Ottawa: National Museum of Canada, 1947.

Teale, Edwin Way. *Autumn Across America*. New York: Dodd, Mead, 1956.

————. *North with the Spring*. New York: Dodd, Mead, 1951.

————, ed. *The Wilderness World of John Muir*. Boston: Houghton Mifflin, 1954.

Thompson, Seton. "Seal Fisheries," in Tressler, Donald K., and Lemon, James McW., op. cit.

Tressler, Donald K., and Lemon, James McW. *Marine Products of Commerce*. New York: Reinhold, 1951.

Turner, L. M. *Contributions to the Natural History of Alaska*. Washington, D.C.: Dept. of Agriculture, 1886.

Unna, Warren. "Republican Giveaways: the Charges and the Facts." *Harper's Magazine*, May 1956.

Van Oosten, John. "The Lake Sturgeon." Washington, D.C.: National Wildlife Federation, 1956.

Welker, Robert Henry. *Birds and Men*. Cambridge, Mass. Harvard University Press, 1955.

Wiley, Farida. *John Burroughs' America*. New York: Devin-Adair, 1951.

Wilson, Alexander. *The American Ornithology*. Brewer edition, Boston, 1840.

Wing, Leonard W. *Practice of Wildlife Conservation*. New York: Wiley, 1951.

Wright, Alfred Hazen and Anna Allen. *Handbook of Frogs and Toads of the United States and Canada*. Ithaca, N.Y.: Comstock Publishing Company, 1949.

Young, Stanley, and Goldman, E. A. *The Wolves of North America*. Washington, D.C.: American Wildlife Institute, 1944.

Index

Italic figures, preceded by the letters *ill.*, indicate line drawings.